Robert D Boyd Cpt

A Razor's Edge

To Gary Prosser,
A good friend on excellent
pilot.

Robert Boyd

ISBN: 1-4701-1724-X
ISBN-13: 9781470117245

FOREWARD

I am not a professional writer but have been involved in writing and editing a lot of government reports, documents, resumes, etc. for the last 45 years. What I am though is a retired US Army Major who spent 20 years in uniform (1967 to 1987) and held positions both in flying and non-flying assignments. I was also an OV-1 pilot in Vietnam and with Bob at the 131st at Fort Hood. I also had the opportunity to command an OV-1 Mohawk Company in Korea for a year. The remainder of my time was spent in the Pentagon or "behind closed doors" working in the Intelligence Community.

When I returned from Vietnam in 1973, at the end of the war, it was the worst day of my life. The way we were treated was inhumane. I started having major problems several years later but it took the Army and the VA almost another 20+ years for them to determine that I had something the now labeled as PTSD. Since my return from combat, I have had the opportunity to be seen by dozens of mental health "experts". Very few of them ever really understood until the past year or two. I have also been able to observe and talk to hundreds of other former soldiers, including my own son who served in Afghanistan, who suffered from the same symptoms that I now realize had such a radical effect on my adult life and will until the day I die. I lost my ability to fly after my tour in Korea in 1982. As the pilot in "Top Gun" said, he just "lost the edge." I did as well and it was primarily because of my continued bout with PTSD and the effects that it was having on me and my health.

Bob was a good friend at Fort Hood and he was a fantastic pilot. The exploits you will read about here will amaze and terrify you. I lost track of him during the 80s and 90s but have now regained an even better friend than before and I value his friendship as much as one person can. I am personally amazed that he is still alive but am glad he is. Down deep, Bob was driven to excel. His father was totally disabled from having polio during WWII, at which time his dad put himself and a B17 pilot who was out of work, through medical school. Bob said he never heard his dad complain. Part of his exploits were that need to excel and part were from being absolutely fearless. Bob is now gaining his life back, primarily due to his relationship with his wife Margo who has had a profound effect on him and is still trying every day to add some semblance of emotional calmness to his life. That has been aided by the addition of his grandchildren who look up to him. Most men would not have survived the lifestyle that Bob lived but as he has said, "God must have kept me around for some reason."

I challenge you to read his litany of escapades and see if you don't agree with me that this is a man who has his whole life been screaming for help without even knowing he needed it. He tells it like it is, from being a combat pilot in Vietnam flying missions that had a high mortality rate to traveling around the world as a corporate pilot flying VIPs and corporate bigwigs around for their pleasure. You will also see his unequalled expertise as a pilot at a level few humans ever experience. He was truly one with the airplane, whatever he was flying.

I am still grateful to have him as my friend and hope to for a long time to come.

George P. Davis III, Major, US Army (Ret.)

George P. Davis III

Major, USA (Ret.)
Vietnam Combat Veteran
OV-1 Mohawk/UH-1H Huey Pilot

A Razor's Edge

I wanted to fly since I was twelve years old. A friend had taken me up on a test flight of a DC-3 and I was hooked. I planned my whole life around being an airline pilot. I got a private pilot's license when I was 16 and devoted myself to flying as much as I could with the limited funds I could accumulate. I mowed yards with a push mower for .50 cents, baby sat kids for the same amount. Pretty quick I learned that I would never accumulate enough money to pay the $25 an hour that a single engine plane would cost. I went to funeral homes and asked if they needed any bodies delivered to other parts of Texas. I offered to fly them for free if the funeral director would pay for the airplane. I would then rent a Cessna 172 take the forward copilot's seat out and have the funeral home deliver the body to me at the airport. In those days the body bags were opaque plastic and you could see right through them. Most of the bodies had only been frozen since the particular funeral home was not going to do the funeral. Some of them were a bit messed up having been in car accidents and other nasty accidents or murdered. In order to fit in the aircraft, the funeral director had to fold their hands across their chests, which made a great cup holder for my early morning coffee thermos. As they thawed out some of them made some unusual noises and once one looked like he was going to sit up. Somewhat unnerving and I had to convince myself that the fucker was dead.

Having graduated from high school at 17 I enrolled in the University of Houston. Vietnam was in full swing and without at least 15 hours a semester you were guaranteed to learn how to shit in the jungle. My classes started at 7:00am and ended at noon. I then reported to the airport where I worked on the ramp for Continental Airlines from 3:00pm till midnight. After I got off work, I had an arrangement with a fixed base operator to fly one of his Cessna 172s and get billed monthly. I was very quickly becoming a pauper.

One day my buddies wanted me to take them flying after work. I met them at the airfield which was just across the runways at Hobby International Airport. The fixed base operator had all his planes tightly packed together, with low wing single engine aircraft tucked up close to the high wing Cessnas. I was showing the guys how to do a preflight, check all the parts that moved, drain all the fuel sumps of any water that had accumulated in the tanks and how to check the oil. Many a cocky idiot just got in and fired up only to run out of oil or discover he didn't have enough fuel and then running out of airspeed altitude and ideas planted himself in some field, the last thing to be seen was his ass passing his head.

I always worked around the airplane from the right side to the left. As I grabbed the Cessna's strut and swung under it I hit something that knocked me on my ass. I thought I had miscalculated the height of the strut, the guys were on the other side of the aircraft I picked myself up and continued around the left side to end up under the engine drain it's sump and check the oil. Draining the engine fuel sump one of the guys says "Hey we can't take this one its leaking oil"

"Where," I said.

He brought the flashlight over and pointed the light on his shoes which were covered in blood.

"Son of a bitch", I said "someone has a nasty nose bleed."

We started checking everyone out until they flashed the light on me and exclaimed "Damn Boyd you're bleeding like someone cut your jugular."

When I swung under the strut on the Cessna I ran into the trailing edge of the Cherokee 140 that was tucked up next to the Cessna I would fly. The trailing edge of an aluminum wing is sharp as a knife if your brain dead enough to run your head into it.

"Damn it Boyd, we knew you would fuck up our flight."

"Just hang on a minute while I run into the restroom."

That part of the building was open so I turned on the light and checked myself out. The Texas Chain Saw murderer had left his victims in better shape. I couldn't see the cut, so I wrapped toilet paper around my chin and head until I had enough to stop the blood running in my eyes. Then I took the guys for a tour of Houston from the air at night. When we landed and had secured the aircraft, the guys really took time to check out the cut.

"Shit Bob, this looks deep we better take you to the emergency room."

As luck would have it, my dad, a doctor himself, had gone to Brazoria, Texas to see his dad. This was before the good Samaritan Law and hospitals refused to treat you without parental consent. I had to call my dad at 3:30am which freaked out my mom and ruined their night. It took the doctor 20 minutes or more to clean all the stuck toilet paper off my head and from the wound. The blood had coagulated and the wound was really tender. The doc looks at the guys and says "Will you guys be all right or should you leave the room."

"We'll be fine sir." Famous last words!

Doc says "Bob this is deep and about three inches long. In order for me to sew it up correctly I am going to need to put a bunch of stitches at the bottom of the cut and move up until I get to your scalp. They will be the dissolving type until I reach your scalp. Those stitches will have to be removed in 10 days. Additionally, I am going to have to deaden the wound and that will require sticking a needle into the side walls of the wound and that will probably hurt."

I have always had a high tolerance for pain so I told him to go ahead. Few of you probably realize just how tough your scalp is. The doc got his first syringe and tried to stick it in the wall of the cut. It hurt all right but I wasn't about to say a word. Unfortunately I forgot to tell the rest of my body. My legs shot straight out and shook like I was freezing. Two of the guys puked on the floor and the other one ran out leaving the doctor mumbling under his breath.

The U.S.Army

It was nearing Christmas break, windy, cold, and dreary in Houston, as David and I made our way into the Roxie bar. We were both on our way to English finals at the University of Houston, and it was our custom to have a pitcher of beer before a big test. It drove the other students crazy, when we entered the room smelling like beer. We loved to stir the pot, and we were usually first ones finished, with a 98 and a 94 respectively. We were carrying 15 credit hours to stay out of the draft, going to school 7:00am till noon, and then working at Continental Airlines from 3:00pm till midnight. I was working on a pilot's license and any flying I did occurred after midnight. It was an exhausting schedule and we were both tired.

"You know David, this schedule is killing me. I 'm to the point, that I really don't give a shit if I die here or in Nam. When I finish this test, I'm dropping out."

"Well you might want to look at the paper this morning. Army is running low on draftees and they are going to start at the beginning of the alphabet and send out notices to several thousand more. With a name like Boyd, you're fucked."

"Shit, beat me, hurt me make me write a hot check I'm still dropping out.

One day later I received an Uncle Sam summons for a physical having been reclassified 1-A. Uncle Sam must have bugged the registrar's office. This was December 1966. I showed up downtown Houston to take a physical with about 400 other guys. Most of these guys couldn't come in out of the rain Fat guys, skinny guys, guys who probably couldn't add 2 and 2 and get four absolutely pathetic examples of America's youth. We had to take a urine test and I was approached by no less than 20 guys to piss in their jar for them. I took on all comers until I ran out of piss. The doctor had a huge finger and when he stuck it up my ass to check my prostate, he said, "If you smile, you're out". Then he jammed that prehistoric finger up my ass and rooted around like he was searching for a way out. I actually thought he was enjoying himself. My dad had been a 1st Lieutenant in the Army Air Corps in WWII. He never went overseas as he was caught up in a polio epidemic while at Ellington Air Force Base just outside Houston. Most of his friends died while others ended up in iron lungs for life. Dad spent two years in an iron lung and later was able to live without one but he was paralyzed. Eventually he got the use of his left arm back and could move his hands but could not walk without braces on his legs and something to hold on too. The VA denied his claim saying he had to prove he was disabled. In the meantime, he had to go through rehabilitation at the VA hospital in Houston. They treated those guys like pieces of meat. It was a fiasco with his claim and as a result he became good friends with the guys at the draft board. He told me he could keep me out if I wanted. I refused. I said I have never heard you complain once and I surely won't use you as an excuse to bypass the draft. I loved him.

A week later a telegram came addressed to me that said, "GREETINGS" you have been selected to serve your Uncle Sam and must report to the recruiting center, on 1 February 1967." There it was a definitive statement, no more college, no more dates, no more screwing off and no more anxiety the shit had hit the fan.

1 February 1967, arrived without warning or fanfare, like a thump on your head from your mother when you farted in

church. One of those SBDs (silent but deadly) that floated through the sanctuary while you tried unsuccessfully to smother your laughter. We were all dressed in civvies and you could cut the tension with a knife. We were lined up next to busses and our names were called. Hurry up and wait became the order of the day and continued for the next 7 and ¼ years. There was some commotion way down the line and as I looked out I saw two Marine Corps gunnies walking down the line picking guys out. Oh crap, I didn't want to be a high diddle diddle right up the middle Marine, so I slowly sunk down and crawled into the baggage area of the bus until they went by. The Marines don't draft, but they did during the Vietnam conflict. The Marines are a proud and honorable organization but I wanted to fly if I could and you had to have a degree if you flew for the Marines. I'm as macho as the next guy but hauling a hundred pound pack around through the jungles of Southeast Asia, was not my idea of a fun time. We finally boarded the buses around 3:00pm for the trip to Fort Polk Louisiana a shithole where they breed mosquitoes big enough to screw Billy goats. We arrived at around midnight. A sergeant climbed on the bus and started yelling for us scum sucking maggots to "get off." Everyone was shoving and running down the aisle. Outside we were formed up again and given the proverbial welcome to Basic Training. There were foot prints painted on the ground and we were told to stand on them. My dad had told me what the drill would be, so I wasn't shitting in my pants like the majority of the guys. The sergeant would look at the foot prints and then the guy standing on them and yell in his face, "You're too stupid to insult."

The Army would break us down, and then build us back up in the Army way, so when some Officer said "jump" you would respond instinctively and without hesitation; "how high Sir". We were then given a quick snack and assigned to barracks. As we filed into the mess hall a sergeant was standing at the door pointing out different guys and telling them to be there at 4:30am in the morning for mess hall duties. I got picked. Years later when I was flying with my favorite Captain at PSA, I asked him: "Why do you think I get picked on?"

He looked at me and said, "You have a face that looks at people like "Your ass!"

Well, I may have been picked but I wasn't stupid, so when 4:30am came along, I crawled up into the attic and hid out until mess had started and then joined the line with the other guys.

Basic Training

First morning, all hell broke loose as guys used to sleeping in were yanked out of their beds and given 5 minutes to shit, shower, and shave. Outside we were formed up by height which put me in the middle of the first row. From there we were marched over to supply where we were told to strip to our underwear leave our clothes and then marched over to the barbers, who took great pride in seeing how fast they could shave a head. Bald and nearly naked we were taken back to supply, and walked through the building where there were stations and you were handed pants, t-shirts, boxers, a ball cap, shirts(long sleeve), socks, and boots. Marched back to our barracks with arms loaded with *Army Issue* clothes, we were given five minutes to change, put the remainder on our bunks and form up outside. We were introduced to the Company Commander, our platoon drill sergeants, and the first sergeant. My drill sergeant walked the front line sticking that Smokey the Bear straight brimmed hat in our faces and moving on. When he got to me he stopped and screwed up his face as if trying to remember something. We were the same height and while I was concentrating straight ahead and two inches above his forehead he was giving me the evil eye. I knew they couldn't remember who they had picked for mess hall duty. We were then taken in the barracks and taught how to make a bunk, how to store our footlocker and how to hang our clothes. We were given a battery of tests, psychological stuff like would you rather be a thief or a queer? No other options. We were issued weapons, M14's at that time and heavy. We would never again be without them. We had to remember the serial number by heart and repeat it, while holding our dicks "This is my weapon, this is my gun, one is for shooting and this one is for fun".

Back in formation, several of us were called by name and sent to see the Commanding Officer. He informed us that we had done very well on the recent tests and did any of us want to go to OCS, (Officer Candidate School.) If we did, we could choose from several courses, artillery, infantry, supply, transportation, to name a few. He also informed us that if we wanted OCS, we would owe the Army three more years, instead of the two required of a draftee. That, certainly reduced the men from the boys, and all but 5 of us dropped out. We all picked something other than infantry. Three days later while in formation, OCS assignments were read out. I got Infantry. Wow, what a surprise! My drill instructor then came and mocked me for wanting to go to OCS and informed me that since I was so cocky and gung-ho, I would get up an hour early and in full gear run to the rifle range about 4 miles away. *Oh great the teacher's pet!* Next morning at 4:00am, there was butt breath himself yelling at me to get my OCS ass in gear? In full gear and carrying my M-14 with dick head counting cadence (I had lots of names for the drill sergeant), I ran alongside him with one other recruit while he called us every name he had ever learned that started with an F. I was contemplating whacking him with my weapon and stomping the living shit out of him when we ran right through the arriving busses with new guys. The recruit running with me was totally out of shape and out of breath. He stumbled and fell and passed out sending his helmet and his M-14 skidding right into the new recruits. The butt hole drill sergeant picked up his helmet and his M-14, put his helmet on the guy's head and propped his M-14 on his body and yelling what a " fucking momma's boy", caught up to me and continued his harangue. Seeing the looks on the new guy's faces and them trying to get back on the busses was worth the run. I made it to the range which seemed to piss off scrotum head and he doubled his efforts at trying to get my goat. I would just continue to look two inches over his head and grit my teeth. After several weeks of harassment the drill sergeant gets in my face and says *"Hey scum bucket, I'll bet you would like to try kicking my ass"*

"Actually Sergeant I would like to bend you over and drive you to the prizes." Always get your opponent pissed off.

Then one Sunday, the drill sergeant came and got me and said, "Pick two of your trusted buddies and come with me". We got into a ¾ ton vehicle and with three other drill sergeants rode out to the firing range. Once there, my drill sergeant took off his shirt and said "here's your chance boy, let's see what you got." I figured that was where we were going so before he could get into a stance I launched myself at him like a mad man. I hit him at least three times before he could take a breath and then we were into it. Drill sergeants yelling, recruits yelling and adrenaline flowing, we beat the shit out of each other until we ended up on our knees looking at each other and too tired to swing another punch. He had two black eyes and a badly split lip and my nose was bleeding like a fire hydrant. "Son of a bitch boy, you're a tough little shit", he said.

"Well, I was tired of your crap", and then we both started laughing. The rest of my time at Fort Polk was repetitious training, but I had found new respect and quitting was never in my repertoire.

We had a guy in our platoon that we called, Mouse. He was about five feet tall and probably weighed 110 lbs dripping wet. He had ears the size of saucers and was very quiet and shy. I felt sorry for him not only for his appearance but what the future held for him in Vietnam. There is no privacy in basic training, you live in the same room, you shower together, eat together, take a dump together and train together. One night I had to go leave a leak and got up to find Mouse in the shower. He turned around and I did a double take. He had a dick hanging down past his knee caps. I mean this thing was friggin awesome probably a foot and half long. I couldn't believe it and without a word I went back to bed. If he got a hard on in Vietnam I figured he would pass out from lack of blood to his brain or trip on it trying to run for cover. I sincerely hoped he would be assigned to Supply.

AIT

From Fort Polk, LA I was shipped to Fort Lewis, WA for AIT or Advanced Infantry Training. It was here that I ran into my first race problems. We had maybe 20 blacks in our unit the majority of which had nasty ass attitudes and hung together all the time. My mother grew up in Africa from the age of 3 months. Her parents were Methodists missionaries and her dad a doctor. It took them 6 months from the time they left the states to arrive in the Belgium Congo. Five months of it was in a dugout canoe paddling up the Congo River. The slept on islands in the river and had to stand watch to protect them from crocodiles and hippos. She grew up in a thatched roofed hut with dirt floors. Her friends were all blacks so we grew up with no animosities at all. It came as a surprise when the blacks gathered around me while I was pitching my pup tent. The taunts began and I was all alone. Suddenly one of the bigger blacks kicked me and I went sprawling. The best thing to do in a situation like that is to take out the leader. So with my entrenching tool in my right hand I got up and swung it into the side of his head. I hit him with the blade flat but it still knocked him nearly unconscious and while he staggered I hit him with my left hand hard as I could in the nose. Anyone who has ever been in a fight knows when you get hit in the nose hard you can't see for nearly a minute, and that's when you finish the job or you lose. When he finally hit the ground and called enough I was still breathing like a high school student at the prom with a hot date, and pissed off. I said "Gentlemen, I won't take any of your racist crap" so leave me alone and I'll leave you alone." Mission accomplished and we actually got along fine after that. Following AIT I was ordered to OCS, (Officer Candidate School), which was located in

Georgia. I managed to take three days travel time with a stopover in Houston, where I made one of the biggest mistakes of my life and got married. She was a beautiful girl but couldn't keep her legs together.

OCS

Fort Benning's School for Boys was a snide reference to Infantry OCS at Fort Benning, Georgia. OCS was as much harassment as it was training. The idea was to teach you attention to detail and leadership qualities. The "TACT (short for Tactical) Officers" (previous graduates assigned as Platoon Leaders) used the occasion to play college boy fraternity harassment games. We were introduced to starched fatigues. We each had about twelve sets so that you always had available a clean set of starched fatigues while others were being cleaned. Name tags and patches were sewn on without the slightest frayed stitching or a TAC Officer would notice it and ask if it wasn't a lanyard for a 105 howitzer, at which point you were to answer "Sir Candidate Boyd, yes sir". The key note being that the first three words out of your mouth were always "Sir Candidate Boyd, yes sir". The TAC Officer would then pull it loose at which point you said "boom". Stupid, ridiculous but one soon learned to pay attention to that detail. The six plus months there were packed with infantry tactics, artillery tactics, ambushes, explosives, weapons training, counter ambushes, map reading, radio procedures and the etiquette and responsibilities expected of an officer. Each platoon was assigned a floor on a multi-storied building with about 20 showers and an equal number of growlers (commodes). Each floor had to be spit-shined by hand. You could not slide a foot locker out from under the lower bunks without putting big scratches in the floor so we bought Kotex folded it over at the ends and stapled it to the bottom of the foot lockers. We bought more Kotex than a woman would use in a lifetime. There were twenty commodes but we never used but one because they had to be so spotless. No time was ever allotted for cleaning or spit-shinning boots or floors so we had to find the time at night. We had fun with the prep boy TAC Officers by putting a dab of peanut butter along the back of the porcelain commode. On inspection which happened every day, the TAC Officer accompanied by a candidate would find the dab of peanut butter and ask the candidate what it was. "Sir Candidate Boyd, looks likeshit sir." Then put my finger in it and smell it, "Sir Candidate Boyd smells like a turd sir." Then taste it "Sir, Candidate Boyd, tastes like a turd sir." Where upon candidate Boyd would drop and do 50 pushups. If you ever saw the movie," An Officer and a Gentleman" OCS was very much in the same vein except you never got to leave until you were a senior candidate. It was a stressful time we never had hair on our legs due to constantly *breaking starch* by pulling on stiff as cardboard fresh fatigues. There was a creek running through our area called "Raiders Creek". For harassment purposes the TAC Officers would have us low crawl ¼ of a mile through that creek and then give us 10 minutes to run back to the barracks and change fatigues. That low crawl accomplished two things, it ruined your stiff fatigues and sandpapered the toes of your boots requiring hours of new spit polishing. At one point two months into the program, a candidate kept his M-14 after a trip to the rifle range and disappeared. After a day of waiting for him to come back they lined us up arm length apart and walked us through the woods. We found him sitting under a tree. He had put the barrel into his mouth and pulled the trigger. No movie can duplicate the aftermath of the destruction that that bullet made to his head. It bulged out his head from the eyes up and the top was completely gone. I mean it looked like a volcano that had erupted out of his head. There was tissue and brain matter scattered for thirty yards. It had a very sobering effect on men who were about go into combat.

There was also an accounting for responsibilities. A report so to speak, made by each candidate that was suppose to grade other candidates as to whether one would want that candidate leading your own son. It was a joke. Guys took their animosities out on each other, and it ended up being a farce. Can you imagine guys with grade school educations, college grads, high school tough guys, and guys that simply had the choice of jail or the Army trying to rate each other?

At one point we were given the opportunity to apply for flight school. In order to apply you had to pass the flight physical. Before you could take the physical you had to sign on for an additional three years. Out of 150 plus candidates in my class, 120 raised their hands for wanting to go to flight school, only three took the physical when the additional three years was brought up. What a way to cull a group. I passed the physical and was assigned to Vietnam TDY or temporary duty to flight school.

Two years later I would learn that my TAC officer was regularly playing hide the salami with my wife.

Upon graduation as butter bars or brand new 2Lts I was assigned to the 2nd Armored Division, General Patton's old division at Fort Hood, Texas. While I was there I was involved in a motorcycle accident. I was riding behind another 2LT when he tried to take a corner to fast. The tires slipped out from under us and we slide across the asphalt on our legs until the motorcycle hit a curb and bounced us up end over end into a yard. No helmets *couple of real dumb asses*, but outside of nasty road rashes on our legs we didn't appear to be hurt too bad that is, until I tried to push myself up with my right arm. It was bent 90 degrees at the elbow and while it didn't hurt at all, I couldn't straighten it. Apparently I had over extended the joint stretched the tendon damn near to breaking point and then the arm snapped back. We tried pulling it straight but it was locked. I was in a bit of turmoil as I had flight school orders due any time. Next day I went to the doctor who explained my predicament and ordered physical therapy. Asked how long before it would straighten out, he replied *"might be months"*. I was in deep shit with flight school approaching. I went to physical therapy where a sadomasochistic nurse took great pleasure putting a rolled towel under my upper arm and then pulling my wrist down until tears rolled down my cheek. Son-of-a-bitch that hurt! A week later my older brother Chuck, a year and a half older than me who had also graduated from Infantry OCS got orders to Vietnam. Chuck had bad eyes, something on the order of 20/400. Our mother was beside herself with worry at Chuck losing his glasses in combat and getting killed. So without Chuck knowing, I called the Infantry Branch in Washington D.C. (we had both gone to Fort Benning home of the Infantry), and informed them I knew that two brothers couldn't serve in the same combat zone and that I was awaiting flight school orders TDY to Vietnam so what did they want to do? The Branch Officer says, *"We need pilots worse than we need platoon leaders, I have two flight school classes starting next week, a fixed wing class and a rotor wing class, which one do you want?"* I took the fixed wing course. Next day Chuck got orders reassigning him to Korea and I got orders to report to Ft. Stewart, GA for fixed wing flight school. I figured when Chuck froze his ass off he would just figure it was the idiosyncrasies of the Army. I was elated. My right arm would still not extend beyond 60 degrees, but since that was the arm you salute with, I covered it up well.

Initial Flight School

I moved my wife with me to Fort Steward and found housing in a trailer park just outside of the gate. The town abutting Ft Steward was so small that if you sneezed you wouldn't even see it while your eyes briefly shut. When we arrived in Ft Steward my wife picked up a puppy. It was allegedly a German shepherd male but turned out to be a blondish red dog with pointed ears. We had no yard so we had to leave him in the trailer if we went out. The son of a bitch would destroy anything we left in the trailer. He ate my shiny officer shoes, he ate our luggage, he tore up the couch, he crapped on a rug, and then, just to irritate the hell out of me we came home one evening to find that he had taken the pillows off the bed removed the pillow cases and then turned the entire trailer into a chicken ranch with feathers everywhere. I wanted to choke him until his eye balls popped out, but as the country song says, *"I love children, old dogs and puppies."*

Flight school consisted of ½ a day in class and ½ a day flying. When flying half of the class would fly out to a practice field while the other half road a bus. We eventually would switch with guys who flew out, and they would ride the bus back and vice versa. Stewart Georgia had all the warmth and charm of a child's funeral. Blink your eyes and you were through the town. They had one bar we would gather at and tell our flying stories. It was rundown, bleak, and full of 3" cockroaches. We had one crazy Special Forces guy who was sitting at the bar one night when a huge cockroach came scurrying up the bar. He slapped his hand on it and looked around at all the single green toothed patrons and then stuck it between his teeth and while they looked on in utter disgust he ate it. Another time after most of us had soloed, he found a little bird that had fallen out of its nest. He cuddled it in his hands most of the way back on the bus and then was heard to say, "You know, little bird, we have something in common neither one of us can fly, and then bit its head off and ate it." Strange dude!

I had a commercial license before I went into the service so flying was a snap for me. However, every time a student had a run in with his instructor guess who had to switch instructors? One particular instructor had a reputation of really being a hard ass. I don't think he could get laid with a handful of pardons in a women's prison. One morning I got summoned to the commandant's office and was told I was being transferred to this guy. I fumed and fussed to no avail. Then I grabbed my gear, walked out to the airplane, a T-41 military version of a Cessna 172, did a preflight and got in the cockpit and shut the door. The instructor was looking out the other window with a face that looked as though he just walked in on his wife in bed with another guy. You see, if you have too many students ask to be reassigned you get fired. All the instructors were civilians. I tapped him on his shoulder and said, "Look I ain't happy either, but I came here to be number one in the class. I want to learn every damn thing you know, every pit fall, every hazard, and every trick. You teach me that and you and I will get along just great." It worked and he turned out to be a great friend.

After a couple of weeks of studies the program broke down into ½ of the class flying and the other just goofing off. My section had the mornings off so we went to play golf every day. I didn't know how to play golf, but several of the guys began teaching me. I could hit the cover off the ball but I never could follow through, and I was constantly mocked for not doing so. I ended up under a tree on one shot with a limb above me about 6 feet from the ground. The guys were yelling at me to make sure I followed through. I took a stance and swung hard enough to drill me into the ground and make sure I followed through. I was using a six iron. I followed through with my six iron, the club hit the branch curled around it and hit me squarely on the head and drove me into the ground. I finished the round with blood streaming down my face and back.

Dreaming

One day an OV-1 flew in. It was a twin engine turbine powered aircraft with three tails. One had to climb into the cockpit with the help of a step that slid out the side of the fuselage and was later replaced by a crew chief once you were settled in. Since no one was around we climbed up to look inside. What awaited us was the equivalent of you walking into the cockpit of a modern day airliner. There were electrical on/off switches everywhere, circuit breakers, gauges and instruments, and did I mention, ejection seats. The whole experience left us wondering if we would ever be able to fly something that sophisticated. For days after we were depressed from the sheer magnitude of that cockpit.

Following initial flight school we were transitioned into the Army's Birddog. It was a single engine tandem seat small aircraft used for spotting and marking targets in Vietnam. It was also a conventional gear aircraft which means it had a tail wheel. The saying goes: **"There are *those flying a tail wheel aircraft who have ground looped it or, are going to ground loop it"*** In other words if you ain't extremely careful it will turn around and bite you in the ass. Half of the class was flying one day when a line of thunderstorms appeared on the horizon. They were extremely black and building fast. Those of us flying were ordered to immediately return to base. A gaggle of us headed for home. However, the winds preceding the storm were blowing faster than we were flying and we ended up flying backward. We were blown past our practice field and we ended up landing on roads or fields, anywhere we could find a safe place to put down.

Following several months at Ft Stewart we moved to Ft Rucker, Alabama where we flew a twin engine Beech Barron for instrument training. We didn't rely on a co-pilot, we had to learn everything ourselves. Front course ILS, back course ILS, VOR approaches front and back course, ADF approaches front and back course, and instrument approaches with only one engine. I loved it and studied hard. Graduation day finally came and being in the top 5 guys I got to pick my choice of aircraft. I picked the OV-1.

The OV-1

Built by Grumman, it sported two turbine powered engines, a bubble cockpit, two Martin Baker J5D ejection seats, and three tails. The ejection seat was what they called a 100 knot seat. In other words, if you weren't right side up, and going at least a 100knots, you would eject, hit the ground and road rash yourself into a bloody pile. It also blasted you out of the cockpit with a 105 howitzer round, so you had to strap yourself in real tight, or the force of ejection would fracture your back. The reason for possible fracture was no padding on the seat that could compress, so you flew with sweat running down your crack and you couldn't even lift a cheek to scratch. Furthermore, it was not air conditioned, so summer flying in the Deep South was like flying a 230 knot sauna without wings. I excelled in the transition and learned the dynamics of single engine work, and what could bite you in the ass or cause you to eject and end up as a pile of teeth, hair and eyeballs. The great thing about flying; if you screw up is that you are the first one at the accident. The OV-1 was a blast to fly. It was fast, ugly, sophisticated, and an all weather aircraft, and had four different kinds of radios in it. It had twin ejection seats, but the one on the right was for an enlisted man to ride and man the sneaky Pete stuff we carried, like IR (infra red), SLAR (side looking airborne radar), and a camera mounted in the belly that could take vertical pictures or side pictures in a 30 degree or 60 degree angles. It also had a nose camera for BDA or bomb damage assessment. It took four pictures a second. The printed pictures came out about eleven inches wide and two feet long but the actual film was 70mm by 12 inches. It looked like the curvature of the earth, but the center of the picture was amazingly clear and detailed for fast low level photos. There were twelve of us in the transition to OV-1s. Our class leader was a Major, we called Uncle Jim. We had several captains and lieutenants, of which I was one and several Warrant Officers. Upon completion of the transition course, we were ordered to Ft. Huachuca, Arizona where we were to continue polishing our flying skills and learn the sneaky Pete intelligence gathering capabilities of the aircraft. We flew four or five hours a day and then retired to the Officer's Club. This was our last stop before Vietnam, so concluding we would probably get killed over there, we drank copious amounts of beer and ate polish sausages, pickled eggs, popcorn and pickled pig's feet. The next morning, you would find us dragging ass and carrying our oxygen masks out to the aircraft where we could hook up and breathe pure oxygen; a great hangover reliever.

OV-1 Last one is a SLAR Model

I had an incredible time flying low level and snapping pictures of moving trains, mountains, sheep, etc. I found out that the Highway Patrol was laying speed traps on pay day between Sierra Vista, (home of Fort Huachuca), and Interstate 10. This was a road running north out of Sierra Vista for approximately 40 miles and it was a very rolling highway almost like a kid's roller coaster. The fuzz would wait on the opposite side of a hill and give tickets to the enlisted men as they made their way up to Tucson. In my opinion, this was a shitty way to make their quota on our service men and women. Being the savior of all good causes, I would fly at about 5000', and find all the speed traps. Then, making sure no cars were coming the other way, I would fly back to Sierra Vista; reverse course and fly low level, and I mean low level back down the road. I would trim the aircraft so that if I hit a bird or some other alien flying down in my six foot area of operation off the highway, and it startled me, the aircraft would zoom up and keep me from spreading my teeth, hair and eyeballs along the highway, along with a very expensive aircraft. In those days the radar that was used looked like a speedometer; and when one was speeding, the needle on the speedometer would indicate the speed of the offender, and then the face of the speedometer would snap forward and hold the needle in that position against the glass. It is important to note that the OV-1 could not be heard when it was approaching; only when it had passed. Flying at six feet off the ground at 230 knots, while making sure your propellers never kissed the earth, was an exacting science and there was no room for error. On the other hand, it was an exhilarating rush of adrenalin. The cops would note a speeder coming, and start opening their door to step out and flag you down. When I would pass them at warp speed, making sure not to hit them with the props, the energy and compression of air that the aircraft generated would blow the cop down the road about 15 feet. By then, I was over the next hill and out of sight. It is a rule of law that no good deed goes unpunished, so I found myself invited to the Commanding General's office. My ass was chewed into what looked like some old fart's cigar but, as I was on my way to the government's free vacation in Southeast Asia I think the Commander was somewhat amused by my explanation of events, as he could barely keep a straight face.

Vietnam June 1969

We graduated, Uncle Jim, I and another student named Bob agreed to meet in San Francisco for a night of fun, frolicking, and serious drinking, prior to departure from Travis Air Force Base the next day.

San Francisco, at least the parts we went too, must have been built to the specs of Sodom and Gomorra in the Old Testament. We went to see Carole Doda, allegedly a woman with the world's biggest breasts. Drinks were 8 bucks a shot and tasted like horse piss. All in all a wasted night and not my idea of the last meal for condemned men.

The flight over to Vietnam was made with a stop in Hawaii and Guam for refueling. Disembarked for a quick stretch of our legs and then on again for another 8 hours. Time in which one comes to terms with one's own mortality, bravado and bullshit take a back seat. I thought about my family and what they would think if I got killed. I hoped if I got killed my body would not be a mess for my mom's sake. I wondered what I would think if I got killed. I wondered if I would freeze up chicken out or otherwise embarrass myself in combat. Nearly twelve hours of flying leaves one to think a great deal.

Coming in over Vietnam we strained to look out the eight inch plastic window. The ground was hazy and green. The lower we got the haze turned to smoke and heat waves. We landed in Bien Hoa. Exiting the 720C Boeing aircraft the heat hit us like a heavy wet blanket. Vietnam attacked our senses with the rancid smell of smoke, cordite, rotting jungles, and human feces. We were edgy and out of our element.

We fell into formation and they divided us between Officers and enlisted men. Further, broke us down into Officers with command status and those that would do the heavy lifting, ground pounders. And, finally into helicopter pilots and fixed wing pilots. Our names were called and Uncle Jim was pulled off somewhere else. This would be his second tour. That left 12 of us who were fixed wing pilots. They marched us over to a Quonset hut and had us sit around a long table. A Major came in with a big stack of what looked like files. He began his welcoming speech: *"Gentlemen, look around you. There are 12 of you and this time next year only three of you will be going home. Three of you will be killed by Charlie, and six of you will kill yourselves in stupid accidents. Which will you be?"* He then picked up nearly 50 8X10 color photos and began passing them around. They were photos of accidents and death from aircraft crashes. There were severed limbs, bodies dismembered, viscera strung through the jungle and twisted sheet metal. Heads with the splattered gray material that had once been thinking brains and blood, lots of blood! Some of the guys puked and couldn't look. The destruction of the human body was nearly beyond comprehension. Sobering was the understatement of the day and probably the millennia.

As zombies we were given our assignments followed by a bus ride to Hotel 3 which was the vast helicopter staging area in Saigon. I had been assigned to one of the OV-1 units designated the 73rd SAC or Surveillance Airplane Company located in Vung Tau about a 40 minute flight from Saigon. I was to be flown down to Vung Tau on an OH-6. The OH-6 was a small highly maneuverable egg shaped helicopter. The pilot looked to me to be 13 years old which was saying something since I was only 19. He pulled us into a hover and got clearance out of the area. Once clear he dropped down to treetop level and headed for the South China Sea and Vung Tau. Now I had no problem with low level flying as long as it was me at the controls. But having a 13 year old dusting the trees with the skids (or the landing gear of a helicopter), especially having just come from the morbidity of aircraft accident pictures left me just a bit puckered up and to be honest pissed off. On top of that it was twilight. Not wanting to rock the boat, I casually asked the 13 year old if his low level flying was standard operating procedure. "No way man, I'm just having some fun." Trying to keep my voice under control, and being senior to him, as he was a Warrant Officer, I replied "well get this son-of-bitch up to at least a 1000 feet or you're going to be pulling my boot out of your ass when we get on the ground."

June 1969

It was dark when I arrived. None of my former classmates were there. The Officers of the 73rd were billeted in a former French Villa away from the airfield. I was driven there in a jeep and dropped off into the company area. No one was there to meet me. On the second floor I could see officers hanging out in a covered patio area. I made my way up there and found that the area was their club. It had a bar, plants and poker tables. Someone finally noticed me as an FNG (fucking new guy), took me to a room and left. I opened the door to complete darkness. It was blacker than a coal mine at midnight. I felt along the wall for a light switch and turned it on. There were two beds and one was occupied. The other bed looked to have been slept in. The guy in the occupied bed turned over and asked me who I was.

"New guy I said, I must have been given the wrong room, sorry!"

"Not the wrong room that guy is dead and won't be coming back"

Sleeping in a dead guys bunk made for a restless night. In the morning someone told me I needed to report to the airfield and the CO. I hitched a ride to the airfield. Looking for the CO, a Staff Sergeant directed me to a waiting helicopter. Once on board we took off and I asked the Sergeant where we were going. "It's all in the folder Lieutenant." I opened the folder and the first page blared out at me, **Duties of the Accident Investigating Officer.** Son of a bitch I hadn't been in country 24 hours and I was already assigned to investigate an aircraft crash. We flew out to the side of a mountain and set the Huey down. The Sergeant and I got out and were met by a Captain commanding an infantry platoon assigned to secure the site. The air was stifling, humid and it was absolutely quiet. There was the sickly sweet smell of death in the air, something I would learn to recognize for the rest of my life. The aircraft had buried one prop into a tree and the rest of the aircraft was some 400 yards away, strewn through the jungle for another 400 yards with bits and pieces of bodies and wreckage. The Sergeant handed me a body bag, looked directly into my eyes, and said "Not my job Lieutenant"

When I got back to the company area I was introduced to the CO and given Supply and Pay Officer as additional duties. Those would be jobs above and beyond my job as a pilot. I went and met the supply Sergeant an E8, which meant he had been in the service at least 6 or 7 years. One thing I learned early on was that Sergeants were the backbone of the service and to consider them just enlisted men would be at my own peril. I informed him that I knew exactly" jack shit" about supply and would appreciate his help. *"You take care of me Sergeant and I will take care of you."* That was not to mean that I would shirk the responsibility just that I would need some help getting my feet on the ground. It was to be a winning proposition. I had to account for and sign for a $150 million dollars worth of equipment.

Back at the Villa I began to meet the other pilots. A group of them were outside in our compound playing volleyball. I put on some cutoff blue jeans and went out to watch. When I emerged outside, the cackles and good natured harassment started.

"Look at that fat son of a bitch", one remarked.

"Looks like an fucking Whale", replied another.

With no sun tan, another remarked, "He's an fucking white whale".

Followed by, "He's got freckles too, so he's an fucking freckled white whale."

And that became my nickname for the rest of my time in the service, **Whale.**

Apparently, all the beer pickled pig's feet, popcorn and pickled eggs had enhanced my school girl figure, and with a lack of time in the sun, my FNG status became cemented.

I found we had other carefully constructed nicknames. We had "The Possum Fucker" named after Denny Walsh, who with his brother had run a mortuary. Denny had several pictures of dudes they had fixed up for the funeral. One had he and his brother with arms around a guy wearing a top hat and smoking a cigar There was FLUF," Fat Little Ugly Fucker", named after my classmate Bob Larvie who eventually got assigned to the 73rd. There was Terry Turner we called

"Animal" truly a man after my own heart and just as crazy. We had "Bentley", a warrant officer given the esteemed privilege of serving or going to jail for specializing in stealing Bentleys. "Rooster" the name given to an excellent Warrant Officer on his third tour who would stand up to anybody and specialized in keeping me alive! Rooster had some nasty ass looking legs thanks to an AK47 from a previous tour. Mike Blacker called"Lizard" a good friend and Captain. "Max" a good friend of Rooster also on his third tour. On a previous tour Max had been flying along in a Huey about 5000 feet when he saw his tail boom slide up next to the cockpit. The tail boom keeps a helicopter from trying to catch up to the rotor blades. At any rate the tail boom flew back to where it belonged and fell off. As Max and crew were trying to kiss their ass's goodbye the cabin of the Huey was trying to spin to catch up to the rotors. Max bottomed out the collective taking the pitch out of the main rotor and the Huey started a falling leaf descent pitching up every now and then. With Angels riding on his shoulder the Huey did a pitch up just as it contacted the top of the 200 foot jungle and stuck in the top of a tree. With the sudden stop, the transmission and main rotor ripped loose from the Huey fell to the bottom of the tree and started burning. Max and crew had a long rope and the only injury came from one of the crew who went down first to hold the rope away from the fire so the others could climb down. He rope burned his hands. "Mild mannered McBroom", a huge muscled dude with a hair trigger for anger (especially when drunk) and "Shadow" our only black pilot and a good friend. Shadow would check in on the radio at night with *"Who knows what evil lurks in the minds of men, the Shadow do!"* Additionally, we had the *Gorrilla*. That was the name I gave my roommate the first night I was assigned a room. Rick Demarche was covered in hair. I told him to stay away from fire and guys smoking.

With the sneaky Pete surveillance equipment we carried on the aircraft, most of our flying was at night. However, since I was an FNG my first flights were daytime orientation. I was shown the borders between III Corps, IV Corps and II Corps with our primary mission being in III Corps. I also learned the borders between III Corps and Cambodia, and II Corps and Laos. The entire area of operation was subdivided into artillery areas of responsibility in which one had to coordinate exactly where that area might be firing big guns, to prevent momma's little boys being blown out of the sky by our own artillery on the ground. My orientation took about a week and then I was assigned to the SLAR platoon.

The SLAR (*Side Looking Airborne Radar*) Platoon flew at night. The SLAR OV-1s had a big cigar attached to the right side of the aircraft. It was a SLAR antennae and our mission was to fly search missions back and forth on a grid in which the SLAR could pick up anything moving on the ground two miles an hour or greater and present that information on a moving slate in the cockpit much like a negative. An enlisted man watched for targets, plotted them on a map, and then called them in to one of the artillery units controlling that particular area. The theory was that, Charlie thinking he owned the night hustling along some jungle route, all of a sudden found heavy artillery raining down on his head. My job as pilot was to keep the aircraft upright and in a straight line on autopilot despite the weather.

I soon became an old FNG, and molded into the click of the unit's Officers. First night I made an appearance in our club, I noticed several guys playing poker. A Major at the table asked me if I played.

"Sure," I said, and started to go sit in.

I was grabbed by a warrant officer sitting at the bar. "Whale, take a minute, have a drink with me and I'll clue you in on whose playing." Peter had been in country nearly 5 months. He said, "Whale these guys play for big bucks and its payday poker. You can play on an IOU but if you lose it has to be paid on payday. Some of these guys couldn't play hearts, but there are about four who know the game and how to bluff, I know I lost a lot. The Major, bluffs a lot, and he's good at it. Captain Mike will call you no matter what. Gary will hold his cards really close if he has a good hand. George will lean back in his chair if he has a load of crap, and start whistling if he has a decent hand. "

He was a wealth of information so I watched for several days. When I was in the eighth grade, my older brother Chuck and his buddy Kenny taught me how to play. Chuck and Kenny were cheaters. I was pretty good at the game so they would use code signals when one of them had a good hand they would conspire with hand signals to build the pot up and then split their winnings later. I was therefore, very cognizant of most of the ways to cheat. Watching the guys play I learned a lot from their facial expressions and body language. I also learned that on especially stormy nights I would be asked what time I had to fly my mission. If it allowed time for me to fly their mission as well as mine, I would be offered money to take their mission too. Most of our missions lasted 3 and half hours. With moderate to severe turbulence accompanied by the formation of static electricity in the guise of St Elmo's fire dancing around the props, the windshield and the fuselage, a mission could be somewhat exciting. I wanted as much time in the OV-1 as I could get in order to be competitive for the airlines So, I would take their missions as well as mine and very soon I was flying a 110 hours a month. I mentioned earlier that I was also Pay Officer and Supply Officer. Pay Officer required that I pay some 180 guys in cash or MPCs, Military Pay Certificates (the funny money we used instead of American green). That situation required that I sign for tens of thousands of MPCs and in order to sign for the money, I had to count it by hand. I then had to arrange every guy's pay into the correct amount in small stacks. If I made a mistake after signing for it I had to make up the difference. Our company enlisted men were scattered throughout III Corps. In order to pay everyone I had to fly to other bases like Phu Loi, Xuan Loc, Cu Chi, Phuoc Vinh to name a few. Do you think I could use an OV-1 to fly to these bases? No friggin way I had to get checked out in our U-6 Beaver. A single engine conventional gear aircraft that you usually see mounted on floats and flying in Alaska! It took off at 60mph and flew at 80mph and landed at 40mhp. In other words it took me all day to go pay all the troops. I was greatly relieved when another FNG showed up and I could pass off that duty to him.

Emergency Leave

The Warrant Officer who had given me the inside scoop on the "poker players", got a letter from a friend back in the states, stating that he needed to get an "emergency Leave" and quietly come home. He requested and received a two week emergency leave. Once home he hired a taxi to drop him off down the street from his home. Prior to leaving for Vietnam he had purchased a new home for his wife and their two year old son. Arriving at his house he heard loud music and laughter. He crept up to a partially closed window and looked in. There on his carpet were several guys smoking dope and cooking hot dogs on a hibachi. He didn't see his wife. He went to his garage opened his gun safe took out his .12 gauge shotgun and loaded it with number 8 shells. He then let himself in his back door walked into his living room fired a round into the ceiling and stated "any of you scum buckets still in my house in 30 seconds, is a dead man" They apparently got jammed up in his front door trying to get out, so he fired a round into them and blew them out into the front yard. He then bounded up the stairs to his bedroom where he found another guy standing stark naked next to the bedroom window and his wife screaming, *"Please don't kill me."* He told the guy to get out. The guy was apparently born a few bricks short of a full load. He said, "I'll leave when she tells me to leave." Another round was fired and the guy was blown clean out the second floor window. My Warrant Officer friend called the police. When they arrived no charges were filed and his mom and dad took custody of his son. No one died!

Supply Room

One day while working in Supply a Major walked in. He was a "REMF". We called them REMFs or *rear echelon mother fuckers*. They got that under your breath nomenclature because they were the ones who got the first camouflage fatigues instead of the troops in the field. They had them immaculately tailored and wore them as a badge of honor even though they had never seen a shot fired in anger and didn't want to. They would also show up at a unit that had just had a major engagement take all the captured weapons the troops had collected as souvenirs claiming they needed them for intelligence, as if we didn't already know what type of weapons the VC and North Vietnamese used. Anyway this Major walks in Supply sporting two ivory-handled .45s and announces he is there to inspect our supply room. He then slaps his pistols to emphasize his importance and to make sure we saw the pistols. There is a huge boom and the .45 on his right side goes off and shoots him in the leg. "OMG, I think I shot myself" he says and crumples on the ground. The supply Sergeant and I with tears running down our cheeks from laughing ran to his aid as the Major had passed out. I learned later that he put himself in for a purple heart. John Kerry must have told him how to get one without actually being wounded by the enemy.

After I had been in country about a month, **FLUF (Fat Little Ugly Fucker)** my classmate showed up. Another classmate, Bob Merrill, a Captain was attached to a Cobra outfit. Captain Merrill was on his 2nd tour and really wanted to fly the OV-1 but, because he was also an instructor in Cobras he was shuffled off to a Cobra outfit. He wasn't there one night when they were mortared and he took a good deal of shrapnel in his head and was sent home. Uncle Jim likewise was shuffled off to command a Birddog outfit in IV Corps, the 121st. He was extremely disappointed but as a Major he needed the command time.

I flew SLAR for about three months and then moved over into the IR platoon. Because Infra Red was affected by clouds we had to fly under the clouds. Normal mission altitude was a 1000 feet but on bad nights it could be lower. Just like SLAR, we flew grids back and forth using the early inertial navigation system (INS) to stay on grid. Programming the INS with one number off could cause you to fly into a granite cloud. You weren't considered a *real* infra red pilot until you had *shot the gap.* With your cockpit in the clouds and only the belly of the aircraft in the clear the *gap* was a small area between Black Virgin Mountain (Nui Ba Din) and a smaller hill right next to it. A saddle, for you contour map readers. That one number mistake in programming your INS could result in the sweet smell of death hovering around what used to be momma's little boy.

During this time I got word that my high school friend Teddy had been killed. He had been in country a very short time and was flying front seat on a Cobra getting an in-country checkout. Cobras had tandem seating, one in front and one in back, the guy in front being the guns and rocket operator although they both had a set of controls. Teddy was involved in a fire fight when a Huey carrying the entire Ninth Infantry Division staff, Officers who wanted to watch the action and write themselves up for a hero badge pulled up into Teddy's Cobra. The Huey's rotor blades slapped into the 7.65 rockets attached to Teddy's Cobra and the collision caused them both to explode sending Teddy's Cobra crashing to the ground. Likewise, the Huey lost its main rotor and crashed. I flew to Saigon to check on Teddy at the morgue make sure it was really him. It was a gruesome sight. The crash was so appalling it made the front cover of Life Magazine.

Loser Buys

One night I heard another OV-1 checking in with an artillery base. The pilot, Chris, was close to Phuoc Long province where I had just completed my mission. Our call sign was "Uptight" and a number which would designate who was flying. We had a private frequency that we could BS on, so I called Chris.

"Hey Uptight 23, I'll meet you over Rang Rang and race you home. Loser buys."

"Ok Uptight 21, I'll meet you at 5000 feet."

We hooked up and started our race south to Vung Tau. Since, both aircraft were the same, neither one of us could pull ahead of the other, so we started a shallow descent to build up speed, and raced on side by side. It wasn't long before we couldn't go any lower, so we started increasing the prop rpm and pushed the throttles full forward, and ran side by side about 500 feet off the jungle at night.

"Uh, Uptight 21 you're trailing a 100 foot long flame out your right engine."

"Good try, Uptight 23, but I ain't falling for that."

I asked my TO, (technical observer), the enlisted guy manning my IR, to see if he could see anything out the right side. We had no indications in the cockpit.

"Can't see anything sir, but it looks light over there."

Chris called back, "Uptight 21, you are going to melt that wing off."

We were over the airfield and the tower called and said "Uptight 21, you appear to be on fire."

"Roger, Vung Tau, declaring an emergency!"

By declaring an emergency Uptight 23 had to take second place. I pulled the right engine back to the stops feathered it and pulled the fire handle shooting a bottle of fire retardant into the compression area. I then flipped open the speed brakes waited until I was under 150 knots, dropped the gear and started the flaps down. Did a decent landing and taxied to the revetments on one engine and shut it down. I quickly secured the ejection seat and hopped out in time to see Chris taxiing in.

"You are one crazy SOB, but I'll buy."

Lower Whale, Top Chris

Anything to get home

We had a CW3, a Warrant Officer, on his third tour. He was just shy of going ape shit, feeling this tour would cost him his life. He developed a nasty ass rash on his feet, full of pus and disgusting to look at. He was sent to Third

Field Hospital in Saigon, where, after several weeks his feet cleared up and he was sent back to us. Within another week, his feet exploded into another nasty rash. Sent back to Third Hospital again, his feet cleared up within a week. He then had his record state that he could no longer serve in Southeast Asia. He was soaking his feet in hydraulic fluid every night.

Monsoon Season

During the monsoons a company notice was put out warning the pilots to watch for snakes in the outhouse. Our outhouses had two seats side by side and underneath there were two fifty gallon barrels cut in half. At the back of the outhouse were two doors that could be opened to pull the barrels out. Then, some enlisted guy would pour JP4 (aircraft fuel), into them and fire them off to burn up the political donations deposited. Most of us always wore our underwear and side arms to go to the john. With wild hairs crawling up my butt I got a long switch and waited behind the john until I saw one of the pilots come out to make his deposit. I would then open the rear door and when I saw his ass sit down, I would tickle it with the switch and hiss. It is amazing how fast your legs can tear military underwear in two.

One day "Possum Fucker" was giving an FNG a checkout ride. They were low leveling out in the "Rung Sac "area of western III Corps when a huge crane, as in bird, lifted off from the grass and they hit it. It came through the pilot's little bubble window on the side. This is a major reason that you trim an aircraft to zoom up when low leveling. Possum Fucker had shit and intestines hanging off his mike, blood all over the place and feathers. When he got back to base he smelled worse than a greasy dog turd in the hot sun that had just been stepped in.

Radios

While flying one night I realized that there was a HF or High Frequency radio in the aircraft. We never used them so I turned it on. Playing with the frequencies I heard ham radio operators talking. I decided to try and talk to one of them and came up with the call sign" Snoopy 33 Alfa Victor airmobile".

After several tries a guy answered me from Oregon somewhere. I asked him if he could patch me through to my dad and he readily agreed. Next thing I know I am talking to my dad while flying in Vietnam.

War No Problem On Phone Calls

The loudjangling of the telephone broke the silence of the night and brought Dr. Charles D. Boyd tumbling from his bed in sleepy response. He glanced at his wrist watch. It was 1 a.m., Sunday.

"Dr. Boyd? This is Ray Carnay in Eugene, Ore. I'm a ham and I've got a man on short wave who wants to talk to you," announced the voice on the phone. "Hold it a minute. I'll hook you in."

Dr. Boyd held the line while the phone call was "patched" through the short wave and soon a familiar voice came sparking through.

"Hey, Dad. This is Bob. I'm flying high altitude over Vietnam on a combat mission. Everything otherwise fine here and I presume it is the same with you and mom. But I'm calling to find out whether you can tell me where Gary is now."

Bob and Gary are sons of Dr. and Mrs. Boyd.

Bob is Capt. Robert D. Boyd of the Army Air Force. For nine months he has been flying a Mohawk plane in surveillance over ground troop action. He is 23, a Houston native and 1965 graduate of Jones High School.

After three semesters at University of Houston, he joined the Army and went through Officer Candidate School to get his commission. He is married to the former Paula Ferguson, now living with her parents, Mr. and Mrs. William B. Ferguson Jr., of 7526 Dixie.

Gary is 21 and a 1966 graduate of Jones High School. He attended San Jacinto Junior College before joining the Navy and is now a fire control officer on a destroyer in the Gulf of Tonkin.

His wife, Becky, is awaiting his return at the home of her parents, Mr. and Mrs. Robert T. Sivers, 5945 Willow Glen. Gary is now in his third year in the Navy.

"He and Bob haven't been able to get together over there yet," said Dr. Boyd.

His third son, Bryant, 25, only recently returned from Korea where he served as a lieutenant in the Army. Also a Jones High School graduate, he attended Texas Lutheran College for two years before enlisting.

He is now back at Texas Lutheran with his wife, the former Ann Dunford of Houston.

"I wasn't really surprised over the call," said Dr. Boyd. "Bob has done this twice before when he goes on those high altitude missions. Hams are always ready to relay the message.

"I've got mixed emotions about this dad-burned war. But I'm proud of these three boys for doing their duty as they feel they should."

FALL 1969

By fall of 1969 enough new guys had arrived that I was able to pass off Supply and Pay Officer to one of them. I then got Physical Security Officer for our side of the base. I had to supervise bulldozing the perimeter and making sure the observation bunkers were constructed to specs. I also got to put in new Claymore mines and run the detonator wires to the bunkers. Most of the troops didn't like to sit in the bunkers, as "Charlie" (the enemy), was very good at targeting them with B40s, a shape charged bazooka. The Army didn't like to broadcast it but there was also a big drug problem in Vietnam. Walking the rounds when I was on guard duty, I could see the red tips of cigarettes flare up and I never knew what kind they might be. Not wanting to get killed by a stoned enlisted guy, I would sing or whistle when approaching. The gooks, my non politically correct word for them at the time, could make a pack of Marlboros complete with filters and cellophane that looked perfect. However, the cigarettes had the most potent grass you could imagine laced with heroin. I heard of entire platoons wiped out due to their LPs or their OPs (listening posts, or observation posts), stoned to the gills while "Charlie" snuck in and turned their Claymores around.

This brings up an important point. The VC and the North Vietnamese were called all kinds of names from Americans. Slant eyes, gooks, fish heads and cowards. However, they were creative little fuckers. They used camouflage to great advantage. They could dig up and rig a dud bomb with trip wires. They would take our discarded c-rations and fashion a propeller on a wire that would use the down draft from hovering helicopters to fly upward and discharge a dud bomb. They knew our tactics and would place punji sticks in ditches exactly where our troops would dive to avoid their programmed mortar attack. The punji sticks were covered with their own shit and once impaled our troops would get vicious infections, if not die. Our SOG troops (special operators who went out in 6 to 7 man groups to gather intel) as well as our LRRP troops were hunted with dogs. Hard to cover a scent from dogs! They were excellent tunnel builders. I highly recommend you read the "Tunnels of Cu Chi". After the war it was discovered that they had built an entire city under the 25th Infantry Division's base at Cu Chi. They had hospitals, classrooms, sleeping areas, and a myriad of ingress and egress tunnels. Truly amazing!

Uncle Jim's 221st Birddog Company

I flew down to see Uncle Jim one day. He was located on a little strip in IV Corps. I called him on the radio and said "Hey Uncle Jim, be at your house in 15 minutes. Would you like to have a picture of your company with the nose camera on this Hawk?"

"You bet, let me call a formation, and call me when you are in the area. I will have them formed up in front of the hanger."

When I got down to his company he had them four deep in a formation in front of his maintenance hangar. I started at about 1500 feet and started a dive right at them. I passed over his hanger with the rotating beacon on the bottom of the aircraft barely missing the roof and then pulled up as I flew past.

"Son of a bitch Whale, you nearly took the top off my hanger"

"Sorry Uncle Jim didn't mean to scare you. I'll get the photo shop to print me up some copies and get them to you."

When I got the pictures back there was an absolutely clear picture of Uncle Jim and his company. On the last row of enlisted troops was a guy in the process of trying to run. I was doing 275 knots when I went by so maybe I cut it a little close.

Me Before the Mustache Grew back

C Day Conversion

Believe it or not, every so often without warning, the Army would call a "C Day Conversion." Everything in the war stopped and you had to turn your Military Pay Certificates in for new ones of a different color. The reason was the black market that developed with the Vietnamese. A gook would offer you $50,000 if you would trade in his $60,000 dollars for the new colored currency. Most of the gook's money came from whore houses, dope and drinks from his bar. If you tried to turn in that amount of money, you did so at your own peril. The Army took a very dim view of such a transaction. At any rate, the war ground to a halt. You didn't go flying, you didn't leave the base, and nothing other than money transferred on that day. Since that was the program, we decided we might as well drink the day away. Twelve of us drank ten bottles of Mateus wine. I will never forget that day. They say every time you get drunk you lose a million brain cells. That left me with three, and two of those were highly questionable. The next evening I heard guys offer a $1000 for someone to take their mission. Hurt city was the understatement of the day.

Relaxation

Whenever pilots get together, it is evitable that whiskey, porn and bullshit abound. The only porn we had was a black and white film with no sound. I was elected to narrate the film. We called it the Phantom Fucker film. I think I narrated it at least 20 times.

We also had a copy of the Beatles "Yellow Submarine". I was also the projector guy. One night we watched it forward three times and then were in the process of watching it backwards, when those of us who could walk, decided it would be a cool idea to take the little chutes from night time flares, tie stuff to them and throw them off the roof. We had great fun until we ran out of stuff to tie to them and started on the furniture. Chairs, bedside desks, you name it. Drunk on our butts, Animal was about to throw something off when he fell through the roof. He fell through the third floor, the second floor and came to rest next to a full Colonel, (a woman), who was visiting. I don't think "hiya" covered it. In the confusion Animal jumped up hauled ass out of the room and then jumped in bed with Mild Mannered McBroom, pulling the covers up. That Colonel could have eaten broken glass and nails, she was so pissed, but she never caught anyone.

When Animal was ready to DEROS (date to return from overseas), we had a tradition for the pilots. We would get a big magnum of Champagne. All the friends of the pilot would gather on the flight line. The departing pilot would open the Champagne and pour everyone gathered a drink. Anything left, the pilot had to chug. Animal had lots of friends but was still hung over from the previous night.

I've seen guys dead three days that looked better. He was to fly a Mohawk to Saigon to catch his "freedom bird". He couldn't even climb up the side of the aircraft to get in his ejection seat. The crew chiefs hauled his ass up and into the aircraft. Once there, the crew chiefs helped him start the engines and make sure he had his hatch locked. While he was doing this, I was to do a high speed low pass. The CO had given me direct orders not to do any aerobatics. What the hell were they going to do, send me to Vietnam? So, down the airfield 10 feet off the ground with balls to the wall, I over flew Animal and pulled up doing a series of rolls. Animal in the meantime, was trying to synchronize his eyes to his brain. His eyes looked like those little steel balls that you try to tilt into slots on a game.

Drinking with the Aussies

There was an Australian base on top of a mountain just to the southwest of Vung Tau. One night we got a ¾ ton truck and drove up there. The Aussies are not pussies and don't ever let anyone tell you different. We started a drinking game with them. Four guys would get on their knees on each side of a bar stool. Beers, Aussie beers, something like 30% alcohol compared to our 6%, were placed on top of the bar stools. When the signal was given, guys would start chugging and when they were finished they had to put the empty beer can on their head and stand up. Let me just say that the Aussies were pros and they could finish four beers while our guys were still working on the first. As if that were not enough, we started playing 21. You take five dice and each guy around the table gets to roll once. Each time an ace (or a one) came up, that was one number. When, we got to the eleventh ace, it was taken out of play leaving four dice. Whoever rolled the fifteenth ace got to name the drink? Such things as scotch, milk, bourbon, triple sec, etc. the most God awful combination you could come up with. Each time an ace was rolled after that, it was taken out of the game, until the guy who rolled the 21st ace had to drink the nasty combination. Everybody then began to chant "down—down- down, drunk last night, drunk the night before, gonna get drunk tonight, like I never been drunk before." After several hours of this kind of macho bullshit we called it a night. I was outside leaving a leak and watching the distant lights of Vung Tau going round and round, when our guys left the top of the mountain. I walked, well, ok staggered to the locked front gate and told the Aussie sergeant to let me out. Reluctant to do so, I apparently pulled rank and started off down the mountain to make the five mile journey back to base. Walking along I kept hearing sounds in the jungle, probably rats, but who knew. So I started singing "You can't roller skate in a buffalo heard". My muddled thinking was that the gooks wouldn't shoot an idiot. At any rate, at some point, realizing my brain would only function for awhile, I decided to just head straight for Vung Tau, instead of going round and round the mountain on the road. That meant I had to go straight through the jungle. Rats, snakes, and gooks be damned. The next morning they found me passed out in the hall, my hand on my door knob, and my fatigues ripped to shreds. Later, retracing my journey, the Aussies found that a drunken idiot had traversed three mine fields and three areas of concertina wire proving once again that God protects drunks and fools.

NSA

Another night we decided to go across our airfield and drink with the NSA guys. These guys flew the U-21, a military version of the King air. It was loaded with antennas and they basically flew round and round in a holding pattern and listened. Walking into their bar I was immediately accosted by a Major who informed me that I couldn't drink in their bar without first stopping the ceiling fan with my head. It was a huge metal fan and it was turned on high. I was about to turn around and leave, when the Major offered to show me how it was done. He jumped on a barstool and slowly put his head into the fan blades until they stopped. Quick note here, the fan was blowing the air down, so by going slow the blades just slapped his head until he brought them to a stop. I figured if that ball headed fucker could do it I could, so not to be outdone and having just left our bar I climbed on the stool and just stuck my head in the blades. I was knocked to the floor with a nice deep gash in the side of my head. Bleeding profusely I got a standing ovation and was allowed to drink with them. What a fucking idiot! A perfect example of bravado, alcohol and stupidity.

Christmas 1969

Nearing Christmas of 1969, I was assigned AOD of the airfield at Vung Tau. AOD was "Airfield Officer of the Day". Your job was to check the security and the guards and monitor the tower. Around ten at night two Air force enlisted crew chiefs decided that they would go for a joy ride in a Cessna push pull spotter plane, an 02. The push pull was the result of a prop on the front and a prop on the rear of the aircraft. As crew chiefs they knew how to start and taxi the aircraft. Flying it was a different matter. I was called to the tower when their flight became known. They were panicking as they were a little drunk and the wind was blowing creating a crosswind on the runway. They made three approaches but at the last minute they would pull up and go around. I tried to talk them down by remaining calm and guaranteeing them they could make it," just do what I say". They were doing great until just at touch down they caught a gust of wind and panicked. They pulled abruptly up, stalled and came down on the nose, and burst into flames. When you hear, "burned beyond recognition", it means you just turned into a charcoal briquette.

LRRP

During this time while paying the troops at Phu Loi, I met one of my class mates from Infantry OCS. He was with a LRRP (Long Range Recon Patrol) group was going up near Song Be to have dinner with the Montagnards. They asked me if I wanted to go. Well does a frog bump his ass when he jumps? The Montagnards were a tribe of people who were usually referred to as hill people. They were extremely tough little fuckers and fought hard. They were experts with a cross bow. The Secret SOG guys used them, as well as Special Forces. We landed in a Huey just outside their village and the LRRP guys led us over to an old Poppa Son. It's a good thing the women looked like him because he looked like he had just crawled through a yard of dog crap, and ate some on the way. But boy could he smile. He seemed to take an interest in me, or maybe I was set up. We sat around this fire pit and he was telling his tales as the embers died down. *(I couldn't understand a thing he was saying)* Then, they brought over this table with a hole in the middle and little holes along the edges of this hole. On some signal from the old poppa son, a frigging monkey was brought over. They had cut off its head placed it in the middle of that hole and shoved bamboo pieces through the little holes and started to bar b que the head on the spot. The burning hair smelled like I figured the old poppa son's breath must smell. I screwed up, and must have made a face of disgust. Poppa Son looks at the LRRP guys and says "Dai Wie baby son" (which meant the Captain is a pussy) or something to that effect, and laughed like crazy. I smiled back and said" tell poppa son he smells like the south end of a north bound donkey". He got a great laugh out of that, and signaled about the monkey head. Another guy comes over and with a little hammer and a machete cuts the top of the monkey's head off revealing the smoking brain. Poppa son gives me some kind of chop sticks and indicates I should eat. Not to let the little troll get the upper hand, I get a big bite looking him right in the eyes and shove it in my mouth. You would have thought I just married his ugly sister. He clapped his hands and nodded approval. Actually, it wasn't all that bad, but I think I will get naked and howl at the moon before I try it again. Don't hold your breath on that account. My buddy looks at me and says now you're in for it. Next thing I know they have a LIVE frigging cobra brought over. They removed the table and all the American guys scooted back a few inches. Poppa son gestures to one of his guys who grabs the snake and stretches it out from head to tail. The guy then cuts a hole underneath the neck and pulls out its poison sack, and throws the rest away. Poppa son has some kind of drink delivered (I later learn is their equivalent of liquor). With a big show he drops the sack in the drink and chugs it down. This has become a contest. Crap, I would rather have married his ugly sister. A clap of his hands and another cobra appears. What the hell, do these guys grow cobras! Another drink is poured, and the sack dropped in it. With that little fucker smiling like a baboon eating banana goo he shoves it toward me. Well, if that little troll could do it, I can too. I chug it down. Ten seconds later I see the Fourth of July fireworks show. My skin tingles my nose runs, my eyes water, I think I'm having a heart attack, and I hear "Whale, you alright?" I later learn that if you have any cut or a stomach ulcer, you get a free ride to the promise land, and at this point in my life I may turn into a briquette.

As with my friend Cunniligus 29, (more about him later) I rode front seat gunner on a cobra with a friend from Phu Loi. A real adrenalin rush and I loved it. One day they asked if I wanted to fly door gunner on one of their company's Hueys. I parked my OV-1 at Phu Loi and went with them, figuring I could make an excuse later. They were going to be flying supplies up in the Straight Edge woods area and would be covered by their Cobras. We were also taking some replacement gooks up that were working with American advisors. After so many helicopters were downed by either hand grenades or turncoats the rule was when you leave the helicopter don't turn around or we would shoot you. We sat down just outside the wire of their camp to let the gooks off and unload the supplies. One gook ran out about 15 feet turned around and shot at me. It missed me but hit the crew chief on the other side of the Huey. I was so surprised I hesitated, a heartbeat and then shot him with a burst from my M60. I knocked him down but he was crawling toward his M16. Pissed off I jumped out of the Huey with my knife and ran to him before he could get to his rifle. He saw me coming and had his knife out. I had hit him in his legs. As I jumped on him his knife sliced a small area of my ribs. I managed to quickly cut his throat, a scene I will always remember as cutting someone's throat results in a monumental spray of blood. I got drenched and can still smell that blood today. The crew chief survived but I gave up flying with them.

Moving to Long Thanh

Our company was ordered to leave Vung Tau and move some 40 miles up into a rubber plantation called Long Thanh. I was designated Moving Officer. As I said earlier the company was worth some $150 million dollars, the majority of which was contained in the aircraft and the test equipment necessary to keep the sneaky Pete stuff working. Most of the move went according to plan, but one tractor trailer carrying about ten million dollars worth of test equipment managed to fall off the side of narrow road and turned over. Our CO was frantic as night was coming and the tide which normally penetrated this part of the Rung Sac area would ruin the test equipment. I told him to take the rest of the company and I would stay with the trailer until equipment could come and pull it back up on the road. So he left me with one enlisted man, an M60 machine gun, and my side arm. It's amazing how alone and vulnerable you feel out in no man's land. I got on the radio and called "Rooster". He was not only an OV-1 pilot, but he was also a Cobra helicopter instructor and Huey pilot. Rooster managed to get the loan of a Cobra and flew cover for me. At one point we were screwing around and I was bugging him to buzz me. After several passes with me deriding him like "Is that the best you can do?" He came around and put both skids on either side of my head while I was standing on the trailer. Son of a bitch that was close.

Long Thanh

David(Cunnilingus 29) and Whale

While I was in Long Thanh I learned that my high school buddy David was next door at the Bear Cat base flying Huey's with the 335th. His mission was to fly the South Vietnamese troops into and out of IV Corps. This was part of Nixon's Vietnamization program, making the Vietnamese take over the war in IV Corps. Americans could fly there but only Vietnamese troops could be on the ground. I asked David if I could fly door gunner for him if I got a day off. He said absolutely, door gunners only had an expected life span of six weeks. As with us, the 335th had their nicknames too.

David's was "Cunnilingus 29". I'm sure the politically correct group of cowards we have today would have had a heart attack. These Huey drivers started their Hueys at 5:00am in the morning and didn't shut them down until dark. Fueling was what we called "hot refueling." The pilot stayed in the aircraft to control the rotors and everyone else got out while they fueled the aircraft as it was running. We flew the South Vietnamese troops in and out of what they called a "clover leaf" search and destroy missions. Each Vietnamese platoon would hit the ground and spread out into one blade of a clover leaf and then return back to where we dropped them off. The movies I have of these missions show grinning Vietnamese troops with no shoes, grenades hanging everywhere, and rusty rifles. In fact so many Hueys were brought down from grenades going off, that David made me check every gook and make sure we had the firing pin taped down with electric tape. Going in to a hot LZ (landing zone) the Hueys formed up in a line. That way, if one got shot down, the others could slide off to either side and take off. We dropped off a company one time for their search and destroy, and unable to get them back on the radio for pick up, we flew back to the LZ and found them mutilated and hanging in the trees. All their weapons, clothes and radios were gone.

Scroungers

We had no club or bar in Long Thanh so we decided to build one. We had an old building we could use but it was screened in and would be very hot. I called David and told him I needed a pallet of plywood. He managed to snag a Huey and we flew to Saigon into the P G and E compound (Pacific Gas and Electric). We scouted their compound and found the plywood back in a far corner, (far corner being at the back of some 30 acres) which couldn't be seen from the front. It was a huge compound. David flew in and we sling loaded a huge pallet of plywood flying away north to outwit the MPs. David dropped it off behind our hanger and I set to work sanding off the stamps that were on each piece of plywood. We painted each piece and set to work building our club. The club was basically a big L-shaped building. We put the plywood on the walls. We stole a big freezer, an air conditioner, and we built a stage. We were hardly finished when the MPs showed up and asked to see our club. They went over it with a fine tooth comb looking for the tell tale stamps. Finding none they left. I managed to get an old ejection seat from one of the crashes and mounted it on the corner inside the club. Then, I got the business end of our control stick also from a wrecked aircraft and mounted it on a commode plunger we stole from the Air Force. Mounted in the floor it could move like a real control stick. When guys got drunk and wanted to tell a flying story we made them put on a harness, get into the ejection seat, put their hand on the stick, and begin their heroic story. We would all stand around and if we didn't like their story, everyone would piss on the story teller.

I managed to get a group of Philippine singers, (all women), to host our first opening. With the luck of the draw I got the first mission that night. A little pissed, I did a mission brief and took off. I called the tower and asked for a low pass over the "Hawks Nest". I went up to two thousand feet and made a diving run on the club leveling out just over the roof. I heard that the guys thought the aircraft was crashing. Later that night, "Rooster" came into my hooch and told me to get up and come with him. I was a commissioned officer, and "Rooster" was a warrant but I respected him so I jumped up and followed him. He took me to the side of the mess hall, and there stuck through the side was the cowling to one of my engines. It had somehow come off on my high speed pass.

"You better get that out of there and the side patched up before the old man sees it"

He helped me get it out of the side of the mess hall and replace the siding. Then, he helped me take it to the maintenance hangar run over it a couple of times with a dozer and throw it in a trash pile.

Vertigo Crash Site

Another of our pilots takes an evening mission during the monsoons. He developed vertigo, lost control of the aircraft, swore he told the TO(technical observer) to eject as he ejected. Anyone can get vertigo but the TO is your obligation. They found the aircraft completely destroyed in a sixty foot wide by 30 foot deep hole. The pilot had ejected, they found his chute and they had recovered him. They couldn't find the TO, they found his chute near the crater but couldn't figure out if he was captured. That didn't make sense though, as the pilot wasn't captured. An enlisted man was walking around the crater and stepped on a boot.

"Would you look at this, some dumb ass lost a boot out here in the middle of nowhere"

A recovery team member went over and ran his hand under the boot and found a leg. The TO had ejected seconds before impact, he got seat separation just before he hit the ground. The incident created trust issues within the pilot and TO group. The only positive thing, if you could call it positive, was that the TO never felt a thing. However, it bugged me for a long time.

Visual Platoon

I had by this time transferred to the Visual Platoon. We flew during the day and checked trails and the country side for signs of recent activity. I usually flew up north in III Corps and along the border with Cambodia and Laos. I liked to fly alone as I figured if I got shot down I could take care of myself better than taking care of an enlisted man too. The border region with Cambodia and Laos was unusually full of recent activity every day. What they called the Ho Chi Minh trail ran along that border and then branched into III Corps. I was flying down the border in an area we called the Fish Hook, when I noticed two bodies on a trail. Not knowing what side they belonged too, as well as knowing the SOG teams operated in the region I decided that I would try to use the nose camera to get a close up picture. The trail the bodies were on ran perpendicular to the Cambodian border, and the trees were very tall. My first pass was done at 250 knots but was too fast and there was a high tree right before the bodies. I stayed low level and banked hard left before crossing into Cambodia. You were never suppose to fly or walk the same route twice, but it was the only way I could see the bodies, so I made another pass at tree top level at 200 knots. That one wasn't good enough either, so again I banked hard left and came around again. This time, at 150 knots, I lowered the landing gear, put down full flaps, opened the speed brakes and tried to knife edge myself between that tree then quickly level out and get some pictures. The picture shows the tree higher than I was but a nice picture of the bodies. I immediately pulled up the landing gear, put the speed brakes back in, increased the power and was reaching for the flaps as I started my hard left turn to avoid the border. As I leveled off about 100 feet off the ground, I noticed movement out the right side. A huge bamboo cover was being raised exposing a quad .51 caliber machine gun. I knew if I pulled up I would slow down and they would have me, so I slammed the throttles full forward increased the propeller pitch and dove down to 25 feet to try and increase speed. The quad fifty was leading the aircraft for a 250 knot speed and I was just barely increasing to 200 knots. I was also over a meadow of sorts about 10 acres. Watching the fifty's big green basket ball size tracers closing in on me, I was inadvertently banking left. All of a sudden I heard the distinctive sound of AK47s and looking down and left I saw about 75 North Vietnamese troops emerging from the trees and all shooting at me. I took a powerful hit from the right that nearly rolled the aircraft upside down and a bunch of small arms fire hit the aircraft like gravel on a dirt road. I reached the end of the meadow and stayed low over the trees and started checking the aircraft. Everything seemed to be okay so I started climbing and called a mayday. An OV10 Bronco, a twin boom tandem

River border with Cambodia and open Field I flew across at 25' after nose camera pictures of the unknown bodies

Seat, Air force close air support aircraft was nearby and flew over to me.

I said "Hey buddy I think I took a big hit on the right hand side. Can you look me over?"

"Sure thing, hang on a moment."

He then flew up beside me on the right, and then slid underneath me onto the left side.

"Don't see a thing. I'll check the top."

"Oh buddy, I suggest you head for the barn. Your smoking and you have big holes in your fuselage"

"Thank you, but do you have any ordinance on you?"

"Yep, I have about 36 Willy Pete rockets on Board."

Willy Pete was code for white phosphorous. If you got any on you, it would burn until you cut it out. I explained what had just transpired and asked him if he was willing to unload on the Quad fifty and the tree line from which the troops had emerged. I told him I would fly into Cambodia then fly over the quad fifty perpendicularly, and across the tree line. When I got over the quad fifty, I would radio, "now." He could then loiter up high to the north and then unload on the area.

"I'll do it if you got the balls."

"Ok done, salvo the whole load into the tree line."

Like I said, you can't hear an OV-1 until it passes, so over flying the quad fifty was little risk, and the troops would be surprised as well. That was my plan and I would execute it by staying low level until I was lined up. That way no one could see what I was up too. It worked great and afterward I headed for home. When I got back to Long Thanh, everyone came out to see the damage to the aircraft. The aircraft had taken a fifty caliber round through the last bulkhead taking out some radios, splitting the bulkhead destroying a battery and nearly both cables that ran through that bulkhead to the elevator. One was completely into and the other had only one strand of the cable left and there I was pulling G's on that sliver of cable. I was flying a brand new OV-1 "A" model that had dual controls and one "Rooster" used to give check rides. The aircraft had to be sent back to the states and my friend "Rooster" was pissed at me for a long time. Rooster probably never knew how bad I felt when he chewed my ass. He was an excellent pilot who I truly admired. After the fan fare and pictures I retired to my hooch where I sat down and started shaking. I relived the whole flight and after seeing the damage realized just how close I had come to being a number on a wall. It was very sobering.

North Vietnamese Troops

Following the attack up near the Fish Hook, I began to spend a lot of time up on that part of the border, as Command kept denying there were any North Vietnamese Regulars in that part of Cambodia. I would fly along our side of the border and could see them moving down the Ho Chi Minh trail. They would wave at m as they knew Americans were too stupid to fire on them and we were not supposed to cross the border. It was frustrating and irritating that Westmorland couldn't see the forest for the trees. I was flying down our side of the Ho Chi Minh Trail when I spotted a huge mechanized convoy of North Vietnamese Regulars brazenly coming down the trail. I picked landmarks, dropped to the nap of the earth, crossed the border, came up out of a valley, and headed toward the convoy at tree top level. As I caught up to the trailing element I used the nose camera to take pictures. What I got was a North Vietnamese soldier asleep on a quad .51 caliber machine gun. I immediately banked left down into a valley and got the hell out of there.

Landing back in Long Thanh the photo imaging guys developed the film and I had a perfect picture of that North Vietnamese Soldier asleep on his machine gun. As I said before, no good deed goes unpunished, and the brass confiscated the picture. Probably hanging on some REMF's den today!

Bentley, my jailbird escapee due to a beneficial judge's "go in the service or go to jail", did not want to be out done.

So, the next day he decided to go get a picture of a .51 caliber machine gun nest that we were all aware of. Our "rules of engagement" stated that we were not allowed to fly below 1500 feet in the vicinity of known .51 caliber guns. Bentley came back later, with a line of bullet holes 3" apart all down the side of his aircraft. He apparently, did not see the gook standing in the jungle with an AK47, prior to his low level photo pass. We got our asses chewed but by that time in my tour I didn't give a rat's ass.

Another time, we got reports that there was a suspected POW camp up in Long Khanh province. The camp was supposedly in a valley between two big hills, and the valley was cloaked in low hanging fog. The commandant of Third corps wanted photographic proof before he would send in a rescue party. I volunteered. The mission called for pin point navigation as I would have to let down into the valley through the clouds. Any mistake and I would be splattered. I used a combination of time and distance and inertial navigation. I flew by myself. I found the camp but the gooks had already abandoned it.

We got reports that there were Migs in Cambodia flying into and out of Phnom Penh. So with David flying with me, we flew up to the airport there. I flew up at 10,000 feet mapped out an approach, picked out guide lines and then we dove down and low leveled across the entire length of the runway. We saw no Migs but David did get a great picture of tracers crossing the airfield hoping we would run into them. Not one touched us.

David invited me to come over to Bear Cat and play poker with the other Warrant Officers. I had made Captain in February and only had four months to DEROS. (Date to rotate overseas) David agreed to pick me up in his Huey and fly me over as it was about a mile through the jungle to get to

Bear Cat. We started playing poker and I introduced the guys to "flaming blue Mimi's". It was a shot of Drambuie in a shot glass that you set on fire and had to drink while it was burning then blow it out and turn it upside down, if more than three drops came out, you had to drink another one. I was a master at drinking those having learned to breathe out my nose to keep the flames away from my mustache and just pour the drink down my throat. There were some tricks too, you didn't let it burn too long or your lips would melt to the hot shot glass. You also didn't try to throw it down or you would end up blue flames all over your face. Several Warrants learned the hard way. We started playing "in between". A game in which everybody put in $20 dollars for ante, and then you were dealt two cards face up. The idea was to draw another card that was between your two cards. The problem was the rules. In order to build the pot, the guys decided that, if you had a Jack and a two and you drew another jack or a two, you had to double the pot. If you got a three or a Queen, cards outside your two cards, you had to equal the pot. The idea was to either say "Pot it" which meant you were so sure you would get a card between your two that you were betting the entire pot on doing so; or, you had the choice of betting just part of the pot, or just passing. If you bet just part of the pot and won, you could take out of the pot what you had bet. After hours of playing and getting completely hosed, I was dealt a 3 and a 5. There was probably $7000 in the pot and I said "Just Pot it". I drew a 4 and won. Next thing I know, I woke up in the drainage ditch running through our base. I was cold, muddy, hung over and pissed. I noticed written on my hand," I Owe U $785, David." I also noticed I had a huge wad of MPCs in my pockets. When I sobered up I called David and asked about the $785.

"Brother that is null and void, because I saved your ass."

"What are you talking about?"

"Well the guys were so pissed off that you won that last hand they wanted to throw you out of the helicopter into the jungle. You took everyone's pay for the month. Consider the $785 a service fee."

What David didn't tell me at the time, was that he and the other warrants would have drinks in front of them, but that was just a decoy. Being plastered I didn't notice several of the guys get up, allegedly to go leave a leak, but in reality to go light up one of "Charlie's Marlboros". They would be bright eyed and bushy tailed in the morning while I was making sure I had at least one round to kill myself.

The Good Life and Idiots

David and I had been good friends since high school. We were both in flight school at Fort Rucker for a time. Housing for married couples was in trailers. My trailer and David's trailer were catty cornered to each other. I went to his trailer one afternoon and banged on his door. His car was there but no one came for several minutes. I was about to leave when his wife opened the door. She was foaming at the mouth and yawning as though she had just woken up. She said David would be there in a minute. When David came to the door he was grinning like a baboon eating banana goo. He said nothing just opened his house coat and his groin was covered in cool whip. Foaming at the mouth and napping time, right!

David was hot refueling his Huey down in IV corps. With hot refueling the Hueys are lined up in a straight line cockpit to tail. The engines are still running and the rotor blades still turning. The South Vietnamese troops are lined up to one side of the Hueys waiting to board after the refueling. David would stay in the cockpit holding the cyclic (control stick) to make sure a gust of wind wouldn't flap the rotor blades down and ruin your whole day. I and the other crew had to stand outside. It was meant to protect us from a possible fire. The Vietnamese troops were each assigned a Huey to board. We called them "Chalks". With a main rotor turning the tail rotor is spinning ten times as fast. One of the Vietnamese decided he wanted to get on board. He dashed between David's Huey and the one behind completely forgetting about the tail rotor. He ran right into it and it split his head right down to his neck in two halves. One of his buddies saw him fall and immediately ran to his aid only to make the same mistake. David felt the vibration and was trying to shut down when the third Vietnamese ran to help the other two and suffered the same fate. Unbelievable! Both of those helicopter rotors can cut down a 6" tree.

Flying along the border of III Corps and IV Corps I heard a Mayday from a Bronco aircraft. The bronco was a twin turbo engine aircraft that the Navy and the Air Force flew. It had two ejection seats and a twin boom tail, along with rockets. It was used for surveillance and marking targets. By the time I got to their position they had ejected and were floating toward the ground. A Huey pilot had also arrived and in his hurry to pick them up he maneuvered toward them before they had released their chutes. The rotor blades sucked the two parachutes along with the pilots up into his rotor blades and decapitated both of them.

Around March of 1970, we got a new kid. His name was Mark Wilson. He was the epitome of an FNG. I liked him immediately. FLUF and I had him move in with us and I proceeded to corrupt him. His first experience with the Whale nearly killed him. I got him so drunk he was physically ill for three days. Right after I went home Mark was checking out a Captain on a SLAR mission. They had an unsafe right main gear light but after checking with the tower that it was down they landed and taxied to the company area. Before Mark could shut it down, the Captain jumped out of his seat and walked back to look at the right main gear. That in itself was amazing because if you were to lean way out of your seat you could touch the spinning 10 foot diameter props. Then without thinking, the Captain walked back toward the front of the aircraft and right through the prop. Mark wound up with brain matter, tissue and blood thrown into the cockpit and all over him. Mark was devastated and to this day has nasty nightmares.

Sight Seeing

Our visual Platoon leader George and I decided to fly up north one day to see where he had operated as a platoon leader on his first tour. We took turns flying the nap of the earth all the way. I have great movies of flying the South China Sea four feet off the water. We flew all the way up to Da Nang, refueled and headed further north into the mountains George had operated in. We crossed over to the Laotian border and flew next to the Ho Chi Minh trail back down over Dak To and down to the middle of III Corps and came home. It took us most of the day. The area George operated in had radar controlled .23s, .88s and .51s. However, flying low level we never took a round which was beneficial as we hadn't told a soul where we were going. *Stupid!*

MP's

I had to drive up to Saigon because no Hawks were available for me to fly. As I passed Bien Hoa, I could see a good number of "REMFs" playing tennis dressed in tennis whites, behind a nice hurricane fence. I was becoming more and more agitated at the insanity of the war and the corruption. On my way back, I stopped the jeep I was driving and got out to take pictures of these fucking REMFs. Next thing I know, I was slammed against the fence, my camera ripped out of my hands, opened, and the film unrolled on the ground. I was then released, and as I turned around, I came face to face with two E-5 Sergeant MPs, grinning.

"Geez guys, what the hell".

"We thought you might be a gook sniper."

I was so pissed off I could have killed them but I played dumb.

"Well you guys sure scared the shit out of me."

"I'll bet we did" and they started laughing. Apparently being big guys and MPs they were used to people cow towing to them. Unfortunately I failed cow towing. Before they knew what was happening I hit one in the throat as hard as I could and kneed the other in the balls. I yanked out my .44 magnum which I had sent to me, cocked it and while one gasped and the other was turning blue, I relieved them of their weapons and hand cuffs.

"You boys seemed to have failed stupid training, you can't manhandle an officer. Be kind enough to handcuff one of your hands to the others ankle and vice versa but first hand me your IDs. Just for fun, I will keep these and if I ever see or hear of either of you again next time you go to the john or take shower watch out for flying grenades or a flying cobra wrapped around your neck. I know lots of guys who would like to take out an MP. You'll find your .45s a half mile down the road."

I then took an alternate route to Long Thanh. I asked for the early mission and made sure the belly camera was loaded. Then, I flew back over the REMFs, and took their picture. I returned back to base and had the II (imagery interpretation section) make me a hundred copies. Next day I flew over Bien Hoa and Saigon and dropped the photos out.

Captain White

Our CO was approached by a Navy Major, who asked for permission to fly with one of our pilots down into IV Corps. It was pretty hush hush as this particular Major was in charge of and knew all of the Operations and current Missions being planned and executed by the U.S. Navy. They got shot down. When they didn't return a rescue mission was formed. With air cover and troops they went back into the area. This was not allowed under the Nixon Vietnamese takeover agreement. WTF, they did it anyway. They found two ejections seats and two sets of boot prints running down the beach with lots of barefooted prints right behind them. They were both captured. The Major was killed trying to escape and Captain White was held in the same area for three years. If you go to back issues of "Life Magazine" during 1973, you will find a cover with a Captain leaning out of a line of POWs coming down the airliner steps , to hug his wife; Captain White.

Night LS59

Almost near the end of my tour, I took a night mission to try and capture photos of suspected movements on the canals south of Cu Chi. I took Sturtevant, a TO with me. We mounted an LS59 flasher pod under the right wing. The LS59 was a powerful strobe light synched to the camera in the belly of the aircraft. It had one major drawback, there was a small propeller on the front used to create the electricity necessary to run it, and you could hear us coming from a mile away. We navigated to the selected area and made a pass at 1000 feet. The LS59 lit up nearly a square mile. We flew southwest until we ran into the river made famous by that coward Senator John Kerry when he supposedly powered up it in a river boat to Cambodia on Christmas Eve and watched the alleged tracers flying. As we turned around and started back home the air exploded with tracers. There were the big green basketball size .51 calibers and hundreds of red AK47 tracers. Keep in mind that every fifth bullet was a tracer. When you can look straight down into muzzle flashes without seeing tracers, you are right on top of the shooter. I could see about 20 guns firing at me and not realizing it, I was making a slow bank to the right. Sturtevant was too scared to yell so he was beating me on my right arm. I finally looked over at him just as a bullet took the VHF antenna that was mounted just above his head, off. I could see 15 more positions firing off his side. I quickly turned off the navigation lights, as well as the instrument lights. I stayed level and ran for it. I was pissed. I called looking for any aircraft in the region that had any ordinance. I got a call from a "Yellow Jacket". Yellow Jacket turned out to be the call sign of a F4 outfit out of Phan Thiet. He said he was a flight of two and was carrying "crispy critters", slang for napalm. I said if you will follow me I will fly over the area again and turn my LS59 on and then bank hard left out of his way. Sturtevant, who only had days to go on his tour was a little apprehensive but agreed to go again. We started at 5000 feet and did a dive down to about 800 feet turning on the LS59. No sooner had I reach the coordinates indicated on our inertial navigation, when Yellow jack called "bank left and climb". Zooming up, I looked back over my shoulder and watched a tsunami of flames engulf the area. All tracers stopped. The aircraft only sustained several AK47 hits.

Night Mission with David

My buddy David asked me if I wanted to go on a night fire light mission with him. It entailed me firing the .50 caliber at targets that might present themselves to us. The trick was that David had to fly down to a particular area and pick up the Province Chief. Carrying the Province Chief, we would fly along with a huge spotlight that could be adjusted from two feet to the size of a football field. If we flew over a sampan or any Vietnamese people and illuminated it, the Province Chief would let us know whether we could shoot or not. It all depended on which ones had paid him their taxes. I wanted to watch the old geezer do a gainer out of the Huey but such was not to be my luck. I made several of those missions with David. Another time doing a Vietnamese troop insert, a Vietnamese soldier grabbed David's cigarettes and lighter and quickly jumped out of the Huey. Unfortunately for him, he caught his back pack on the tie down ring on the left skid as we were taking off. David was really pissed. He got out of his seat came back to the door beside me. *"Little shit stole my cigarettes and lighter. I'm over here risking my life for this little prick and he steals from me."*

He reached out grabbed the guy with one hand, pulled him up took his cigarettes back and then tossed him out the door. We were only ten feet off the ground over flooded rice fields. The other Huey pilots behind us started making comments, "7", "6", "8" rating the gainer that he did out the door.

Going Home

After 365 days FLUF and I got our orders to go home. I called Uncle Jim and suggested he come stay the last night with us and we would catch the Freedom Bird home together. Uncle Jim showed up and I was so happy I told him I could drink him under the table. Bad mistake! Uncle Jim was a bull of a man the kind that led from the front and didn't take any shit. I love that guy. We both got a bottle of Ten High bourbon and retired to our hooch. I poured for him and he poured for me. With the bottles empty we decided to run in place and see who could last the longest. I woke up and couldn't see. The other guys had come and broken a dozen eggs all over me and my eyes were glued shut. One of our traditions was when a guy was going home everyone who liked him would meet on the flight line to open a bottle of Champagne. The Officer leaving would pour the Champaign into little white cups and then had to chug the rest. I was so hung over I wanted to go back to bed even if it meant another tour. Sober minds prevailed and we were driven to Saigon. Once in Saigon we learned that our Freedom Bird was going to be several hours late. What could we do but go to the Air Force Club and try to drink off the hangover. I ordered a Bloody Mary. My head was pounding like a sledge hammer. I hurt and I hurt badly. I ordered a second Bloody Mary and started to feel better. Five more and I was ready to roll. Our Freedom Bird arrived and they loaded it from back to front, enlisted were boarded first, and then officers. Uncle Jim, FLUF and I ended up sitting in the front row right next to the "biffy" (lavatory). An hour into the flight I started to sober up and get another vicious headache. The plane was full. They had no magazines, no booze and to top it all off the lead flight attendant was either pregnant or having her period, because she kept running into the biffy two feet in front of us, and puking her guts out. It was a miserable ride home but with the prevailing tailwinds we did the flight in one leg. For entertainment we discussed how to assimilate back into society. We were told not to ask mom and dad to "pass the fucking butter and not to respond to questions with "No shit".

In San Francisco we parted ways. Uncle Jim to see his beautiful wife Fran, FLUF to go see his wife, Jinx and me to fly back to Houston and see my parents and my wife Paula. I had to walk nearly around the whole San Francisco airport to get to the United Airline counter on the other side. We had to travel in uniform and the looks I got were anything but friendly. Arriving at the United Airlines area there were a bunch of hippies accosting every service member they saw and throwing red tomato juice on them calling them "Baby killers", "Nazis", and "Pigs". I walked way around the side trying to stay away from them. Suddenly, a group of skinny long haired hippies spied me and ran over. They were led by a screaming flower girl with beads in her hair and a loose fitting moo moo dress. The skinny boys were holding a box with jars of tomato juice. The girl got right in my face and started screaming her shit, not only to intimidate me, but to make sure everyone else there heard her. There were security cops but they just watched. I said "Don't throw that shit on me" She looked at me with a wicked smile and turned around to get a jar of tomato juice. When she turned back around I hit her in the nose hard as I could. Her feet went up even with her head before she ever started to fall. The cowardly skinny guys dropped their jars and high tailed it leaving her where she lay. I filed that experience as wrong place wrong time which was just the beginning of 35 years of being trashed and abused. If you happen to read this, and you were that flower girl, *tough shit,* there are consequences for certain actions and you were no lady.

Coming home to the USA

Coming home to the USA was a real ball buster. No ticker tape parades, no high fives, no thank yous, just intemperate rage, a profound intellectual hatred of the men that had taken part in a devastating war. One's pride at having done a job in hell's backyard was completely overwhelmed by the intensity of the cowards left at home. The inconceivable lies of the likes of John Kerry, himself a coward in the face of combat, quickly metastasized throughout the nation. Kerry, who thinks of himself as a Combat Veteran testified before the Senate in 1971 on Vietnam. His testimony designated *"Winter Soldiers"* was a massive misrepresentation as far from the truth as his forehead is from his chin. He made all kinds of claims gleaned from other cowards who claimed to have served in Vietnam, none did so. Kerry had three purple hearts from wounds so small even his CO couldn't see them. A soldier with three purple hearts in a year could go home. As a result of his testimony we were publicly criticized and called names usually reserved for murderers, rapists and pedophiles. I am one of many who would have loved to make Kerry walk point.

A simmering hatred began to fill me. I became devoid of any emotions involving trust, loyalty, or love. So as not to bore the reader, I will explain these emotions and you can decide how you would have reacted. I came home a Captain with several hero badges. A hero badge is for something that you receive for something completely stupid that you managed to live through. Those badges and .75 cents would get you a cup of coffee in America. As an officer you took your turn as escort duty for the remains of fallen soldiers, those that gave their all. It required you to put on your dress blue uniform and escort the remains to the home of the deceased and present the American Flag to the surviving member of the house hold. It was an honorable and patriotic duty. However, with the unbridled hostility and rage that was afflicting America, I was spit on, eggs thrown on me, slapped and even had dog shit hurled at me from grieving family and friends. This was endured without the slightest emotional expression or retaliation. These were U.S. citizens and I hated them with every breath I took.

First Day Home

Arriving at the new Houston Intercontinental Airport that had just recently opened, I found Paula and my folks. There seemed to be some kind of tension in the air. I shook my dad's hand, hugged my mom, and Paula drug me behind a big pillar. She looked like a million bucks, had a nearly see through blouse, and was beautiful. She said:

"Glad you made it back okay."

"Me too, I really missed you."

"Well, I'm not going home with you, I've changed."

With that she walked away leaving me stunned and my guts ripped out. Mom and dad took me home in a daze. My folks didn't drink and when I asked to stop and buy some Scotch my dad refused, saying I knew his rules. So I went down the street to my dad's best friend, Bill Jones. Bill had been a B17 pilot in WWII. Released from the service with several hundred thousand other guys, he couldn't find work. My Dad, a 1st Lieutenant in the Army Air Corps, caught polio while stationed at Ellington Air base in Houston. He spent two years in an iron lung and was eventually confined to a wheel chair. He could move nothing. He wanted to be an automotive engineer but changed his mind when he got polio. He wanted to research what had happened to him and become a doctor. Unable to write, he hired Bill to be his hands and they went through medical school together. Dad eventually got the use of his left arm back and his right arm from the elbow down. Other than that he was confined to a wheelchair.

I rang Bill's door bell and he invited me in. He poured us both a scotch and started to talk.

"Son, I know this hurts but your mom and dad and I knew this was coming. I passed Paula on the freeway, I knew your Dodge Charger, your officer's sticker, and your license plates. She was giving some guy a BJ. She had a restraining order against her for screwing around with another woman's husband. I hate to be the one telling you this, but your mom couldn't do it. Just remember if it wasn't that guy, it would have been another."

"I don't know what to say Bill, but thanks."

Fort Lewis 1970

I divorced Paula and telling my folks I just couldn't stick around, I headed for Ft. Lewis, Washington. I was pulling a 1970 Correct Craft boat. Van the father of my friend Teddy, who was killed along with the entire staff of the Ninth Infantry Division had a friend sell me the boat at cost. It had a 440 Chrysler marine engine, the boat was powder blue and powerful. When I was 12 years old, Van, a pilot for Trans Texas Airlines took me up with him on a maintenance test flight and I was hooked. The aircraft was a DC-3. Trans Texas Airline became Texas International Airlines and then was merged into Continental. Ft Lewis was the home of the 184th Military Intelligence Company flying the OV-1C aircraft. An air conditioned version with more powerful engines. When I checked in, there were only 5 pilots of whom I was one. Two were in company headquarters and three of us to fly. I could fly any where I wanted, in order to burn our fuel allotment and not lose any. The transition from hot and humid to the cool of the Northwestern Washington was like heaven. The base was absolutely beautiful. I was however, still depressed over Paula. There was no housing on the base for bachelors so I found a very nice two bedroom two bath apartment just outside of the base. I would go to work and come home and brood. My parents, worried about me, flew up for Thanksgiving. Later, my mom would laugh because I served them chili and crackers for Thanksgiving. When they left my dad talked to me and said I was very different and should seek some counseling. I blew him off and let it slide. I stayed in that apartment for nearly 5 months except for work. I went through three emotional phases thinking about my marriage. The first one was, it was my fault and I just wasn't attentive enough for her. Having only been together for approximately four months, before leaving for Vietnam, I then decided that it was her fault and she was what Bill said she was. And finally, I decided it was both of our faults we were too young and had spent too much time away from each other. Couple that with a war for me and a bunch of ass wipes hustling her, it was a no win situation. After that, no matter who I was dating I would always tell them what I was doing and they could accept it or hit the road. I began to come out of my funk and it was grand, or so I thought.

Ft Lewis had two officers clubs. One was a formal club located on base and the other was a lakeside club located on American Lake. Once we started to get more pilots, we would all eat lunch at the main Officer's club. We had a huge round table that would seat 15 or so. We would wear our flight jackets, with our *"I was alive in 65 patches",* and our wings. We made for a great clique, and intimidated other officers. Any women that would come in usually wanted to sit with us.

I met Paul there. He was also a Captain and a pilot, but of Hueys. He was basically pretty quiet. Apparently, he had lost a good friend in Vietnam who was flying with him. Further, he had gotten shot down and had the VC chasing him and his copilot through the woods before Cobras could cover for them while another Huey picked them up. When he arrived at Ft Lewis, they told him to go find housing and they would get back to him for assignment. Three months later, Headquarters discovered they had this Captain but no one knew where he was. They tracked him down to an apartment off post and rang his doorbell. No one answered. They continued to ring his door bell for another week before they had the manager open it for them. There in a corner, covered in cases of beer cans, they found Paul. The Commanding General didn't want to court martial him as he had a great record in Vietnam, plus they had told him they would get back to him, so they restricted him to living in the BOQ. (Bachelor Officer Quarters). I met him at lunch, we hit it off right away and I asked him to move in with me. He checked with the Commanding General and was allowed to move off post with me. He also got assigned to our company as Supply Officer.

Paul advised me that he didn't like to shop, and would I buy his clothes. He said he would pay extra for the service. I agreed to do so. We discovered that there were two good looking girls living below us. Paul decided to go check them out. He was gone for over an hour, so I went down to see what was up. They were both flight attendants for Flying Tigers Airline. One was married to a 1st Lieutenant serving in Vietnam, which immediately put her off limits to me. The other was a pretty bleach blond having what I referred to as big hooters. There was a guy with them who turned out to be a Captain for Flying Tigers. He was as full of shit as a Christmas goose. He told us, referring to the blond with big hooters, that "this girl, has everything I own except my last name."

"No shit and why doesn't she have your last name?"

"Well, I am in the process of a divorce, and then I will fix that."

"Paul and I are going to dinner at the McCord Air Force base, why don't you guys join us?"

"Great", says the blond obviously a little too quickly for Captain Ass wipe.

I had a 1969 Dodge Charger, bronze with a black vinyl roof and nice mag wheels, so we all went together.

McCord was located right next to Ft Lewis and had a really nice Officer's Club. We ordered dinner and the nice blond girl who I will refer to as J.J., spent the dinner rubbing my leg under the table. Captain Ass wipe tried to entertain us with his daring do stories until Paul decided to flip for dinner. Captain Ass wipe lost the toss. He tried to grab JJ and leave but she wanted to stay, so he left in a huff. On the way home, Paul drove while I sat in the back and got to know JJ. Things were looking up.

We had another pilot in the company George. We would take two airplanes and fly all over the Cascade mountain range. The snow covered mountains rendered us a great opportunity to create avalanches by pulling one prop slightly out of sync and creating a frequency that would start the avalanche. I loved flying more than anything in the world. I never tired of aerobatics and flying tight formation with George. On one flight I pulled into formation with George while I was inverted, and when he finally asked where I was, and I said "your left side", he looked and nearly went nuts. Another time, I flew past George and pulled straight up. I continued the climb until the aircraft ran out of speed and started a tail slide backwards. George started yelling "eject eject" as I slid backward in a nose high tail spin. All I had to do was pull the power off and the nose snapped over. I got really good at four point rolls, a split S, and inverted flying. I loved it better than sex.

It wasn't long before we had a full complement of pilots. Because of the political atmosphere in the country, we were not allowed to wear our uniforms off post. There were no ticker tape parades, or bands playing when the Vietnam veterans returned. The Army was cognizant of the problem and tried to help troop morale by making available to us new "Head" skis, poles, boots and a courtesy bus whenever we asked.

Growing up in Houston, I never really saw much snow. I could water ski better than anyone I knew, so I figured, how much different can snow skiing be? Hello, does complete idiot come to mind? About six of us took the bus and drove to Snoqualmie pass, outside of Seattle. I didn't know jack about snow skiing or having the necessary equipment. I was dressed in my blue jeans, with a couple of shirts, my flight jacket and my new Head skis, poles and boots. I took the chair lift to the top with the rest of the guys. Trying to get off the ski lift, I fell on my ass. Then, continued to fall on my ass every ten feet down the slope until at one point one of my skis came off and like a rocket ship headed down the hill at warp speed and into a draw. I was exhausted from picking myself up, my face was covered with snow and nearly frozen, and I was breathing like a wounded bull. It was suppose to be *cool* to have a wine bag, so I had one around my neck with Merlot in it. Every time I fell down I would take a sip. My hands were friggin blocks of ice, my socks looked like a pirate costume, full of snow and bloused out. I staggered down the mountain to find my other ski amid sour looks from the other skiers. Reaching the draw, I stepped over the embankment and sank clean up to my neck in the soft snow. I had to swim over to my other ski and swim back to the edge. I was so exhausted I could hardly walk and shivering with cold. I made it to the lodge and made my way to the huge fireplace that was burning. My teeth were chattering and I was sopping wet. Steam rolled off me like a locomotive engine. Unknown to me, all the heavy breathing had melted the snow around my mouth and then frozen over on my mustache. The wine had dyed my mustache purple and the ice was about an inch thick. I couldn't pull the ice off as it was embedded in my mustache hairs.

"First time" I heard someone say.

"How could you tell?"

I could barely speak my face was so frozen from falling down.

When the other guys came in, they found me with about six good looking girls laughing about my day with purple wine running down my face. Life was good and getting better.

My friend George was not enamored with black folks. He had a beautiful and I mean a drop dead beautiful, Taiwanese wife. George lived back in a forest with about a quarter mile road. Paul and I hired a black guy to walk back out down his road when George came home. It was almost a disaster as George nearly went completely ape shit when he saw the guy. Such was the nature of our humor.

Paul's parents lived on the Sacramento River in California and were fairly wealthy. Since, I could take a Mohawk (OV-1) and go anywhere I wanted, I took Paul and we flew down to see his parents. His Grandfather was an amazing guy and had built big cannon to shoot grapefruit out into the river. Paul had introduced me to Scotch, so we were drinking and shooting that cannon, when we hit a pleasure cruiser with a grapefruit at about 200 yards. That took an amazing amount of fast talking and BS.

One of his parents introduced Paul to a beautiful red head which I shall refer to as Chris. I didn't want to interfere so I was going to stay home until everyone forced me to go along. I drove and Paul and Chris sat beside me. Paul was still dealing with his Vietnam stuff and was pretty shy unless the two of us were drinking Scotch. Unfortunately, it was obvious Chris was not all that enamored with the situation. A couple of weeks after we got home Chris called and wanted me to call her if we came back. Paul and I scheduled another flight to Sacramento the following weekend. Paul was going to spend time with his dad as he would be going to work with his father when he left the service. So I rented a car and went to Sixth Army Headquarters in the Presidio to see my friend "Rooster." Rooster was out of town, so I called Chris. She was happy to hear from me, but she had a date for the evening. She begged me to come along.

"Damn Chris, I don't want to be a third wheel."

"Don't worry about it, meet us at 7:30pm at the San Francisco Country Club, it's up on the hill south and west of the Presidio."

Well what the hell, I bought a pair of nice slacks and a decent Long sleeve shirt and went to the club. Chris shows up with a real ringer for a date. Judging from his diamond Rolex, and $1000 suit, I was not in his league. Chris does the introductions all around and we walk into the club. The Maître d' asks if he could speak to me a moment and had another tuxedoed guy seat Chris and the ringer. So as not to embarrass me he takes me around a corner and says:

"Sir, all guests are required to wear a coat and tie."

"Well, that's no problem, would you just inform Chris that I forgot an appointment and had to leave."

'Sir, there is no need for that. I can outfit you with a coat and a tie and I think Miss Chris is looking forward to your presence."

He picked out a nice coat and a tie to match my shirt and escorted me to the table. Chris and Mr Smug were both waiting for me. Smug made a little smirk as I sat down and called for a wine list. He made a big show of picking an expensive wine, told me not to worry about it as the dinner was on him. When the wine came, he made a show of sniffing the cork, smelling the wine and swirling the wine around in his mouth. I don't think I spent that kind of time on a set of new bristols. To the Maître d he says:

"That sir, will not do, as it does not have the right ambiance for what we will be eating."

"Well dumb ass why did you pick it?" He ordered another bottle and held Chris' hand to indicate ownership. The next bottle of wine came and he repeated his earlier routine and turned it down as too acidic. He ordered again, same scenario, and turned this one back as too warm. The Maître d' was getting a bit pissed but he could say nothing to a member. When he brought the fourth bottle, before he could open it I said, "Sir, if he turns that one down too, please, just bring me a Goddamn beer." Chris laughed and Smug wanted to shit in my mess kit. I thought he might be foolish enough to make a scene. I later thanked him profusely for the dinner, and Chris took me home with her.

One weekend Paul and I flew down to Sacramento to see his folks again. His sister from Stanford University was also home. I was spellbound. She was the epitome of a southern California girl, beautiful, long waist length natural blond hair with intelligent azure blue eyes. She was vivacious had a quick smile, and loved to do everything I did like scuba diving, running, jumping out of perfectly good airplanes, laughing and water skiing. She took me water skiing on the Sacramento water. Ah, now here was where I could shine. It was a hundred degrees and the river looked like a mirror. I grabbed her ski and jumped into the river. I nearly had a heart attack. The river was colder than a well digger's peter. I lost all ability to even speak. Paul and Marylou thought it was extremely funny.

Back at Paul's house we warmed up with a couple of Scotches and then went out to a local restaurant. I had a wonderful time. We had left the aircraft at Travis Air Force base. When I was strapping in the ejection seat I discovered I had Marylou's keys in my pocket. We discussed our options, and decided that we would buy one of those fold up plastic containers you use for packing your soap bar, put Marylou's keys in it, tape it up and fly back to Paul's house and drop them to her. The OV-1 had a three inch tube just below the ejection seat for dropping messages or photos to guys in the field. The bottom of the tube had a small door that I could pull to drop stuff out. We bought the soap bar container at the PX, dropped the keys in it, and taped it up. We called Paul's parents and told them what we were going to do. Flying back down to the house we buzzed them to let them know we were there and then dropped down to fifty feet. I had the flaps full down, the landing gear down, and the speed boards out. I flew directly over the front yard and dropped the keys right into Marylou's hands. I cleaned up the aircraft and wiggling the wings as a goodbye gesture, Paul and I headed back to Ft Lewis.

It was about a three hour flight back. Approaching Portland Oregon, air traffic control called me and told me there was an inversion layer forming over Seattle and fog was starting to form. We passed Portland and fifty miles south of Ft Lewis, air traffic control again called me and said that Seattle was now zero visibility, Ft Lewis was zero visibility, and McCord air force base was zero visibility. The airports were all closed, what were my intentions.

"What's open within 100 miles of Ft Lewis," I asked.

"Nothing, all airports are reporting zero visibility with no improvement forecast for 12 hours."

"Well you better notify Ft Lewis to get their best GCA (Ground Controlled Approach radar) man up to the tower, because I don't have but 40 minutes of fuel left."

I told Paul that we were a little short of options. I said I am going to shoot a GCA approach. If I have to miss, I'll take you back over the field and you can punch out. A GCA was a ground controlled approach. A controller would set you up on finale with a line depicting the center of the runway, and another line depicting at what altitude you should be at during the approach. It sounded something like this:

"On course, on altitude, slightly left of course, slightly high on glide slope. "

A good GCA controller could talk you right down to the ground. Of course the whole thing depended on what kind of pilot you were, and whether you could keep the airspeed of the aircraft and the descent following the controller's instructions. The controller got on the radio and made a radio check. He advised me to "dirty up" or get the gear and flaps down and the airspeed on my final approach speed. When I acknowledged that I was ready, he reported no more calls were necessary from me, and guided me to the initial approach point from which we would begin our descent for a final approach. I told Paul to keep his eyes outside and tell me when he saw the runway. We shot the approach, and when the controller said "Over the runway, take over visually to land." Paul said he saw absolutely nothing so I pulled up and went around, to try it again. We had no more than gotten to 1500 feet when the low fuel light came on. That could mean anywhere from 5 to 20 minutes of fuel left.

"Paul we're screwed, I need you punch out. If I have to go around again, I'm going to fly out over Puget Sound and punch out myself. I can't afford to let the aircraft crash any-where on post."

"Fuck You! where you go I go. Those waters are too cold for me".

I called the controller and advised him of our situation. "This time buddy I need you to take me clean down to the ground. I'm counting on you. "

We were lined up and shot the approach. "You are on lo-calizer, on glide slope. You are over the runway, you are on the ground." We hit the ground. Paul said "I can't see any-thing." I pulled the props into reverse and added brakes. I gave it full reverse and the engines flamed out. Not know-ing where on the runway we were or how much of the run-way might be left, I braked hard and silence enveloped us. I requested a tow truck and we had to open the windows and yell for them to find us. Arriving at the hanger I found the CO, XO and most of the pilots who informed us that they had been advised we were out of fuel and coming in, and ran to the airport. They fully expected us to crash or punch out.

It wasn't two weeks later that we were again flying back from Sacramento. I heard approach control trying to raise a small aircraft that was apparently lost. Control called me and asked for help in relaying a message to the pilot.

"Cessna 5468 Tango, this is Hawk 347."

"Uh, Hawk 347, read you loud and clear, I think I'm lost."

The pilot's voice was high, full of fear, and panicky. I called approach back and asked if they knew whether this guy was instrument rated.

"Negative, Hawk 347. Not rated and very scared. We have no idea where he is and would appreciate any help."

'Cessna 5468 Tango, the weather is marginal at best and due to decrease further. Can you tell me what your heading is and your altitude?"

"Uh Hawk 347, we are, (he had three other people with him) 3500 feet and heading Southwest."

"Cessna 5468 Tango what does your VOR indicate from the McCord VOR?"

"I don't know, I'm not instrument rated, and don't know how to read it."

"Cessna 5468 Tango, turn the knob on the VOR until the little bar in the middle lines up with the McCord frequency, and tell me where the TO FROM arrow head is pointing."

"Hawk 347, it indicates FROM and a heading of 265 degrees."

Fuck me, the guy is heading right into the mountains, and I have no idea how close he is.

"Cessna 5468 Tango, please make an immediate left turn of 180 degrees and line up the little bar on the VOR where it shows a TO heading. I said, it happens to me all the time. Just watch your altitude and let me know when you are turned around."

I contacted approach and told them where to look on their radar. They couldn't believe that he hadn't impacted the mountains yet. I told them I would get back to them when I had him turned around.

"Hawk 347, (*I could hear crying in the background*), I have a TO indication and the little bar is lined up."

"Okay Cessna 5468 Tango, just stay on that course until I can get Approach Control to hear you. Where did you take off, and how much fuel do you have?"

"Forgetting his radio procedures he replied, "We took off from Puyallup and I have a quarter of a tank left."

"Well, Cessna 5468 Tango, you won't need that much, your almost home. However, I will get clearance for you to land at McCord, and you can take off again when the weather is better."

I could hear cheering and hand clapping.

Ten minutes later I made sure he had Approach Control's proper frequency and handed him off to them.

Approach Control asked, "Is that you Captain Boyd?"

"Approach, please don't tell my mother, but to answer your question, yes it is."

"Thank you Captain Boyd, I'm sure you just saved several lives."

Back at Fort Lewis, I was requested to go see the Commanding Officer of the base.

Once again, no good deed goes unpunished.

I reported as ordered, and was ushered into his office.

"Well, Captain Boyd, it seems you finally managed to pull your head out of your ass and do something admirable. I just got off the phone with McCord Approach Control, followed by a call from four very happy people. It seems that you have been offered the chance to sleep with the pilot's wife. She is of course 56, but what's a little age to a hound dog like you. Approach gave me the story, and you are to be commended. You are dismissed." After plotting out on the radar, where Cessna 5468 was in comparison to where he first told me his VOR indicated, he was less than a ½ mile from kissing a big granite mountain.

PT22

PT22 Before Crash-Notice Front Seat has a Cover

I wanted to own an airplane and use it to fly down and see
Marylou. I found a guy who had a reconditioned PT22. It
had a brand new Kinner engine, brand new wooden prop,
a flush riveted metal fuselage, new wing spars, and he had
an FAA approved double layer of Mylar on the wings. The
double layer so that he could sand the fold-_over edges
and make it look like a piece of glass. The interior was done
by the guy who had done Air Force One. The PT22 was a
WWII pilot trainer and was cursed with a heavy wing load
and high stall speed. Both of those design features aided
the Army Air Corp in teaching bomber pilots how to take
off and land. It was beautiful. Ft Lewis however, required
that any airplane flying on post had to have prior permission and a check for airworthiness. I asked the owner if he
would take me up and let me fly it. Turned out, he didn't
have a pilot's license but knew a friend who worked for the
state of Washington, who would give me a ride. On the se-

lected day, Paul and I drove down to the Chehalis dirt strip the owner lived on. There were high tension wires running across the north end of the strip unusual but not necessarily a no-go feature. The Washington pilot shows up and says lets go. I told the guy that I was experienced in conventional, (tail wheel), aircraft but had not been flying any, for some time, so if he wouldn't mind, would he take it off and land it, I just wanted to do aerobatics once we were in the air. I was still in uniform having come straight from work. As we walked to the tandem seated aircraft I was pulling on my Army helmet.

"WTF are you doing?"

"It's open cockpit, I don't know you or your ability, so I think I will just wear this."

"What a pussy."

Another entry in my record of **Famous last words!**

The engine fired up and ran smooth as glass. We taxied out to take off towards the high wires.

"If you want to fly this thing, then you take it off and I will land it," he says.

I took off, climbed to about 5000 feet and did a loop, a slow roll, a spin, and then buzzed Paul on the airstrip. I shook the stick, (the universal sign for the other guy to take over), and sat back to enjoy the view. It was a beautiful day, and I had my arms out the sides of the cockpit. Mr. Washington Ace (spelled with a double S) starts a downwind, from which, I thought he was just setting up to buzz the airfield. If we landed the way he was going it was going to be with a 15 knot tailwind. Next thing I know he pulls out the carb heat and cranks the aircraft over into a near 75 degree bank. The aircraft did exactly as it was designed to do, and we got a high speed stall. The nose flipped up and over into a spin faster than you can read this. It made the 1000 feet to the ground faster than a girl could tell you "NO" on a date. We hit nose first, left wing low, and proceeded to turn over about 6 times. We landed in a Christmas tree farm. The trees were small and young but the dirt was black. Looking from the airfield, the dirt made it look like we had caught fire. Paul took off running to see if he could pull me out. As it was, we stopped upside down, one wing folded against the fuselage, and my eyes full of dirt. I was momentarily disoriented hanging upside down in my seat belt. I couldn't see and my neck was bent down where I could kiss my ass goodbye. I managed to unbuckle my seat belt, then feeling along the side of the aircraft, I dug a hole and crawled out 90 degrees to the fuselage. Paul was a heavy smoker, and almost gave his life for me, being so out of breath as he arrived on scene. The aircraft was a total loss. I had a chipped a bone in my elbow, the top of my helmet was crushed, and it took 30 minutes to get the dirt out of my eyes so I could see. On my enlistment physical I was 6 feet tall. Now I am 5' 10". I found out later that the Washington pilot had killed a guy the previous year, trying in a hurry to takeoff downwind and crashed into some trees.

The Boat

I mentioned driving to Ft Lewis in June of 1970 pulling a brand new Ski Antique. It was a competition Ski boat powered by a 440 Chrysler inboard engine. The Antique, made by Correct Craft, was the finest ski boat around. (You Master Craft owners were number two and I will explain later). The

Nautique would attain speeds of 55 mph from which I could spin the steering wheel as far as it would go and the boat would literally swap ends. Most of our group would meet out at American Lake, ski all day, lie in the sun, and perform what the guys called "punishing Whale's boat". Punishing my boat referred to speeding around the lake and then swapping ends with a high speed turn. I was dating Suzy, a Captain's sister. Suzy was a tom boy and nothing bothered her. We stayed at the lake one day, had a picnic and a couple bottles of wine. I left my boat parked just off shore, while Suzy and I went skinny dipping. We ended up on shore half in the bag, laughing and having a good time. As it was late we took two of my big towels and crawled into a huge barbeque pit. That might sound weird to the uninitiated but nothing in the Army is left dirty, so the pit was absolutely clean. Around 2:00am I awoke to a flashlight in my eyes and somebody speaking.

"What are you doing here?"

"Get the fucking light out of my eyes and tell me who you are."

"MPs, Sir!"

"And your rank?"

"Sergeant Sir."

"Well Sergeant, I believe a Captain out ranks a Sergeant. Why are you here at the Officer's Club?"

"Part of our patrol area sir."

"Sergeant my ID and wallet are out there on my boat and Suzy and I are both naked."

"I believe you are who you say you are sir, but you can't sleep here."

"Come on Suzy the Sergeants want to see your naked ass and be embarrassed by mine. Let's swim back out to the boat."

Suzy crawls out gives them a bow and swims to the boat.

Standardization Instructor Pilot

I was sent to Standardization Instructor Pilot School located at Ft Rucker, Alabama. The SIP was responsible for periodically giving check rides to other OV-1 pilots. My selection was in anticipation of the company receiving the new OV-1D model aircraft. Instructor pilot school was absolutely heaven to me. My instructor was Jerry Thorpe, a civilian and former instructor for guys going through transition to the OV-1 following flight school. Jerry quickly found out that I could fly the OV-1 as well as he could, so our training consisted of normal procedures required of an instructor pilot followed by the two of us trying to outdo the other. One of our procedures was making a short field approach. This entailed "dirtying up" the aircraft, (gear and flaps down) and basically hanging the aircraft by its props in a very slow flight approach. The idea was to come in as slow as possible and the instant you touched down, go into full reverse coupled with hard braking and stop. *(Reversing an engine is kind of a misnomer, as you don't really reverse the direction of the engine, especially one turning 1600 rpms, but rather, the blades of the props suddenly are made to twist from pulling air to pushing air.)* With ten foot diameter props it like sticking a sheet of plywood out into the airstream. Jerry had a white line painted on the approach end of the runway and I was supposed to try and make the landing gear land right on that line. I could do it every time. He then had a circle painted on the runway. He would pull one of the props back to idle (Army's way of simulating a single engine) and tell me to land in the circle. It was a circle of about three feet.

"Which landing gear do you want me to put in the circle?"

"Well, the left engine is out wise ass so put the left gear in the circle."

I made it perfectly. Jerry then taught me how to land the aircraft on one wheel and keep it on that wheel all the way down the runway. He taught me how to "bow" the aircraft. Taxiing along I was to pull the engines into reverse and gently touch the brakes and the nose would bow down. Again we had a blast challenging each other. We did what we call a 360 overhead approach, landing in that circle. You come across the approach end of the runway at 1000 feet yank the throttles to flight idle, and start a 45 degree bank using the speed boards, flaps and eventually the gear in a continuing circular descent ending up just leveling out prior to touch down. Trick was, to end up right in the center line of the runway without dragging a wingtip. Following a day of flying Jerry and I would retire to the Officer's Club. At one point in Jerry's career while teaching a new guy how to shoot a single engine approach, the guy lost control of the aircraft and they had to punch out. Jerry ended up in a barbed wire fence but survived.

The OV-1D

Meanwhile, back at the ranch we got news that our first OV-1D was ready for pickup. It was a greatly sought out mission to go with me and pickup the new aircraft. It paid $32 a day in per diem and you got a commercial flight to West Palm Beach, Florida to pick up the new aircraft. However, before I signed for the aircraft, I had to test fly it and make sure every system was working as designed. Signing for a new aircraft from the manufacturer, that was being delivered to the U.S. Army, was not to be taken lightly. Additionally, one could only fly a "new" aircraft during the day. Well, beat me, hurt me, make me write a hot check, I guess I will have to fly back avoiding all weather and it just so happened my flight back took weather detours into every city that I had a girl friend in or a buddy. I would also make it mandatory that I made an overnight in San Francisco. I would land at the Presidio, a short strip running along the ocean. I had to come in over the sailboat marina facing west, and later take off heading for the southern end of the Golden Gate Bridge. Rooster was stationed there. His boss, Colonel Rose, was one of the finest Officers I had ever met, in the same league with Uncle Jim. Max was also there. He held the same rank as Rooster and had served with us in Vietnam, a great guy. Unfortunately, there were no Mohawks anywhere near the Presidio so Max and Roster had no opportunity to fly one. I would call in to the Presidio and have the tower inform Mr. Rooster that I was on approach. Rooster and Max would meet me at the airport, I would climb out and they would climb in. They arranged a car for me, and while I left the base for arrangements with the opposite sex, Max and Rooster would fly the Mohawk until their hearts were content. Not only did I love and respect those two but I also felt it was a small payback for Rooster and Max having taken care of me in Vietnam.

On one trip back with another new D model, I was flying over Crater Lake when my window blew off. The cockpit windows were designed like gull wings. Once secure in the cockpit, you could actually see straight down. They rarely came off, but if they did, they normally took the left vertica stabilizer with them. At 230 knots cruise when the window blew off, everything in the cockpit went with it. Maps, approach plates, hats you name it were sucked right out.

Another time Barry, another warrant officer was allowed to go with me to pick up another D model. Barry was an excellent pilot and I trusted him implicitly. There was only one set of controls in the D model so I did all the flying. That is, until I decided that Barry deserved to fly some. Flying along at 10,000 feet we safely unarmed our ejection seats and very carefully changed seats. That in itself was a job as we were both 6 feet and 180 pounds. Once Barry and I got settled back in, we were going to make a fuel stop in Dallas. The weather had turned to shit so we pressed on to Shepherd Air Force base. We picked up extensive headwinds and were advised that there was another front moving toward Shepherd with lots of lightening, and if we intended to land we had better hurry. Barry wanted to know if I wanted to change seats back and I told him no, we didn't have time. Coming up on Shepherd there was indeed a massive thunderstorm just off to the west. They were advising 40 knot crosswinds with gusts to fifty.

"Barry, I want you to do exactly as I tell you. If we break this grass hopper spit colored airplane, we are going to be in deep dodo."

"Yes sir."

All bullshit ceased and we were back to Captain and Warrant Officer.

"Barry you are going to have to crab into the wind. Don't let a gust take your attention from flying the aircraft. Close to touchdown I want you to add left aileron and cross it with right rudder like slipping other planes. You will be landing on the left main gear. Watch that you don't drag the left wing and whatever you do, don't stop flying the aircraft until we stop." We were 20 miles out on final and the rain started in earnest along with unbelievable lightning. Of course no good deed goes unpunished, so the low fuel light came on.

"Don't even worry about it, just fly the plane."

"Yes Sir."

Barry made an acceptable landing and we taxied to a hanger. Never again would I allow someone to switch seats in flight with me not having any controls. Once the storm had passed, the airmen were allowed to refuel. The OV-1 holds 297 gallons of fuel in the main fuselage tank. We took 295 gallons. Someone loved me, despite working my way through the Ten Commandments.

Training the OV-1D

We decided that to train our pilots on the extra weight of the OV-1D, we would only use three quarters of the power on a dual controlled OV-1C. In essence that made for a longer takeoff roll, and a hazardous single engine simulation. As I said earlier, we never shut an engine completely off unless we were up at altitude. To simulate a single engine on takeoff, I would simply pull one of the throttles back and the pilot would compensate by using rudder and pushing the good engine up to max power. It apparently, was interesting to the other pilots as they would all line the runway in front of our hanger and watch the show. I was training one on the pilots on this technique, when he immediately jammed the good engine to the stops. If one engine was not producing (X) amount of power on takeoff, and the good engine was shoved to the stops, the aircraft would automatically shut down and feather the non producing engine. It worked exactly as designed, and I found myself ten feet off the ground with a real dead engine, and right at stall speed.

"I have the aircraft. If I tell you to eject, do not even hesitate, go."

When I gave him the simulated single engine, he let the aircraft wander nearly twenty five degrees off course, which put us heading for the barracks and below the roof line. If, I let go of the control stick to eject the aircraft would roll into the dead engine and I would punch right into the ground, something they learned the hard way in Vietnam. I remained calm, my ass had a tight grip on the ejection seat, and did what you are always supposed to do and that is *Fly the damn airplane.* I got every bit of power I could out of the good engine and finessed the aircraft over the barracks roof with inches to spare. Still low and slowly building airspeed we passed over the freeway, awing some and getting the finger from others and stayed at tree top level until we got to American lake and I told him to start the dead engine. Once that was completed, we were back in the guaranteed land of the living.

Sometimes Your Luck Runs Out

Around this time Lt. Cossey and Captain McBride, classmates of mine and recently returned from Vietnam, went out on a familiarization flight. They never returned. With every available pilot looking for them it was still three days before we found them. They had apparently crashed nose first into an area normally covered by water due to the tides on Columbia River basin just before it emptied into the Pacific. Our XO, Captain Olney a good friend and an excellent pilot, was tasked as Investigating Officer. It was tough duty as both men were nearly side by side in the wreckage. Further, the crabs had been at them. It's one thing to see dead men, but quite another to pickup what's left of friends and inform the survivors. They were both married.

Crash of LT Cossey and CPT McBride

Wild Men

Paul and I were constantly having parties and a grand time. We were going out constantly. No sooner would we agree to stay home, than someone would call and say it was happy hour somewhere and away we would go. I would sometimes wake up and Paul would be on the couch with some rather large Kmart girl snapping his bean. Next day I would say:

"Paul, what the hell were you doing, that girl was four times your size?"

"Yes, but she was so appreciative. She washed my clothes, cleaned the kitchen, and took care of me."

"Well listen, Paul, if I see some KMart plus shopper sitting on you again, I will get out the vacuum cleaner and start vacuuming the house."

A Shallow Gene Pool

While I was in Vietnam I had my Smith and Wesson model 29 .44 Magnum sent to me. I figured it was a shade better than the .38s that we were issued as pilots. I was bored one day and had just finished cleaning my .44 when another Captain stopped by. Pete needed to use my bathroom and I directed him to my bedroom informing him that my .44 was laying on the bed loaded and not to pick it up. Three minutes later, **"boom".** Can't tell you how loud a .44 sounds going off in a closed space! I ran to the bedroom expecting to see teeth hair and eyeballs all over my bed. Pete was standing there looking sheepish surrounded by smoke and a strong smell of cordite.

"WTF Pete, which way did the round go?"

"Out the wall behind your headboard"

"SOB there is an elderly lady living in that apartment!"

I ran next door and pounded on the door. Couple of minutes later a frail and scared little woman appeared at the door.

"Maam, are you all right? I had a mental retard next door play with my weapon and it went off."

"Yes, please come in."

She had been sitting on her couch watching TV when the round came through the wall missing her head by 6". It then crossed the room hit her fireplace and ricocheted out her sliding glass patio doors through her wooden railing, splitting it wide open, and departed to parts unknown. I was so relieved to find her unhurt I would have married her. Maybe that's a bit much, but you get the idea.

Army Navy Game

We were invited to the Army Navy football game by the pilots at Whidbey Island Navy Base. Shadow our only black pilot, myself, and Bats (Bill Belfy) rode together for the trip up to Whidbey. We had on

Army Navy Game Whidbey Island

our party suits from Vietnam. Mine was red with patches all over it like Laotian Border Patrol, I Was Alive in 65, 1000 Mission Red Haze Mission and others. A good time and good drinks. Later on our way back to Ft Lewis we had to take the ferry across Puget Sound. In front of our car was a good looking girl talking to some guy. Since it was a 20 minute ride we got out of our car and wandered close by to check her out.

She was intrigued by our party suits and made a comment. Well that of course, demanded a face to face reply. We wandered over to her car while the first guy walked away. We flirted away the ride and when I asked for her phone number she said "You guys are Military Intelligence, find out yourselves." Around 1970, the Army transferred the OV-1 into the Military Intelligence Branch from the Infantry Branch.

That statement turned out to be prophetic. Monday morning rolled around and the four of us were called in to George's office.

"Sir, reporting as ordered."

"Under the Military Code of Justice, you have the right..............."

"Hold it right there sir, what the Sam Hill is going on?"

"You gentlemen have been charged with drunk in public, and conduct unbecoming of officers."

"Who in hell made those accusations"

"Apparently, an officer on the ferry who claims to have observed the behavior,."

We started having an adversarial discussion when in walks Dan Klobucher, a young Warrant Officer I had met at the officers club at Ft Rucker. Sir, Warrant Officer Klobucher reporting.

"Uh Mr. Klobucher, we are having a private discussion here. This is Captain Boyd and,..."

"Oh, I already know the Whale."

I could see steam coming out of Major George's ears. Timing is everything.

The 184th Military Intelligence Company was made a part of a Signal Battalion. That had never happened before and the Signal Battalion Commander didn't have a clue about how to handle an aviation asset. Couple that with the fact that the Signal Battalion Commander was a real prick our CO was just following orders from the "Richard head".

I said, "Sir I won't take this laying down, and walked out of his office."

I contacted the ferry operations office and asked to talk to the Captain that had been on duty on that particular day. I then ran home and dug through all my crap and found the girl's license plate number that I had written down. I called the State Highway Patrol, and after telling the story to dispatch and who I was, I managed to get an address and a phone number. I called the young lady and inquired if we had harassed her, insulted her or made her feel in any way uncomfortable. She was delighted to hear from me and equally impressed that I had found her. She said she would be willing to come to the base, sit on the Commanding General's lap and tell him what great guys we were. I told her I would get back to her. I then demanded to know who the Officer was who had made the accusation. George was reluctant to tell me. He then showed me his OER (Officers Efficiency Report) written by Colonel Richard Head. It was bad.

"This is bullshit George."

"Just please stay out of it and let it slide."

" If you won't set this straight, then I'm going skiing for the day."

I walked out of his office again and headed home. I was beyond pissed. I had promised myself that if I made it out of Vietnam alive I would never again let some incompetent bastard tell me what to do. When I got home I picked up the phone and called the Commanding General's aide and asked for an audience with the General. I was given an appointment. Later that evening I got a call from George's wife who pleaded with me to not to interfere. I called the General's aide and told him to cancel the appointment.

Next morning I was still pissed off, drinking coffee and just laying around when the phone rang.

"What," I yelled.

"Uh, is this Captain Boyd?"

"Yes, who is this and what do you want?"

"This is General so and so. Is this a good time?"

"Uh, yes sir, how may I help you?"

"Well Captain, I see that you made an appointment to see me and then canceled it. It has been my experience that when such an occurrence happens it is usually the result of the officer in question, having been threatened or otherwise intimidated. If you can tell me right now that neither of those scenarios applies to you, I will let it go."

"Uh........"

"I will see you in my office at 10:30 sharp, Captain"

Oh shit, I thought and started scrambling to get out my dress uniform, polish all my brass, make sure all my hero badges were in place and properly aligned, and polish my shoes. At 1030 sharp, I arrived at his aide's desk.

"Send him in."

I walked into the General's Office, stood three feet from his desk, stood at attention and gave him my best salute. "Captain Boyd reporting as ordered sir."

"Sit down Captain Boyd and tell me what this is all about."

I had notes, the address of the Captain that had been running that particular ferry, the name and base from which the accusing Officer had come and the name address and phone number of the young lady involved. Then I told him about the OER that George had been given and expressed my utter disdain for Colonel Richard Cranium and George for not fighting back. I explained my desire to get out of the Military as soon as possible if such were to be the results of future commands. I took great pride in my uniform and had a good number of hero badges the result of stupid things accomplished and lived through, which I noticed that the General had taken note of.

"Well Captain that's quite a story. Let me do some checking and I will see you here again tomorrow at 1030 hours." I left his office and felt a little better.

Next morning at 1030 sharp, I again appeared outside the General's office.

"Send Captain Boyd in please."

I walked in to the General's office and stared like a stupid deer in the headlights. There sitting on his lap was the young lady in question. Obviously, the General had a sense of humor.

"At ease, Captain Boyd." Miss Sherri was just explaining what a great guy you were, courteous, handsome, debonair and very intriguing. I bought the very intriguing part, so one out of four ain't bad. I also talked to the Captain of that ferry and no complaints were ever alleged. I also have talked to the Commanding General at Fort Rucker as to the allegations made by one of his officers. Miss Sherri, if you could leave us alone for awhile, I'm sure Captain Boyd would be pleased to meet you at the Officers Club and buy you lunch. Thank you very much for coming in."

I escorted Sherri to his door, made sure she knew how to get to the Officers Club, and then closed the door behind her.

"The Commanding General at Ft Rucker has indicated that he will hold a conference call with us in 10 minutes. What are your wishes?"

"Sir, jealousy usually runs right off my back. In fact in our company, we have all agreed that if any of us are ever dating a girl, and she appears to be interested in another one of us, then rather than get pissed, we say, "**You Got to Share!**" To me it beats this kind of situation, but I would like an apology. Other than that Sir, I really don't give a big rats butt." I should also point out that Colonel Scrotum Head used this alleged incident to hammer my CO, and while I am not on my CO's social roster, it still pisses me off that the Colonel tried to ruin his career. Additionally Sir, I would be remiss if I didn't tell you that George told me to just let it ride and then his wife called and begged me to leave it alone which was why I canceled my first request to see you."

"All right Captain, let's take our conference call, and then we can discuss your future."

His aide called and said that the Ft Rucker General was on the line, and transferred the call to us. They knew each other by their first names, so a quick update ensued, before we got to the meat of the matter.

"General, I assume you have Captain Boyd in your presence, and I have Captain Idiot with me. Captain Boyd would you like to say anything to Captain Idiot."

"Sir, had we been civilians I might have made some remark as to the marital status of his parents and let it die. However, we now find ourselves where neither one of us really wants to hang out with the other, so if your Captain Idiot will just apologize, I'll consider the matter dead and buried."

I could hear Captain Idiot blubber an apology and the two Generals signed off and hung up.

"Okay, now Captain Boyd, I assume you will be worried about your OER and your future."

"Sir, with all due respect the only way an OER could hurt me would be if it was rolled up tight and stuck in my eye. I have no intention of making the Army a career. I think you can see that I am not cut out for a military career."

"Point well taken Captain Boyd, but we need people like you, especially in war time. I hope you reconsider. Now as to your CO, I will personally review his OER and if what you say is correct, I will have the other OER written by Colonel Richard Cranium destroyed. Will that suffice?"

"Yes Sir and I appreciate your time."

Friends Departed

My friend Paul was getting out of the service when I left for Instructor pilot School. I really missed him. There were so many girls and just so much time. When I got home, (home being Ft Lewis), I went to the Officers Club to have lunch. The usual group of guys were there sitting at our table. Alone at another table, I saw a young Second Lieutenant. I said" hey, let's invite the guy over". The other pilots didn't want too as the Second Luey was not a pilot. I said screw it, and walked over to his table. His name was Mark Corwin, a kinky haired Jewish boy, with a since of humor that I would come to love and appreciate. I brought him back to our table as Kathy, a Brigadier General's daughter sat down, and following her, was her dad's attaché. The attaché was a Captain who was not particularly amused by our gregariousness or humor. He was wound so tight you couldn't drive a ten penny nail up his ass with a sledge hammer. I started flirting with Kathy, and as the Captain got more and more pissed, the guys said **"Hey you got to share."** Bye Bye Captain! I asked Kathy out for that evening and told her I would pick her up about 1900. *Seven o'clock,* for you civilians.

DATING KATHY, THE GENERAL'S DAUGHTER

This was 1970, bell bottom pants were in and wild shirts. I had a 1968 Corvette I had won in a poker game, so I show up on post where the Brigadier Generals were housed, dressed in a long sleeve pastel purple shirt with huge butterfly wings on it, a purple tie, grey bell bottom slacks, and wearing white shoes. WTF, Pat Boone wore white shoes. At any rate, as I was driving up to her house and trying to check my tie in the rear view mirror and maneuver to park too, I noticed her Dad in the front yard with a hose watering his grass. I drove right over the curb and parked on the sidewalk. Not wanting him to think I didn't know what I was doing, I turned the car off and got out.

"Captain Boyd is it, please come in." He had a look like I had just farted.

This was old school. You had to meet the parents first, especially in the service.

"Kathy will be down shortly may we get you a drink."

"Yes Maam, a scotch with a dash of water would be nice."

We sat awkwardly in their sitting room and made small talk for about 10 minutes until the appropriate time arrived for

Kathy to come down. Kathy sat on the couch with me and her mother said,

"You know Kathy, perhaps Captain Boyd might have a friend who would like to help us next week with our dinner party, and tend bar."

"Sure mom, he can get Mark, and I'm sure they will do a great job, how about it Bob?"

"Yes maam, I would enjoy that."

The General looked like someone had just shit in his mess kit but said nothing.

I escorted Kathy outside, opened the door for her, and drove off. I had a couple of tumblers in the car and a flask of Scotch. I stopped, poured us both a drink, and then drove off to go to the McCord officers club next to Ft Lewis. In order to get to McCord, I had to make a clover leaf right turn up onto Interstate 5, drive three miles and exit into McCord. On post I had to drive 25 miles per hour which really affected the carburetor on the Vet, so I decided to blow it out on the quick drive to McCord. I looked left as I entered the freeway and not seeing anyone I floored it, shifting into 4rd about 110mph, and then left it there as I exited at the McCord entry point. The Corvette had a 427 cu in engine with three deuces putting out 480 horse power. What an absolutely exhilarating ride, that is until the red and blue rotating lights caught up to me.

"Here Kathy put these on the floor."

"May I see your driver's license and registration please? Captain, I noticed your sticker. Have you been to Nam?"

"Yes Sir, got back couple of months ago."`

He squatted down and looked in the car seeing in an instant the drinks and Kathy.

"Why good evening Kathy, how are you?"

I'm screwed he knows Kathy and obviously her dad.

"You know Captain Boyd (reading from my ID) I know the General and if I told him I caught you going, I don't even know how fast because you pulled away from me at 90mph and that you were drinking with his lovely daughter on board, well, I would hate to see you cleaning the latrines for the rest of your life. So here's what I am going to do. Hand me the two drinks, be glad there is a God, and be on your way." Unbelievable!

At about 2300 hours (1100pm) I asked Kathy if she was expected home before midnight.

"Are you serious, I am 21 and do what I want."

There went another entry in my *famous last words* diary.

We went to my apartment and played suck face and I got her home about 0300. When I parked, correctly in front of her house, I noticed the front porch light come on and her dad step out. He looked at his watch and went back inside. So much for, *I do as I please.*

Kathy, General's Daughter

Next day Kathy calls and informs me I have been uninvited to bartend. I called Mark and he said " I hope you got your bean snapped because you really screwed the pooch."

Somehow, over the next week, Kathy managed to get us reinvited to bar tend the party for her dad.

This time we both wore pressed white shirts with black bow ties.

They had a receiving line and first in line was the commanding General.

"Why good evening Captain, good to see you."

Kathy's dad heard that and I could hear the conversation later, "How do you know Captain Boyd?"

BATS

My friend Bill Belfy was not at all enamored with the Army. In Vietnam he flew the U21, a military version of a Super king Air. He was taking two enlisted men from Da Nang to Saigon to catch their Freedom bird home when he turned around and found a full Colonel and a snot nosed teenager occupying the cabin. He said, "Who are you and where are the two enlisted men?" The Colonel informed Bill that the snot nosed teenager was Senator so and so's son, and that he was escorting him on a tour of Vietnam and further stated that the two enlisted men had been bumped off. Bill packed up his briefcase and started back down the aisle. That's when the Colonel stopped him and wanted to know where was going, Bill curtly replied "If you can fly this tub have a good trip." The Colonel and the idiot pampered kid got off. Bill found the two enlisted men and flew them to Saigon. Bill was my kind of guy, never get bullied and never compromise your principles. When he got to Ft Lewis, Paul having left, I asked him to move in with me. His Name was William Belfy, but we called him Bats.

We were out at the American Lake Officers Club, drinking and having a good time. Kathy was there, when her Dad's attaché showed up. He was a slow burning fuse, and about as much fun as a child's funeral. Bats had let his hair grow longer than was truly authorized, but didn't give a big rat's ass. Bats was standing at the urinal when the attaché walked up next to him. Unzipping his pants, the Captain looks at Bats with distain and says, "Kind of long don't you think Captain?"

"You should see it when it's hard", snapped Bats.

The Officers Club

Fort Lewis, had two Officer's Clubs; one big one on the base, and another log cabin style club on American Lake, which was within the boundaries of Fort Lewis. The main base was huge and had its complement of senior officers. These are officers my age now, and men who had grown up not only with a sense of personal responsibility, but with integrity, honor, respect, and a code of conduct towards women and their wives, which obviously seems to have died somewhere between our respective time periods.

The Commanding General called a meeting for all officers on the base to meet in the Officers Club. As ordered, several hundred of us, reported.

"Gentlemen, we have a situation here involving the support of this club. The club is virtually empty during the evenings, which, if it continues will require me to shut it down. The floor is open and I'll take any suggestions."

The room erupted with cross talk, but no one wanted to confront the Commanding General. That was, until some idiot raised his hand, that idiot being me.

"I recognize Captain Boyd"

A hush fell over the club like a child's funeral. Apparently, my reputation preceded_me, as everyone noted my one lone hand hanging in the air. I stood up.

"Sir, I think I can shed some light on this situation. The American Lake officers club is usually packed. It is packed with junior officers, such as me. Most of us have recently returned from Vietnam, and being 22 to 25 years old, we need to unwind. The problem is two- fold, one, the officers club on American lake is only open on weekends, and two, the main club, is home mainly to senior officers. With no disrespect, our two generations are vastly different. Officers of my generation, Vietnam era officers, can be ordered to come and promote this club, but I doubt that we would voluntarily come with a date, just to have dinner and listen to Joe Nose and his five pickers. Further, if we were allowed to listen to current music, your generation would find us irritating. "

"So Captain Boyd, what is your recommendation?"

"Sir, I would suggest that we divide the days of the week into a four-three allotment. It would be published, that my generation may entertain four nights a week with our brand of music and fun, and your generation would be allotted three nights a week to listen to the Big Band music of your era. While three nights may seem unfair to some of your officers, you started this meeting with the fact that the club was not sufficiently being attended to generate enough funds to keep it open."

"Excellent idea, Captain Boyd! All in favor of Captain Boyd now running the club raise your hand."

Well beat me, hurt me, make me write a hot check, and paint me with brown mahogany, I stepped in it clean up to my arrogant neck. The response of course was unanimous. As I was leaving a full Colonel stepped up to me, *"You arrogant little prick you will fall flat on your ass."* That's what like, a challenge.

I put the word out that our first Junior officers night would be held the following Saturday night. I rounded up other single officers who only had enough blood to run one appendage at a time, which left their brains in idle a good deal of the time. Together we started hitting the clubs in Tacoma, looking for a decent band. After several bad hangovers, we settled on a band called KID AFRICA. I wrote up a contract; how long they had to play, how many breaks they could take, and other rules and regulations befitting an Army officers club. I made it perfectly clear, that I held the purse strings, and any violation would result in zero pay. We signed, shook hands, and went on our way.

My next step was to get some women to attend. I made flyers and proceeded to pass them out to every nurse's station, every hospital, every gym, every college, everywhere you could remotely find women. The real kicker on the flyers was that only women were invited. If guys wanted to come, **JOIN THE ARMY!**

I had to curtail my usual routine of cheering up lonely girls, but I had a challenge. Saturday arrived, and I spent the afternoon polishing the basketball size dance floor. I made arrangements for numerous bars around the room and plenty of seating with 8 person tables. As I was polishing, that Colonel showed up to harass me. My guess was he either had an ugly wife, or he was single and couldn't get laid with a hand full of pardons at a women's prison. However, RHIP (rank has its privileges), I told him to come before 8 o'clock if he wanted a seat. He stormed off muttering something about the marital status of my parents. By 8:15pm, the club was packed. There were women everywhere. So many to help and so little time. The club, after expenses, made more money in that one night than in the previous few months.

Sixth Army

Following the bullshit with the Captain from Ft Rucker, I think I could safely say that I wouldn't be invited to George's funeral. I was running Operations, when we were advised that a surprise inspection team from Sixth Army Headquarters were due in 30 minutes. Our CO gave me specific orders, *not to be at operations when they arrived*. It was going to be Colonel Rose, Rooster, and Max. They started their inspection but were looking around for me.

With my CO standing there, Colonel Rose inquired: "Major, where is Captain Boyd?"

"He is not available Sir."

"Well make him available Major."

I was called back to Ops and introduced to Colonel Rose, Rooster and Max. My name was on the paperwork, so the CO couldn't hide me forever, besides I knew they were coming and were going to stay with me.

"Major, I would like to have Captain Boyd for awhile, is that a problem?"

"No Sir, I will have your bags taken to the BOQ."

"No need Major, Captain Boyd will drive us."

We left and went to the Officers Club for lunch. Colonel Rose asked if by any chance I had room for them in my apartment.

"Yes Sir".

"In fact Colonel, if we won't be breaking any protocols, I have a little party lined up tonight."

"Excellent Captain Boyd"!

I had invited lots of girls. Bats and I had approximately 20 bottles of Scotch and lots of ice. At one point, I noticed one of our warrants had Colonel Rose by the lapels and was yelling in his face how he wanted the fuck out of the Army. *Fools and drunks, what a combination!*

The next day I took the group for a ride in my boat. As a courtesy the Colonel invited my CO George to go with us. You wouldn't know it, but George had been a wild man as a junior officer. He got toasted one night and his buddies put him on an airplane to Hawaii. As luck would have it, he met his wife on the flight as she was a flight attendant. Now that he was Major and in a command situation, he was all business. George showed up on American Lake dressed very sharply in a pale green cashmere sweater. We all got into my boat and I gave them a tour of the Lake and the Officer's club. After that I showed them how the boat could swap ends doing 55 mph and turning the steering wheel all the way to the stops. The Colonel really liked it and wanted to try it himself. After failing several times because he couldn't bring himself to fully turn the steering wheel to the stops, I instructed him again and he finally got the hang of it. Everyone was laughing except George. He was seated on the rear seat which would get covered in water as the boat swapped ends. His cashmere sweater had stretched out to three times its normal size. He didn't say a thing but I was sure he was contemplating roasting me over a small fire.

Summer 1971

Puyallup, Washington was having an air show on a Saturday. I wanted to fly over and see it as it was just a 25 minute flight over. I took a Super C, staying up at 8500 feet and 10 miles away. I didn't know if they were having jumpers or any other programs going on, and I didn't want to disrupt anything. I was tuned to the tower frequency and listening to the activity. During a break, I called the tower and asked them if it would be all right for an Army OV-1 to make a high speed pass. Absolutely, was the reply, let me get it set up and I will call you back. So, I orbited around and waited. Five minutes later, the tower called me and said that all aircraft were already on the ground and the airspace was clear. Call us one mile out. I set up for a diving run, which would put me at nearly 300 knots when I leveled out over the runway. I trimmed the aircraft nose down, and when I hit the boundary fence, I rolled inverted and flew down the runway upside down at about 10 feet. Trimming nose down allowed the aircraft, while inverted, to pitch up, if some unforeseen situation like a bird or big bug impacted the windscreen. At the opposite end of the runway, I pushed the aircraft up until the speed dropped off, lowered the gear, speed boards, and flaps while trimming the aircraft back to normal, and did a split S back to a landing on one main gear and held it on that one gear with the other gear and the nose wheel off, most of the way down the runway. I then exited the runway onto a taxi way and proceeded back to the center of the field. Turning towards the crowd, I pulled into reverse, touched the brakes and bowed to the crowd. *Good ole Jerry Thorpe and his training.* With the tower begging me to shutdown, I declined and took off back to Ft Lewis. The Canadian Snowbirds, their aerobatic team, had given me a white Nomex flight suit. I ran home put it on with a blue ascot, and drove back to Puyallup to watch the rest of the air show. Standing around minding my own business, I was grabbed by the arm from the Signal Battalion Commander, the one who tried to screw George on his OER.

"I got you now Captain, I'm going to hang your ass out to dry."

Almost at the same time, I see the Commanding General walking towards me.

"Was that you Captain Boyd? That was fantastic. The service needs more stunts like that. You should have heard the crowd. Great job!"

Saved in the nick of time and Colonel Richard Cranium sauntered off chewing nails, probably even kicked his dog at home.

T-41 Crash

Another Sunday, I was tasked to try and go find a 1st Lieutenant and a Forest Service employee who had failed to return. Their last call had indicated that they were stuck in a valley in the Olympian Mountain Range. I took the Super C and flew up into the Olympian Mountains. I flew above the mountains looking into nearly every valley. Mountain flying is extremely hazardous, especially in a single engine aircraft. Cold air on one side of a mountain may be going up over the top, but on the opposite side it is diving down, and with such speed, that it can drive a small plane right into the dirt. After an hour of looking, I spotted something that gave a quick flash as I flew by. I turned around and flew back for another look. Sure enough it was a T-41 crashed into the trees. I felt sick, just as I did every time I witnessed a stupid accident that caused a death; in this case two deaths. I needed to pin point the location and take some pictures. In order to do that, I had to fly tree top level through the saddle of two hills and then drop quickly into the valley and turn on the camera. Maximum exposure time, maybe 6 seconds before I had to add full power and climb back out. I tried it several times, and finally climbed back up over the mountains and headed back. As I was leaving, I noticed a small fire on a ridge line. Looking closer, I could see little yellow jacketed men on the ridge. The wild hairs on my ass started to tingle and I was sure those little yellow jacketed guys needed a buzz job. Diving down across the top of that ridge, recovering in the valley on the other side, and pulling up and doing rolls, I managed to shave off the wild hairs. As I landed at Ft Lewis, I noticed three MP cars, lights flashing waiting at our hanger. Exiting the aircraft, maps in hand, I was approached by the MPs.

"Sir, you are requested at the Commanding Generals office, please ride with us."

Shit, he is here on a Sunday? I was ushered into the back seat behind the cage, and driven with lights flashing to headquarters, where, I was ushered into the General's office.

"I should have known it was you Captain Boyd, please be seated. I have a report here that says, an Army aircraft scared the shit out of a group of fire fighters, who were monitoring a controlled burn on a ridge line in the Olympian mountains. I checked, and you were the only one flying today. Would you care to elaborate? The Forest Service wants some ass."

"Well, yes Sir, I would. May I approach your desk?"

I still had all my maps, and proceeded to open the one in question, on his desk.

"You remember sir, the 1st Lieutenant and the Forest Service representative who failed to return early this morning? I was tasked to go try and find them. If you look on my map, just to the east of this saddle, I found them crashed down in the adjacent valley. I tried to make several passes dropping down into that valley to get pictures. If you can give me the coordinates of the fire fighters, it's possible that I didn't see them as I was making these passes."

The General sat back in his seat and looked me right in the eye.

"You are a clever, fast on your feet, bullshit artist. But, since I was not given the coordinates where the fire fighters were working, I will have to accept your explanation. You are dismissed."

Engine Failure

My buddy George and I were out flying and landing on every strip we could find in the Puget Sound. The Kitsap peninsula had a nice runway and coffee shop. We stopped for lunch, and were taking off again, with me first in line. I pushed in max power and started my take off roll. Just as I had lifted the nose wheel off the ground, the left engine literally blew up. With such a catastrophic failure, the propellers immediately froze, and the aircraft made an immediate left turn towards their hanger. I yanked the right engine into full reverse, and stepped on the brakes hard. By the grace of God, I missed all the aircraft parked on the ramp and managed to come to a stop four feet from the hanger doors. We went back out on the runway and found bits and pieces of compressor and turbine blades. It could have been really bad.

Helicopter School

Near the end of 1972, I got orders to attend the Advanced Course at Ft Huachuca. The orders were TDY to Ft Hood, Texas which meant I was ultimately assigned to Fort Hood, but before I was to go, I was to attend the Advanced Course for Captains. The Company I was to be assigned to (131st MI Company) had Hueys as well as OV-1s, so I managed to talk my way into Helicopter transition school. Ft Rucker, Alabama was where nearly every nation in the world sends their pilots to learn to fly helicopters. It was a great course and I managed to graduate first in the class. While I was there I met Dan Kloubcher a young Warrant Officer who was finishing OV-1 transition. We hit it off right away and spent a good deal of time in the Officer's club talking about the OV-1.

Posse Comitatus Act

When I got back to Fort Lewis, the company had been asked by the Corps of Engineers to use our SLAR capabilities and map the entire state of California. This would require hours and hours of flying the autopilot along fixed lines up and down the state. The OV-1D model had a remarkable upgraded SLAR which could actually see down into the earth quite a bit. It gave a multicolored map showing fault lines as well as the States Mountains, lakes and rivers. Fortunately or unfortunately as it mapped the San Francisco Bay, it also was able to pick up pipes spewing industrial wastes nearly 100 feet under water. Apparently, the Corps of Engineers brought this to the attention of the polluters, who in turn offered to sue the Corps and our company for violation of the Posse Comitatus Act of 1878. That act had been passed by Congress to limit the Federal Government from using military assets to spy on civilians. As I said *No Good Deed goes unpunished.*

Leaving Ft Lewis

Back at Ft Lewis, most of the guys I trained in the OV-1D had already shipped out for a tour in Vietnam. Paul was working with his brother in their dad's business, Industrial Tank, in Walnut Creek, California. Industrial Tank cleaned up industrial waste, oil spills, chemicals, what have you, and was very successful. Bats, had gotten out and was attending Emery Riddle Aeronautical College in Florida. The advanced course was a necessary step toward making Major and since the airlines were not hiring, I was hanging around the Army, drawing a paycheck until the Airlines opened up. Everything I owned could fit in my 1968 Corvette. The day before I left I sold my boat to a Warrant Officer friend of mine and the guys threw me a going away party. I was presented with a Silver Mug on which the guys had engraved my favorite saying **Fuck it, it don't mean shit.** It was something I learned in Vietnam when guys got killed, and it has stayed with me.

My first stop on the way to Ft. Huachuca was to spend a couple of days at a resort on the Stanislaus River. A friend got me a huge house there that allegedly belonged to Jill St John. It was peaceful there, had a big crystal clear lake, and jogging trails. I had called and invited Marylou to come up and scuba dive the lake, and raft the Stanislaus River. While waiting on Marylou, I went out jogging on one of the trails. I was just shuffling along when a guy on a big black stallion comes running by, and I had to jump off the trail. I yelled some inarticulate profanities at him. He turned around, came back, and started apologizing. I noticed right away that I had seen him somewhere before. As he got off his horse, I remembered, it was on TV.

"Sorry for yelling at you Robert or do you prefer Bob?"

"Robert is fine, what do I call you."

"I'm a Bob too, pleasure to meet you."

"Well Bob, can I buy you a drink, it's almost Happy Hour?"

"That would be great shall I see you in 30 minutes?"

"Yes, I need to put my horse up, and take a shower."

Robert was Robert Conrad of the Wild, Wild West TV show. I took a shower and walked to the resort bar. Robert showed up and we sat at the bar drinking and telling lies. He was not anal about who he was and we were having a good time and getting just a little hammered. Then, I noticed Marylou was standing at the door and Robert's eyes bugging out.

"Son of a bitch Bob, look at the Goddess who just walked in."

"She is definitely a 12. Tell you what, lets bet on who can pick her up."

"Well, what do you have in mind?"

"I'll go first and I will bet you I can put a lip lock on her inside of two minutes."

"You're on. What's the bet?"

"Drinks, for the rest of the night!"

"Done, You get slapped you lose."

I got up, walked over to Marylou, and stood in front of her where Robert couldn't see what I was saying. I told her it was great to see her, and told her not to look around but Robert Conrad was sitting at the bar and I had bet him drinks for the rest of the evening if I could kiss her within 2 minutes. She said okay, how much time do we have? We made what looked like small talk, and then she put a lip lock on me that nearly busted my zipper. Damn she was gorgeous. When she let me loose, I grabbed her hand and led her over to Robert. He looked like a guy who had just stepped into a bar and realized it was gay.

Marilou

I felt bad for pulling his leg, but felt he could afford it. The next day, Marylou and I went on a rafting trip down the Stanislaus River. We came to a deep part of the river with a high rock cliff on the right side. A rope was hanging there and the guides said they were going to climb up and jump; did anyone want to join them. Sure I said, and followed them up. There was a small four inch ledge which the guys balanced on while still holding the rope, before they jumped. No one else wanted to go with them. Both the guides jumped feet first to a roaring sign of approval from the tourists. It was thirty feet down as I looked at Marylou. I did the breast stroke, and was a diver on our high school swimming team; so with more balls than brains, I launched off and did a one and half dive. It was so far down, and I entered the water so cleanly, that I nearly drowned getting back to the surface.

The night, before I was to leave, Robert asked me if I would mind if he asked Marylou out.

"I don't own her Robert, if she wanted to go and I said no, I would be the asshole, so knock yourself out. She's a lady and I really respect her so treat her right." Robert was married.

The Advanced Course

I arrived in Sierra Vista, home to the Military Intelligence Center, in the early summer of 1973. It was all desert and cactus and 100 plus degrees of heat. The humidity was around 8 percent so while it was hot, it wasn't miserable. I reported in, was given a schedule of class times and where to go. There were about 25 of us, most were married.

I went to find a place to live, again no housing for bachelors on post, and found a fairly livable two bedroom two bath place in Sierra Vista not five minutes from work. I went in to work that afternoon and met the other class members, one of whom instantly passed the roommate test and I asked Larry Cassaw to share the apartment.

I love horses and found out they had stables on post. I checked out the horses and decided to come back when I had time for a ride. Saturday, as usual in that Sahara desert, was crystal clear and radiating heat, like Hell must be for atheists. Having been given the proverbial, *you look just like Burt Reynolds* routine I naturally bought myself some rough suede, hip huggin bell bottom pants. *If tight jeans worked for Burt, it would work for me.*

I picked out my horse, checked the saddle and the length of the stirrups, swung up and rode off into the desert, to amaze myself and any others that might be observing. After, about twenty minutes, my shirt was soaked to the bone. I took it off and tied it to the saddle. I decided to try a nice *short* cantor; knowing anything longer would get me bucked off, or kicked in the head back at the barn. As such, I was loping along when a rattle snake decided that the shade looked better under the adjacent cactus. The horse made an immediate exit, stage left. As all the experts, (and probably Burt), would not do, I continued on as if still in the saddle, airborne for six feet. And then, as gravity dictated, I hit the ground, flying ass end over tea kettle, through the cactus and desert rocks, coming to rest with something warm running down my back. I missed the snake, which was probably thinking," *works every time"* got up and realized that I was about three miles from the barn with no shirt. A great deal chastened and with a cut on my left shoulder, I managed to get back home.

My 1968 Corvette

I met a girl, Tina, at the Officers Club. She was in town staying with a friend because she lived 30 miles away in Bisbee, Arizona. Bisbee is the site of one of the largest open pit copper mines in America. In order to date her, I had to drive to Bisbee pick her up and bring her back to Fort Huachuca to the Officers Club and return her home before 1:00 AM. The date sucked, mainly due to friends referring to her as a dumb blond, not to mention the drive. While driving on any Military base a strict speed limit of 25mph is required. My corvette needed to be in second gear to maintain such a speed. It was like trying to hold back a Stud (I mean a horse) and making it walk all day. So when I let her off in Bisbee, I noticed that I was up on a high plateau and could see the lights of Sierra Vista. The road was a straight long shot down the plateau to the base. It was 2:00am and not seeing any car lights, now was the time to blow a little carbon out of my three deuces. I ran the corvette through the gears until I was cruising at 110mph eating up the asphalt like a wife goes through your money. I was about ten miles out when I saw some flashes of light on the highway ahead. Shit someone must have had a wreck. Not being in a hurry to slow down I just let the car slow down on its own until I could make out three cop cars in the middle of the road. *Come on bullshit, don't leave me now.* One of the officers flashes his flashlight at me and indicates I should pull over. I could feel bubba's dong trying to get in. I pulled over and shut it down. The Officers approached my window.

"Good evening gentlemen, how can I help you?"

"License and ID please"

I handed them my military ID and license. The guys were all my age and all smiling.

"What's the joke, I like to laugh too"

"Captain, if you will step out of the car and turn around, you will notice way back towards Bisbee, a set of red and blue lights coming this way. That is our buddy who is driving a Ford interceptor. He radioed us that some asshole in a green corvette pulled away from him at mach one. He was pissed he couldn't catch you, and asked us to come out and hold you for him. What do you have in there anyway?"

"Officers you know a gentleman doesn't kiss and tell."

"At 100 plus miles per hour unless you prefer to spend the night in jail, we will ask you one more time."

"Well Shit gentlemen, let me open the hood and show you."

As I was opening the hood the officer from Bisbee skidded to a halt.

"Son of a bitch you caught the fucker."

Apparently these guys missed the war and grammar school. I made the war, but missed etiquette school.

"Good evening Officer, I was just about to show these nice gentlemen how I managed to coast almost all the way here from Bisbee."

"Great, maybe you can coast all the way to jail too."

"Tom, don't be so hasty. I think we have a plan that will fit this Vietnam veteran."

They then locked me in the rear of one of their automobiles. I had never been in one before but with the nice little fence, no door handles or window handles, I felt very secure. The boys then went and had a conference. When they came back they offered me a $300 ticket, a night in jail, or I could sit in their patrol car while they each drove my Corvette. It was an offer I couldn't refuse. So while I sat in the back of their nice patrol car I watched as each officer sped by me at warp speed. When they let me out they were grinning like they had each just won the lotto. They even said thanks.

When I got in my Corvette, I had no gas left.

"Hey, guys I don't have enough gas to make it into Sierra Vista."

"We suggest you drive slow and be careful."

Big bad ass corvette idled into Sierra Vista, on fumes.

Fort Huachuca `also had a flying club. After class I drove over to check it out. There was nothing I wanted to fly except an old Aero Commander. That particular aircraft was still painted as a U.S. Army aircraft. The Aero Commander is a twin engine high wing aircraft that's makes you feel like you are landing on your ass because the bottom of the aircraft is so close to the ground. I had Kathy coming to see me who would be traveling on Continental Airlines and landing at Tucson Airport. Dressed in cut off blue jeans, tank top and flip flops, I flew up to Tucson. While on approach I informed them that I was picking up a girlfriend from Continental and could they direct me to park right next to arriving gate. I park, shut down, climb out, and can see the tower guys watching the unloading passengers from Continental looking at me like I was choking the chicken. Kathy gets off and thinking nothing of the way I was dressed, climbed in the co-pilots seat and away we went.

The base also had a football team which played other teams like the Marines, the Air Force, and other

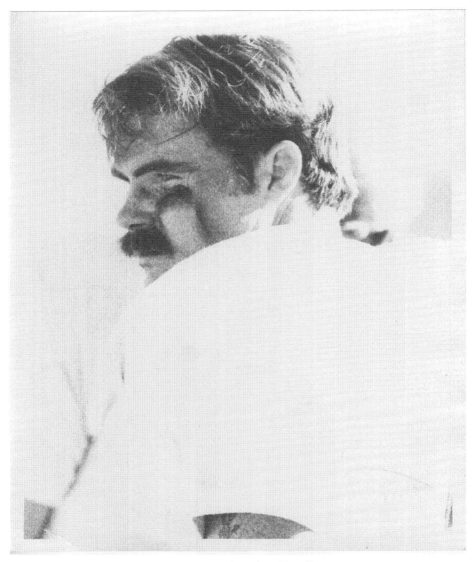

Dressed for football

Military bases.

The coach of the team appeared in our class, looking for players. Being highly aggressive, I volunteered. Practice was after class, and it helped reduce the stress of an eight hour day of studies.

I was out at practice when my classmates showed up at the practice field. They said: "Bob you have to come see this now."

"Guys, I am in the middle of practice."

"You have to come now, ask the coach, it's just over there at Brian's house."

So, I ask the coach if I can be excused for just ten minutes. With his okay, I follow the guys over to one of their on base houses.

"WTF guys, what is it?"

They wanted me to watch the news. As the evening news came on, the camera showed a huge black cloud of smoke boiling up from Tucson. The camera then zoomed in and **Key Corvette** materialized out of the smoke.

"Isn't that where you took your Corvette to be customized?"

I stared wide eyed at the screen, because I had indeed taken my nice 1968 Corvette there to have the wheel wells flared out, and a custom paint job put on it.

Walter Cronkite was announcing, "This is the worst fire in Tucson history."

The camera then went to a Mexican who was being interviewed. "Man, I try get Corvette out, but fire too great. I tink fire start in back of shop, where rags are throw away."

The camera then zooms in on my Corvette. It was sitting in the doorway the wheel wells had been flared out it was primed and ready for the paint shop. Just as they zoom in, the roof collapses on my Corvette, the mags already heated burst into flares like a thermite grenade *(a grenade designed to burn its way through a tank)*. The guys look at me and burst out laughing.

"Fuck it, it don't mean shit!"

I had the Corvette insured with USAA, an insurance company for former officers. I call them and they indicate that they will find me a replacement, or give me $2500. Since, it was my choice, I tell them to find me a replacement, one with the same engine and the same three deuces for carburetion. They agree. At this point, let me brag on USAA for just a minute. They are the finest Insurance Company in the world, and I have been with them for 41 years.

Betsy

Larry Cassaw and I both met Betsy Oar at the same time. She was drop dead gorgeous, living in our complex and teaching school in Sierra Vista. First night I met her, I invited her to dinner at the Officers Club. She was shy, intelligent, talkative laughed easily and was not a push over. I knew I was going to be in deep shit.

The next week USAA calls and cannot find a Corvette equivalent to the one I owned. We haggle and finally agree on a price of $6500 dollars. It was the fall of 1973 and I took Betsy with me down to the local Corvette dealer. *(You will always find fifteen to twenty car dealers wherever there is a Military base)* The new 1973 Corvettes had been out for several months and I wanted one. On the show room floor was a nice silver one. I ask for a salesman.

"Excuse me sir, what do you want for this Corvette."

"Well son, this is nearly our last one. They go out the door like hotcakes at the IHOP."

Spoken like a true salesman.

"The question was what do you want for it?"

"$8500 son, and that's the best we can do."

"Okay, I'll give you $6500 for it."

The guy stammers and guffaws and finally gets his mouth back in working order.

"Absolutely no way, are you crazy?"

"Well, let me speak to the manager."

By this time there is a crowd starting to gather.

"I am the manager, and I say No Way!"

"Tell me sir, do you gamble?"

"Occasionally!"

"Well, I will bet you $6500 versus your $8500 on the toss of a coin, and you can call it."

Betsy thinks I'm out of my mind but the crowd that had gathered, are egging on the manager to do it.

He wasn't really going to lose anything as I had checked with the bank on what it was worth. But, I loved pulling peoples chains and it was fun.

"Okay, I'll do it, you pay me $8500 if you lose and I sell you the car for $6500 if I lose."

There were probably 20 people standing around now. So I pull out a quarter, show him it is real and tell him to call heads or tails when I flip it in the air. He understands and I flip the quarter up in the air and let it land on the floor.

"Heads," he says as the quarter is in the air.

It lands on the floor and comes up tails. I thought he was going to cry but true to his word, we make the deal.

Football Game

Our football games were usually played on Saturday nights. Lots of people would show up. Not much to do in Sierra Vista unless you wanted to watch someone's paint dry. We were playing the Marines. Big time rivalry and they were having trouble stopping me as a running back that is, until a Marine stuck his elbow through my face mask and knocked out my front teeth. I jogged over to the sidelines, pulled out my mouth guard and several broken teeth fell out. He had broken them in half and the nerves were hanging out like little pink worms. Unbelievable pain and sensitivity! Larry agreed to take me to the hospital. Once there, they had no dentists available, so I had to wait two hours for one to show up.

Several weeks later we were playing the same Marines again, and I was running through their line. That same Marine got frustrated, blindsided me and tore the ACL out of my right knee. So much for football! I think the intern on staff was peeved at having to come in and tells me, he wouldn't advise surgery, because you really don't need an ACL. I was put in a cast from ankle to crotch and escorted to the door. That decision would haunt me later.

Motorcycle Accident

Six weeks later I was out of the cast and had proposed to Betsy. We were both excited. Some friends who had two Kawasaki 750 motorcycles suggested we ride double and drive over to Old Tombstone. Betsy had never been on a motorcycle. I instructed her to hold on tight to my waist and lean wherever I leaned. We were doing about 60mph when we crossed a bridge over a dry creek bed, followed by a 90 degree left turn, then another 90 degree turn to the right within 100 feet. We made the first turn, leaning over almost touching my entire leg on the ground, and started into the next turn. There was a couple of handfuls of gravel on the road, and Betsy, having made the first turn, got scared and sat upright, causing the bike to touch the footrest on the ground which made the back tire skip sideways, on the ground. When the gravel ran out, the back wheel caught solid ground and jerked the bike straight up. I had throttled down as best I could but there was an old railroad crossing sign dead ahead, ready to hair lip me. I swerved to the right to miss it and ran right into a washed out rail road track that was some 12 inches off the ground. The front tire hit the track, Betsy and I started a one way solo trip through the air. Betsy pushed herself off the back of the bike as we went airborne, but I held on for another 100 feet before I crashed straight down onto the front tire. I of course, hit the front handle bars, followed by a face first crash into the ground. The bike bounced back up into the air and came down on my back. I didn't lose consciousness, but I knew instantly that I had screwed the pooch. However, I was very concerned about Betsy. I was lying face down in the dirt, but managed to roll onto my back. I could actually hear bones scrapping together as I moved, plus there was blood coming out of my mouth, but instead of it dripping, it was foaming. Guys in combat and Paramedics know that is a sure sign you punctured a lung. I saw Betsy 100 feet back near the rail road tracks. She was lying on her back with a big piece of rebar sticking out of the ground next to her. Great, I've killed my fiancé. I took my helmet off, and started crawling toward her, using only my left arm. My other friends were in a state of shock, just sitting on the road by their bike. I still didn't hurt yet, but the grinding of my bones was somewhat unnerving. I made it to Betsy, and found the rebar was sticking out between her chest and her left arm. As I pushed up her visor, she opened her eyes and uttered the first profane thing I ever heard come out of her mouth, "You stupid Shit".

I was gamely trying to access her injuries when two enlisted guys stop to see what's going on and jump into action. Betsy was well endowed upstairs so they both jumped immediately to help her. I was just another deer that had been shot through the lungs, so I could wait. Think about it, what would you do? You have a beautiful girl with big hooters, and a Captain that is foaming blood out of his mouth, and has hairy legs. That didn't take you long did it?

So they pick up Betsy, laying her gently in the bed of their truck. The Captain, *(we know he is a Captain because he is wearing a flight jacket)*, we throw him over one guy's shoulder and pitch into the bed of the truck. Then they hauled ass for the base hospital, Madigan General. Madigan throws us both on gurneys and roll us down to the emergency room. A doctor comes in sees me breathing foam and tells the orderly to cut off my clothes and get me to X ray. He then walks over to Betsy. Not seeing anything obvious, he tells another orderly to go get her clothes off and get X rays. Both of these orderlies are enlisted men, the one assigned to me is obviously pissed off because the one with Betsy is going to get see her big hooters. Hell, I wanted to see her hooters. At any rate this guy is pushing me down the hall like he had just stolen a car stereo. Of course by this time every inch of my body hurt. I could hardly breathe due to a punctured lung, and he wasn't making any friends.

In a raspy voice I say, "Hey buddy if you want to go see her tits, just push me up against the wall and come back later." Son of bitch, he does it.

Turns out I had a punctured lung which needed a tube pushed through my chest wall, a collar bone fractured in three places, a scapula or shoulder blade fractured in two places, and broken ribs front and back on my right side. They put me in figure eight bandage, which pulled the rib out of my lung, straightened my fractured collar bone, and pretty much kept the scapula from moving. I then went to the ICU, where I had enough tubes and wires attached to pick up radio in the Soviet Union. They would not give me anything for pain because the doctor was afraid I might have internal injuries. I told him I did two hundred sit ups a day and that was why my stomach was so tight. Misery is the brother of stupidity.

Larry brings Betsy to see me at about 7:00pm. She took one look and fainted. She would later learn, nearly two years later, that she had fractured her jaw. It seems she couldn't open her mouth as far as she used too and it was bothering her. So much for military x rays! For the next week the right side of my body turned purple, blue, and yellow. I needed a bath, I always sweat at nights, even if I sleep naked with no covers. *(Never had before, but it started after my return from Vietnam, and continues today)* Frustrated and pissed off, I demanded to be given a bath. An orderly came in and helped me off the bed at around 8:00am. He took me to a room with a large tub, filled it with hot water, and said he would be back later. Later, turned out to be nearly 12 hours later, by which time I was blue from cold, and shivering so bad I was in terrible pain. The room had a door, and the orderly had shut it. I couldn't expand my chest far enough to call out for help and the water controls were high above my feet. Near 7:00pm, a nurse walked in, looked at me and said, "What, the hell are you doing here?" I could barely whisper, I was in so much pain and so cold. Man never screw with a nurse, she was mad, and getting me out of there, took less time than it took to send me a draft notice, once I dropped out of the University of Houston.

The Dentist

Once I got out of the hospital and could walk, I had to go see the dentist, which hadn't happened in about three years. He took X-rays, rooted around in my mouth like a blind man, and whistled through his teeth. The universal sign of stating, *I'm going to enjoy this.* I had four wisdom teeth that had grown in sideways and were crushing my other back teeth.

"Bob, you need to get these out, not only because they are impacting your other molars, but also because in the civilian world they will cost you about $750 a piece to get out."

"Okay, schedule me an appointment."

I went home to my buddy Larry, who, with all the sympathy one normally reserves for the guy who stole his girlfriend, told me how swollen and painful it would be.

Back at the dentist's office, Jack the Ripper was waiting.

We decided to do one side, upper and lower, at a time. He numbed me up, and commenced his dissection of my gum, to get down to the tooth. Once, he was there, I hear this," oh crap!" You're sitting with your mouth open like a crocodile in heat, and you hear that "Oh Crap". I had heard that many times in my life and it always meant that I had just passed the line reserved for normal people.

"Bob this tooth is laying nearly horizontal, which means, I have to break it in pieces to get it out. I am going to have the nurse hold this padded piece of wood under your jaw, while I use this chisel and hammer to break it up. And yes, later tonight it is going to hurt, so I will give you some good drugs."

Well thank you doc that gives me such a warm fuzzy feeling.

You know if you stand in a shower and put your fingers in your ears, it really sounds like it is raining. Think what it sounds like, when some sadistic dentist is hammering on your tooth with a hammer and a chisel. Sounds like breaking glass inside your head.

It took thirty plus minutes to get the first one out, having broken it into four pieces. The upper one took longer, and by the time it was out I could barely open or close my mouth. He gave me some killer drugs and sent me home with another appointment for the following week. When, I entered out apartment, Larry took one look at me and said, "Hey buddy, no one is going to ask you to dance any time soon." Next day I looked like I had tried to see how many golf balls I could put in my mouth. The drugs didn't work all that well and I spent a miserable night.

The following week we had to repeat the procedure. Again, he gave me some killer drugs, but this time when I got home, I opened a bottle of Brandy, and drank the whole thing. Never underestimate the healing power of alcohol. Slept like a baby and never felt a thing.

Marriage

Before I was to leave Ft. Huachuca, I married Betsy. It was a traditional military wedding, Dress Blues, crossed swords, held at the Davis Monthan Air Force Base. Betsy was an exceptional person, beautiful, intelligent, Christian, moral, and most of all loyal. In hind sight, she deserved someone much better than me.

Trip to Ft. Hood

I graduated from the Military Intelligence Advanced Course, and got orders to Fort Hood, Texas. Betsy had to stay until they could find a replacement for her Third grade class. I was so sick of Ft. Huachuca, that once I said good bye to Larry, I got on the road at 3:00pm determined to drive straight through to Ft. Hood. I was cruising along about 11:30pm thinking I must be getting tired because I couldn't see very far. It was mid-January and cold, but I thought I needed some fresh air so I attempted to roll down the window of my **New Corvette**. The window went down about three inches and stopped. *Piece of shit new corvette a month old and the window won't work.* So, I attempted to roll down the passenger window with the same result. That kicked in something my dear ole dad used to say about batteries and cars. *"When your car battery dies, so does your car."* I immediately looked at the battery charge on the dash. Son of Bitch, it was reading a negative charge. I was about thirty miles from Pecos out in the middle of nowhere. I turned off the lights and radio and sped up to 80mph. I would pass the few cars on the freeway and it must have scared them shitless. I saw the exit to Pecos, when the car died. I managed to coast down the exit ramp under the overpass for the freeway, and right into a filling station that was about to close. The owner was an old grizzled guy with a heart of gold. He helped me push the corvette into his station even got a nice big blanket to lay on the side of the car while we looked under the hood to find the problem. Didn't take us long, the alternator belt was gone. Of course, there were belts for the alternator, belt for the air condition-er, belt for cooling fan on the radiator, belt for the power steering, and a belt for the heater and air conditioning fan inside the car. Just to screw with my deteriorating sense of humor, the alternator belt was the last one in line, meaning I had to take all the others off before I could replace it. The old guy had one weak arm, but was determined to stay with me until the problem was fixed. Turned out, he didn't have a belt small enough for this new car but, what he did have was an old tractor outside that had a belt that would fit. I scavenged that belt and was on my way after about two hours. The old guy refused any payment but I stuffed a $100 bill into his coveralls and thanked him profusely.

On the east side of Pecos was a Holiday Inn, where I decided to get a room, get some sleep, and start out early in the morning. I got a room at the back of the motel. The parking lot was damn near a ¼ of mile long and at 2:30am not a car was there. I took my toothbrush, change of clothes, and went to my room and took a shower. Just before I turned in, I took a quick look out my window to check on the car. Coming down the back of the hotel I watched as a sedan slowly made its way down toward my car. Then in amazement I watched as it pulled in right next to my corvette. I watched as the driver's door opened hitting my Corvette enough to make it shake. I was immediately irritated. Wrapping a towel around myself I grabbed the car keys and headed down the stairs to the parking lot. Still wet with wild hair, I stomped across the asphalt toward the car. When I get there I lean down and look at the big nick in my new Corvette.

"Ah, sir do you have insurance, this is a custom paint job and you just put a big ding in my door?"

"Fuck you kid."

Now I thought I had been calm under the circumstances, and this bozo tells me to fuck off.

I had backed in my parking space, so I went around to the driver's door, opened it, got out my 1911 .45 caliber pistol and walked back over to the f…you guy.

His mousy little wife is hiding behind him saying, "Harold he's got a gun."

"What do you think you are going to do with that?"

"Well sir, I figured I would ask you again if you had any insurance. If, I get the same answer again, then I intend to blow several holes in your door you know misfire while unloading."

Out pops a wallet and he offers me $200 to make amends. Then he and mousy jump back in their car and high tail it out of there.

Next morning I am back on my way to Ft. Hood. I arrive late in the evening, report in, and go looking for somewhere to stay. Next day I rent a nice little duplex for Betsy and me to call home.

I was Operations Officer with about 25 OV-1s. Ft. Hood has quite a history. It used to be a nuclear storage facility, with nearly 100 plus miles of underground tunnels. The tunnels have floors smoother than your home. Where a tunnel branches off from one to another the initial tunnel goes on for about 25 feet. A blast will not turn corners, therefore the extension. There were huge rooms with overhanging I-beams for lifting the nuclear weapons. The perimeter outside has three fences, outside one is 10 feet tall topped with razor wire, middle one was sunk into the ground 15 feet with 12" wide reinforced concrete plus 12 foot high fence, the inner one is 10 feet high with razor wire. The fences are about ten feet between each one and guard dogs had walked in there, free to roam, and they didn't bark first. Guard towers were actually underground pill boxes that had to be accessed by the tunnels. Very interesting place!

I was assigned to the 131st Military Intelligence Company (Aerial Surveillance), formerly stationed in I Corps Vietnam. We were attached to the 82nd Airborne Brigade as part of, an IRE *(Initial Reaction Unit)*. As such, we were on a 24 hour alert status to fly anywhere in the world where trouble might break out. With an IRE status we got top priority for anything we needed. We were flying the OV-1D model aircraft, requiring three of the following aircraft to be ready at a moment's notice. Three Infrared aircraft, and three SLAR aircraft, equipped with the latest technology. The Infrared system was 10 times better than what we had in Vietnam and so was the SLAR. The aircraft were also equipped with tape instruments for monitoring the engines. Tape instruments looked like big thermometers instead of round gauges. Like all government crap,they didn't work very well. We also had a new inertial navigation system, apparently designed by someone who smoked some good grass. They didn't work long either. The internal pieces, six inch square computer boards, cost more than a brand new Cadillac. I was constantly ordering new parts. Another drawback was the fact that we couldn't fly nonstop to New York, much less anywhere overseas. I would constantly requisition new parts, and 300 gallon drop tanks, (which only the Navy had), which would have extended our range dramatically. The requisitions would come back denied. Our Company Commander, Norm, could do nothing about it. If he pushed too far, he would be reminded of his place in the hierarchy. I got explosively pissed. WTF did IRE mean, *I remain excluded?*

We constantly had drills, you would get a call at midnight and within one hour you would have to have the aircraft ready, and your personal gear immaculately folded and ready for inspection. The aircraft held 295 gallons of fuel internaly, those drop tanks would have added six hundred more gallons to our distance. After weeks of this we were given one weekend off. Betsy and I drove to Houston to see my parents. While we were there we went out to a Steak House for dinner with friends. Hollis and his wife Jeanette, Betsy and I, Luke and a girlfriend, and another couple were seated at a table in a far corner. We were the only ones in a room fifty by thirty feet across. We were having a good time, talking about had we been girls, which of us would have had the biggest hooters. My mom was five foot two and a double D. We had been there thirty minutes when another two couples walked in and sat as far away from us as they could. These two guys were six foot seven inches and six foot six inches and built like a brick shit house. Ten minutes passed when these two monster men walked over to our table and stood behind Luke, who was only five feet eight inches.

"We don't like you guy's cussing in front of our girlfriends. " Luke sitting at the end of the table turned around and was looking into his belt buckle.

"We don't want any trouble but we weren't cussing."

"Well, what do you call tits?"

Someone said, "Bet you can't eat just one."

It appeared that they were just spoiling for a fight and of course like all cowards, they picked on the smallest guy at the table.

Luke says, "Listen, if we offended you we apologize we don't want any trouble."

"Well, you got it mother fucker."

Betsy had her hand on my leg and squeezed, like please don't get involved. I stood up, "Gentlemen, you talk about our saying tits, then use really foul language which I don't appreciate here in front of my wife."

He then started poking me in the chest, "Oh yeah and what are you going to do about it mother fucker"

I wanted to tell him to keep his mother off the streets.

"Please don't do that" I said, and he immediately started to poke me again. As soon as his finger reached my chest, I reached up with my right hand and broke it with a loud snap. Next thing I knew I was flying backwards across the table, through the wine glasses and food.

Hollis later told me that he never even saw me hit the ground before I was flying back across the table.

This bully obviously didn't expect any retaliation from someone he outweighed by seventy pounds. I knew if he got his hands on me I would get a real pounding. So I grabbed his shirt by the neck and stuck my right hand straight into his mouth. I felt teeth break as he stumbled backward and fell. I stayed glued to his chest and started pounding his face for all I was worth. Blood was flying everywhere and he was choking on it. His buddy tried to kick me in the head, but when he reared back to kick, he stuck his leg through a stained glass window cut the shit out of it and started howling. Mean time, all my friends except for Betsy, filed out through the kitchen and out a back door.

The manager came and grabbed my arm and told me the guy was out. He said he had seen the whole thing, had called the police and perhaps I better leave too. I walked out with Betsy, blood dripping from my arms and returned to my dad's house. Next morning a guy shows up at my dad's and asks for me. When I got to the door, the guy was laughing. He said he had never met someone worth ten million dollars, but he had an envelope for me. The envelope was from the attorneys for the Houston Oilers. Those two bullies were linemen for the NFL football team, I was being sued for screwing up their ability to play for several weeks. Actually, I started laughing thinking about how that would play out in the papers, since I was only five feet and eleven inches and a 180 punds. My father on the other hand did not find it remotely humorous, and once again queried me regarding counseling and whether I had been to any. He said, " Son you came home different, something is wrong, and next time you might kill someone. I blew it off again.

I had flown part time for an attorney, and called him. He was an internationally known Jewish attorney and I laid out what had just happened. He told me to hang tight by the phone for twenty minutes and hung up. Sure enough I get a call twenty minutes later from the Oilers attorneys, who wanted me to drop the whole thing as a mistake. Apparently, they too did not want the publicity and they knew my buddy by reputation. I called Don back and asked him what he said. "I just explained to them that you were my bodyguard and pilot and I had expert witnesses from the restaurant that their big 270 pound guys attacked my 180 pound pilot and you kicked their ass. It will look good on the evening news." They actually asked me if I could consider the matter dropped with their apology. It's nice to have friends in high places.

I wanted it in writing.

Returning to the world's biggest goat fuck at Fort Hood, I was so pissed I would come home and run clean out of town along the highway, until my Betsy would pick me up.

Two days later we get another alert, and have one hour to get into formation on the airfield. They were going to have the Commanding General, his entire staff, and Congressional visitors, Senators and Congressmen, inspect us. It was going to be another giant dog and pony show. I was to be in command of the six aircraft scheduled to be deployed so I stood out in front of the aircraft while auxiliary power units were attached to them in order to make this rat fuck as real as possible. I also had a manila folder three inches thick with all the denials I had received for parts. This dog and pony show covered nearly the entire airfield at Fort Hood, Texas. The General, his Congressional visitors, as well as his staff approached me. I snapped to attention and saluted.

"Good afternoon, Captain Boyd, how much time do you have in this aircraft?"

"2500 hours sir"

"That is impressive, and I see you have a significant number of decorations from Vietnam, impressive indeed. Are you ready to go flying?"

"That Sir depends on where we are requested to go. Right now, we don't have an aircraft behind me mission capable, and those are the best we have"

"Stand at ease Captain Boyd, and step over here by yourself."

I could see Major Norm behind him starting to shake his head. In addition, the General's entire staff, were making *"cut throat"* motions with their hands. What a cluster fuck!!"

The General and I moved out of ear range, and he wanted an explanation.

"Sir, these aircraft as currently configured have a three hour fuel load with a reserve. Not one of them can perform the mission for which they were tasked. The reasons are multitude and serious. In order to say, fly across the Atlantic, we need to have three hundred gallon drop tanks. As they sit, we have 150 gallon drop tanks. The inertial navigation systems are down due to a lack of proper computer cards, which cost about as much as a new Cadillac. The engine tape monitoring gauges are broken on four of the six aircraft. To be honest, Sir, we could not legally fly from here to New York, nor could we perform our tasked mission."

'Would you like to explain to me Captain, why all of that is so?"

"Yes Sir, I would. I was led to believe that our mission held the highest priority for anything we needed, having been assigned as part of the 82nd Airborne Initial Reaction Force. I have here, requests for all the parts needed, sometimes requested three and four times. As you can see, your G4 (*Supply*) denied them all as being too expensive. My CO, Major Norm, is the best there is on this aircraft and he has tried as well, only to be advised not to push any further. As for me, Sir, the quicker I can get out of this cluster fuck, the better off I will be."

"You realize Captain, that you just made a bunch of highly placed enemies."

"Again Sir, and not to be crude, I don't give a rat's ass."

"You are a remarkable young man Captain. If you are threatened in any way please alert me immediately. I would hope that you would reconsider your desire to get out, but if that is your wish, I personally will sign your release papers."

With that, the General dismissed everyone, and ordered his staff to report immediately to his office. I resigned that very afternoon.

You may think that my military career was performed in an arrogant and subordinate nature. Was I arrogant, hell yes, especially if you tried to dazzle me with your bullshit. I also had a quick temper, something eating me from the inside and I never really knew when it would show it's ugly head. Like I said *REMF's, blowhards, incompetents and assholes didn't get the time of day from me.* Additionally, while I was at Fort Lewis the Army RIFed (reduction in force) some 20,000 Captains, just mustered them out with *"Call us if you find work"*. These were mostly combat pilots who, due to flying, had not had time to work in their branch.

A New Start

School was out so Betsy and I packed up and moved back to Houston. We found a nice two bedroom apartment, and settled in. I immediately went looking for work. I was offered a job with Thunderbird Airways, a Lear charter service, if I could get a type rating in a Lear. Leaving Betsy behind, I went to Dallas's Love field, and started a transition with my GI bill. I met a great guy who was in our class. His name was Bill he was a senior Delta Airlines 727 pilot. Both of us finished the course and the FAA check ride in under, 8 hours. I returned to Houston and got a job with the charter service. I was in 7th heaven. I met several Captains there who really helped me with the Lear Jet. They told me the inherent dangers, the wing tanks draining into the fuselage tank if not turned off would drain to the opposite wing tip tank and the next morning you would find your Lear jet resting on the opposite wing tank and a wheel off the ground. They articulated the risks of trying to fly at speeds above Mach .82, and of being cognizant of hypoxia and pressurization. I became very proficient in the aircraft and never forgot their admonishments.

I was flying with my favorite Captain we were up at 45,000 feet when he hears another Lear jet check in with air traffic control. My buddy in the left seat keys his mike and says, "Did you ever get all those pine cones out of your aircraft?" He then proceeds to tell me a story of how that particular Lear and its pilot were asked to be in a movie. They wanted them to fly low level across Lake Tahoe and over a boat they were using in the movie. They wanted them to get permission to fly with only the Captain, and mount a camera in the co-pilot's seat. The FAA granted the request and they set the Lear up for the shot. The Captain comes across the boat with the Director yelling "too high, and too slow."

The pilot pulls up over the rim of Lake Tahoe and sets up for another approach. This time he is lower and a bit faster. The Director again yells "too high and too slow." The pilot is pissed now so he climbs up for another run. This time he is balls to the wall and so low, the wing vortices are creating rooster tails on the lake. He was nearly to Mach speed and when you take a Lear jet that fast, it tends to tuck the nose down as you try to climb up. Lake Tahoe is a former volcanic crater and while it is filled with water, it ain't that far across. As the pilot is trying to pull up over the rim the Lear tucks toward the lake. He immediately reduced power and managed to get the aircraft to start up when he disappears into the trees. Trees are seen shooting up into the air and seconds later the Lear appears climbing back to altitude. It had dents in the leading edge of the wings, but a remarkable story. He told me that Lear jets were designed to be a fighter by the Swedes, and therefore had 8 wing spars compared to a U.S. airliner that only has two. In other words, built like a brick shit house. Bill Lear bought the plans and turned it into the Lear Jet. A little history never hurt anyone except for our revisionist of today.

One of Thunderbird Airways Lear25D

My friends were all jealous so one night about 11:00pm I took them over to see the Lear. We were in the cockpit when two of the partners showed up and were very clearly agitated. Didn't seem right to me, but we left.

We were flying a guy "Mr. Cotton" all over the world. We flew to Bermuda numerous times and while the Captain and I nearly got strip searched by the customs officials, Mr. Cotton and two of his associates were waved right through. This went on for several trips until I asked Mr. Cotton why he got waved through and we got searched. Next time we went to Bermuda we all got waved on through.

The charter company charged $1.85 per statute mile. So a trip out of Houston could cost a sizeable amount of money. Next trip to Bermuda I was flying Captain, when one of Cotton's associates leans into the cockpit and asked me how much Mr. Cotton owed the company. The company had given me an invoice in case I got to talk to Mr. Cotton and it was for $23,000 dollars. Without batting an eye, the associate opens a brief case absolutely filled with $1000 bills, and counts out $23,000 and hands it to me. Some of you may not know, but if you take more than $5000 out of the country you are subject to a fine and imprisonment. I'm a crazy man but I'm not stupid. I tried to give it back to him, but he refused, so I tucked it up behind the instrument panel and left it there. It turns out Mr. Cotton had foreseen the oil industry being greatly expanded and had bought up, all the drill pipe. He was selling it, at a handsome profit.

Flying west out of Bermuda, our Lear was the old 25D model with turbo jet engines, so it ate a lot of fuel. Add to that, the easterly jet stream at nearly 200-250 knots and to make Miami was on luck and a prayer. Once we touched down in Miami, Mr. Cotton took us all out to eat at an Italian restaurant. The Maitre'd, came to take our order. When he saw one of the associates he turned white as a ghost and dropped his pad. He says, "I thought you were dead!" This guy quickly replied that obviously that was not the case. Apparently, the associate was a hit man. Dinner was served with all the pomp and circumstance normally reserved for royalty and it was free.

MIG 21

The Lear 25D which has turbojet engines, actually the same engine as the T38 except for the afterburner, and could easily climb to 45,000 feet. Cruising along up there in route to Grand Caymen, a Mig 21 approached me from behind and pulled up into formation with me.

"Lear 24 tango rrrromeo you are close to Cuban airspace"

"Right you are you brain dead commie, our Navy F14 just radioed the same information. They're a little bored so they are in afterburner coming to see you, be here in less time than you can say Castro."

With that the Mig driver did a hard left descending turn and made like a cow turd and hit the road. My copilot found his voice about ten minutes later.

Mr. Cotton also took numerous trips to the Grand Caymen Islands for the same banking uses. We were there one evening having dinner. We had an associate's girl friend with us, we were doing the proverbial small talk and telling lies. Several blacks were in the restaurant. None of them were appropriately dressed. They were wearing cutoffs and tank tops, but what the hell it was their island. One of the guys kept repeatedly coming over to ask the girl to dance. With all the subtlety of a coiled Cobra, our Hit man would inform the guy that she wasn't interested. Apparently this guy's brain tumor was acting up and he couldn't see the danger. He comes back a third time and informs the Hit man that "he wasn't talking to him". With the speed of a congressman jumping in front of a camera, the Hit man is out of his chair grabs the black guy by his throat and stuffs a .38 down his throat. He hisses into the guys ear, "you don't listen do you asshole?" Even for a macho man like myself I sucked my underwear so far up my ass I could have used them for a hankie. The guy and the others left apologizing like they were in church.

I also flew Mr. Cotton to Venezuela where he was supposed to look at some real estate for future development. When I landed in Caracas there were troops down both sides of the runway armed with AK47s. I started questioning my involvement with these folks although they treated me very well. We met some big wigs and they took us to dinner in a fancy hotel. The women there were drop dead gorgeous, auburn haired, blue eyed, perfect bodies and very friendly. Mr. Cotton was a serious alcoholic. If he didn't have a couple of drinks in the morning he just flat couldn't function. The night we had dinner he had dropped an envelope I found on the floor. It had $15,000 in $1000 dollar bills in it. I don't think he would ever have missed it but a gentleman by act of Congress, and an honorable former Captain I returned it to him at breakfast the next morning.

After breakfast we flew to a barren little Island off the coast, known to most of you today as Aruba. It looked like a forlorn desert Island. If I hadn't spent so much money on women I could be a wealthy guy today.

Back in 1975 the United States was experiencing a shortage of sugar. Ever the entrepreneur, Mr. Cotton managed to buy ship loads of sugar from Venezuela. He then would sell that sugar to the military here in America. I found myself down in the holes of merchant marine vessels in Jamaica kicking rats, stomping on huge spiders and counting bags of raw sugar.

Checking the Books

The fact that the principles of Thunder Jet Charter had been so uptight about finding me in the cockpit late at night had made me suspicious. I had started to check the aircraft log where the time on the engines are recorded due to maintenance requirements. I started watching the two managers after I would land back in Houston and on numerous occasions I would find them immediately leaving in the aircraft for several hours. When I checked the log books, there was no time recorded for the trip. They were taking passengers, not logging it, and keeping the money for themselves. I wanted no part of an illegal operation so I quit.

Oil Service Company

I got hired by a friend whose family ran an oil service company. Oil rigs would be drilling thousands of feet deep and periodically they had to change bits which involved pulling all that drill pipe out of the hole. Before drilling a well they first had to drive a 24" to 36" or larger pipe into the soft mud to keep the well from collapsing before they started drilling. This initial pipe had to be driven below the mud level. My friend's company did both of these events and it was my job to fly out to Oil rigs and try and get the job. Flying out was done in a Cessna 185 on floats which required me to get a type rating in sea planes. He had me fly one of the planes to Baton Rouge, take a couple of hours of instruction, followed then, by a check ride to get my type rating. That was the easy part. Learning to dock a sea plane next to a barge, which all oil rigs have, was tricky and hard. My friend taught me very well. The problem was that a sea plane will naturally turn into the wind when the power is shut down. On the other hand, the current may be going in exactly the opposite direction. If you weren't careful the aircraft could turn a wing into the super structure of the rig and do some serious damage. I learned quickly but most of the drill bosses knew that several companies would be competing for the job and it became who could give the guy the best deal. The deal being new boots or whatever their pee pickin' heart desired. I wasn't real thrilled with the mechanics of the operation but my friend was a blast to hang with and party.

I became good friends with one of the guys I called on. His son was getting married followed by a honeymoon on Lake Travis in Texas. The Dad, my oil field engineer friend, wanted to do something special for the happy couple. *(It's amazing, how happy married couples are in the beginning. However, once the swelling goes down, you realize you are stuck for life)*. We decided that after the wedding I would meet them at Houston Hobby Airport with our amphibious Cessna 185 and fly them to Lake Travis, which was just outside Austin, Texas. I had decorated the Cessna with lots of colored streamers. I flew them to Lake Travis, and after landing I taxied up to the resort hotel putting the gear down and driving right up a boat ramp to their room.

Enterprise Products

I got interviewed and hired by Enterprise Products Company. It had originally been set up as a partnership between my Lawyer friend Don, and Enterprise Products Company, the idea being to share the astronomical expenses of owning and operating an aircraft. Each party would pay his or her pilot fees. We started out with a rice rocket, (a MU2J), a Japanese built high wing twin turboprop atrcraft. We flew it to nearly 100 plus hours a month. The chief pilot discovered that he had a cancer in one of his eyes and eventually they had to remove it which temporarily knocked him out of the cockpit.

The Enterprise Products company was owned by two guys. One was the President, Dan, and the other was Joe. They made Dan President because he never lost his temper, could make killer deals, and had the look of honesty and integrity. After our Chief pilot lost his eye Dan and Joe decided that they needed the MU2J far more time than Don did so they made arrangements to take over the operation totally.

I was flying my ass off nearly 100 hours a month. With a full load of passengers the MU2J would only climb to about 23,000 feet which put it right in the middle of any weather. I hired another acquaintance, Scotty, who was trying to build time to get on with the airlines. After about two months I had Scotty apply for a check ride and get his type rating. Doing so, would give me a break on the number of flying hours I was logging. Once Scotty had his type rating I would switch seats with him during each stopover, or leg, as we called it. We had landed in Austin Texas unloaded our passengers and would be flying empty back to Houston. The weather sucked I had landed with an RVR (runway visual range), of 2400 feet. By the time we were to take off the weather had deteriorated to an RVR of just over 700 feet with fog and light rain. I still let Scotty fly from the left seat while I acted as co-pilot. Our flight director, a small instrument that lets you know whether you are climbing, descending or in a bank had cross-hairs on it like a rifle scope which would sync to the instrument approach systems as well as with take offs, in really marginal weather. If you pushed a sync button for takeoff the cross bars would jump up to a normal angle of attack for a takeoff. However, push the sync button again, and it would drop the cross hairs to a level flight mode. I told Scotty to watch outside on initial takeoff and then glue his eyes to the instruments. We took off and Scotty called for gear up. We started to accelerate past two hundred knots and my mind told me something was wrong. I glanced outside and as I did so, I saw roof tops flying by at five feet. I yelled "I have the airplane" and immediately pulled up hard. Scotty had taken off and once the gear came up he had synced the cross hairs to level flight thus the increased airspeed and the low level. My heart had quit beating and there was some brown underwear. Once again, for whatever reason God had protected an idiot and fool.

I was running around with my hair and my ass on fire and carrying a box of matches in case one went out. I frequented a bar downtown where the women were known to accumulate. As I walked in I noticed a friend from Vietnam, Howard a former Huey pilot. He was sitting with his boss and several ladies. He introduced me to his boss as the best fixed wing pilot he knew, and that I was to jets what he was to helicopters. I told Howard that I had been transitioned into Huey's prior to my last assignment. His boss overheard the exchange and being four sheets to the wind exclaimed.

"Bet you can't fly my helicopter."

"Well, that depends on what kind of helicopter and where it is."

"It's right outside and it's a Jet Ranger."

"Oh shit, I can fly that."

I never could bypass a challenge, so with a cock sure attitude, I was asking Howard if I could fly his helicopter, when his boss spoke up.

"You don't have to ask him, it's my helicopter, knock yourself out."

"Okay, any of you girls want to go for a helicopter ride." Of course there were, so out the door we went to look at the helicopter. I buckled four girls in and then myself. It took me a couple of minutes to remember how to start the damn thing. I cranked it up and was pulling pitch when Howard's boss stumbled out the door waving his hands. The jet ranger was parked right in the middle of four tall buildings. Howard's boss must have had second thoughts but a challenge is a challenge, so I lifted off. I was a little shaky in the initial hover but quickly got my control touch back and climbed out over the shortest of the buildings. The night was clear and Houston is beautiful with all the lights on. I flew the girls around for about thirty minutes then returned to where I had taken off. I walked back in the bar with a guarantee of getting lucky. I had amazed the girls and myself. Howard's boss was by then, completely toasted. Howard asked me how the jet ranger was. I told him not to get too far from a fuel stop.

BELIZE

Don called one day and asked if he could rent the MU2J. He wanted to take a religious group to Belize. I checked with Dan and he authorized it. Don would fly in the co-pilot's seat and his friends would sit comfortably in the back. We left Houston flew across the Gulf of Mexico and into Belize. I was not thrilled to find out I was to sleep in a hut with one of the men. Don however arranged for the two of us to fly out to a small island off the coast. We would stay there scuba dive and fish. The runway was just a crushed coral affair and short. We arrived safely and immediately went scuba diving. The place was a scuba divers dream with nearly un-limited visibility and lots of Conch shells and lobsters. We would pull up a Conch shell cut the animal out and eat them raw. Delicious! After a couple of days of this Don told me he would like to visit a 30,000 acre parcel of land that he was considering buying. It belonged to the Salem Cigarette Company, and Don said it had a small strip on it. He was to meet his friends who had flown with us down to Belize they were renting a jeep and would meet us there. It was just a 20 minute flight to this ranch and we had enough fuel to get there and back to Belize before we would refuel and head home. We took off and headed inland. I was flying about 500 feet off the jungle and spotted what appeared to be a jeep on the side of this narrow road with people waving at me. I kept flying but asked Don:

"Hey Jewish Boy, what kind of a vehicle did your friends rent?"

"I think it was a pink jeep!"

"Well I could be wrong but I just saw a pink jeep on the side of that road we were following and there were people waving at us."

"Oh shit, turn around maybe they broke down."

I did a hard bank and turned around. Sure enough when we flew back over the jeep I had spotted, Don says:

"Oh crap, it is them, what are we going to do?"

"That is a really narrow road but I think I can land on it, pick them up, and then take off again, as long as no cars come along!"

"Then do it, please."

I scouted down the road several miles and then back up the other way. I saw nothing but jungle.

"Okay Don, I'll give it a shot." I set up an approach, got gear and flaps down, and landed on that friggin road. It was not what I expected. The jungle was 100 feet tall on both sides of the road and I had landed on the downhill slope of a long hill. I taxied up to them and told Don to get out, get them and let's get the hell out of there. My landing gear was hanging ½ on and ½ off the cracked and shitty asphalt. With the engines running I told Don he had to get out and direct me back up the road while I backed up it in reverse. Don did as I directed him and I backed up the road nearly ¾ of a mile. I motioned for Don to come get back in. I told his friends that we could use some prayers, held the brakes, pushed her up to max allowable power, and let her rip. It quickly became obvious (at least to me), that the broken down jeep on the side of the road was going to present a major problem. As narrow as the road was I would hit

the jeep with the left wing before I had safe flying speed. I was committed so we roared down that hill with me asking someone upstairs for help even though I knew I was not one of the favorite sons. I got to the jeep, lifted the left wing over it and continued on down the road another couple of hundred feet before I could become airborne. You couldn't drive a ten penny nail up my ass with a sledge hammer. The folks were yelling and clapping, something that was short lived. We arrived at the small dirt landing strip on the ranch and I set it down. As I was turning around a jeep full of black guys with torn undershirts and sporting AK47s skidded to a stop in front of me motioning for me to shut it down, and get out. Five AK47s would have a devastating effect on the thin fuselage and there was no way with them parked in front of me to take off. Don says:

"You still packing that .38 that I asked you to carry as my bodyguard?"

"Yes of course!"

"Well shit can it quick and don't let them see you."

I slipped out of my shoulder holster and shoved the whole thing up under the instrument panel. We deplaned with AK47s pointing at us. Only one of the guys could speak broken English. He directed the women and the other men to get into a second jeep that pulled up and left. I was searched and I forgot I had $4000 in hundred dollar bills on me to pay for gas. (Unless you are previously approved, you can only purchase fuel out of the States with cash). They found it, and it appeared as though they were elated. Don and I were pushed with the Ak47s toward the side of the strip. As we approached the side two of the guys pulled up a concealed grate that covered a 10'X10' hole that was nearly 15' deep. Unceremoniously, we were pushed into the hole. The guys, obviously proud of themselves, replaced the grate and left. Looking at Don I said:

"I feel like dinner at a cannibal's banquet, WTF is going on?"

"The President down here is a friend and I am sure he will come get us."

"Are you sure about that, or are you talking out your ass?"

Friends have such a direct way of communicating!

We spent the night in that hole, along with 50 million mosquitoes, and a chorus of jungle chatter. The next day, late in the afternoon, some soldiers came for us. They allowed us to re-board the MU2 and fly back to Belize. When I touched down the President was indeed there to meet us. My $4000 was returned, so I asked for a fuel truck, and once full we were allowed to depart. Once, I got airborne and filed a flight plan home, I wanted some answers, and wasn't nice about asking. It turned out, that when we stopped for the rest of Don's party, there were some locals hiding in the jungle watching. Apparently, the current President was not all that beloved, and the locals (spelled rebels) had observed our landing on the road, observed us picking up the others with their bags, and concluded that we were drug runners. The $4000 they found on me, confirmed their suspicions. Out over the Gulf of Mexico Don hands me a newspaper on which, prominently displayed on the front page, was a picture of me. It said that yours truly was now **Persona non grata** in Belize and that if I ever returned I would be arrested. Funny how I was the only one mentioned in the story.

Bill

I casually mentioned to Dan one day that if we had a Lear Jet we could cut our flying time in half and fly at 45,000 feet above all the weather that we currently had to fly through. His response was "go find us one". *Dan and Joe had been two salesmen who specialized in Natural Gas. They did so well at it they decided to go into business for themselves. As such, they currently had enough liquefied Natural Gas stored in underground Salt domes to run the entire U.S. for several years.*

I explained to Dan the expense, the need for occasional "hot section" inspections of the engines and the D-Mate required of all Lear Jets every X amount of time or 10 years. A D-mate required removing the wings from the aircraft and fully inspecting the wing roots and fuselage. Dan didn't blink an eye. While I had been in Lear Jet transition in Dallas, I had become aware of a virtually brand new Lear 25D. It had been foreclosed on due to a business failure and was now just sitting in a hanger collecting dust in Dallas. I took the MU2J and flew to Dallas to look at the Lear. It was immaculate. A bank owned it and had for several years. They wanted $1,000,000 for it. I told them I would give them $700,000 or go look for another corporate jet. Of course they pissed and moaned but within 12 hours they called me back and said okay. I called Dan to see if it was okay and he said, "I don't really know anything about the idiosyncrasies of the aircraft. If you think it is a good deal, you being the chief pilot, buy it." I had Scott fly up to Dallas on Southwest Airlines and fly the MU2J back home. Dan faxed me a check, the bank checked it out, and we owned a Lear Jet. I was in seventh heaven but reality soon set in. Scotty was not qualified to fly co-pilot on the Lear and I had no one else. Dan wanted to take his beautiful wife to the Grand Ole Opera that evening. I called my classmate Bill, the Delta Airlines Captain, and informed him of my dilemma. He said, "Can I fly it some of the time", to which I replied, "Every other leg". He said, "I need to call you back." Within 10 minutes he called me back and informed me that he had taken a month long leave of absence and where was he to meet me. I said "Love field and pack to do a lot of flying". I was happier than a politician who had just screwed the public.

Bill and I flew to Houston and landed at the new Intercontinental Airport which was closer to Dan's office. Having let the aircraft sit for so long, we had hydraulic leaks and other minor problems. We were able to get Atlantic Aviation to fix the problems by promising them our future business.

Dan and his wife Billy showed up on time and we flew them to the Grand Ole Opera where they bought us tickets as well. Billy was a beautiful woman, slim, gracious, quick to laugh, and very intelligent. The two of them made a striking couple and I loved flying for them.

Bill was able to fly with me for a month. We paid him the same as me and both Dan and Billy liked him. He was a bachelor and nearly as crazy as me while at the same time being an excellent pilot.

By this time in 1975 Scotty had accumulated enough time to be a co-pilot on the Lear. As I always did, I let co-pilots fly left seat every other leg if we were deadheading back home, until they were comfortable in the Lear. I could fly either seat and was confident in both. We flew to Oklahoma City and were returning empty. I allowed Scotty to sit left seat. We got clearance for takeoff and started our roll. At about 100 knots the aircraft started skidding left and right down the runway. I took the aircraft and had trouble stabilizing the take off roll. Scotty being a GQ dresser had gotten his platform heels stuck between the rudder pedals. I was able to get the Lear in the air but I was furious.

"If I ever even see you wearing those damn shoes again you are fired."

"Yes sir."

I calmed down several weeks later.

Dan and Joe both wanted to fly to Cabo San Lucas. Dan had 8 passengers and Joe wanted to take his maid along, making it 9. I was going to have to make two trips. I had a three person couch that was satisfactory to the FAA. I had to take out one of the forward seats to install it. I planned on doing that on the second trip. I took Dan's group first. I was to fly to El Paso to pick up four of Dan and Billy's friends. There was a frontal system expected to arrive just after I was to leave El Paso. I took off and headed toward El Paso. In front of me the clouds were building faster than anything I had previously encountered. I tried to fly around the building storm but it was building faster that I could get around it in the Lear. I elected to land in San Angelo, refuel and try again. However, upon landing in San Angelo, the weather service was predicting baseball size hail and 60 knot winds within the hour. I started looking for a hanger that would take our Lear only to find there was no space available. I pulled Dan aside and explained the situation to him. I proposed he get a hotel and I would fly the Lear out to save it from certain damage. Dan replied, "Do you think it safe in these winds?"

"Not necessarily but if I don't, we will get our Lear beat to shit"

"Well then, we are coming with you, no argument!"

My plan was to fuel up and try climbing to 45,000 feet to see if we could pick our way through any cells. The takeoff was extremely rough, with gusting winds up to 55mph, heavy rain, turbulence, lightening and wind shear. I burned out the nose wheel steering on the takeoff but otherwise turned east and started climbing. The frontal system was a sight to be seen. It stretched from Mexico to beyond my vision to the north. Arriving at 45,000 feet Dan still wanted to try for El Paso, so we turned to the west and started picking our way between cells on the weather radar. Most were below us, but you could not see out the windscreen and it was rougher than a ride on prom night. I made it down the other side of the front to a clear sky at El Paso. I landed, fueled up, Dan met his people, and we took off for Cabo. Again, I climbed to 45,000 feet and headed south. At the time, virtually no one flew at 45,000 feet except Lear Jets and a few other corporate jets and of course the military. You could usually get vectors from air traffic control straight to your destination. I was above a Continental Airlines DC-10, watching him when all of a sudden he pitched straight up. He radioed air traffic control he had just encountered *severe CAT* (clear air turbulence). I watched him regain control at the same time the Lear started a rough climb to 51,000 feet. The Lear was only rated to 45,000 feet and 51,000 feet is when your blood can boil if you lose pressurization. I ran out the other side of the CAT with a tremendous jolt and returned to 45,000 feet. Dan came up and enquired if everything was all right. Assuring him it was under control, we proceeded to Cabo. I checked the weather on landing and it was forecast to be a return through the devil's den. I told Dan that it just wasn't safe to tempt fate and after 8 hours of flying I was exhausted. I said Joe is going to be pissed if I don't pick him up, but Dan said to tell him to rent another Lear.

Pissed was the understatement of the year. Not only was Joe pissed, he was livid. Other available Lear Jets did not have a couch seat so he could only take 8, and he wanted to take his maid. He told me I was fired the minute I got back to Houston. Well, fuck it, it don't mean shit, there are lots of pilots sticking in the dirt because they couldn't stand up to a corporate bully. Dan asked me what I was going to do the next day. I told him I would return to Houston and await his pickup date in a week. Always thinking of others Dan said, "Why don't you stay down here. I will get you a hotel room and you can go deep sea fishing and just relax." I thanked him for the offer but told him my budget could not afford the deep sea fishing.

"Put it on your expense account, I'll authorize it." Sum bitch what a generous and remarkable man!

Another time I was flying Dan and Billy from Midway down to Miami. We were flying at 45,000 feet above a frontal system that was slowly moving east. North of Hilton Head Island about a hundred miles we ran into some severe clear air turbulence. I never worried about the Lear coming apart as it was designed as a fighter for the Swiss before Bill Lear purchased the plans and made it a corporate jet. It has eight wing spars where a commercial jet only has two. We took such a beating that both engines flamed out. The intakes on the turbojet engines are really not that wide and it doesn't take a whole lot to disturb the airflow into the compressor section and flame the engine out. Quick lesson here, a jet engine will operate at high altitude only due to the compression section squashing the air down to such an extent that combustion will take place. Flame out and you lose that compression which means you are now a glider. You ain't staying at altitude either, so you have to quickly advise center control and find out where the closest place is you can land. Center makes sure you don't glide into another aircraft. While I was taking care of the situation, Dan crawls up and wants to know if everything is all right as it got really quiet back there. I assured him that everything was fine, that the engines flamed out in the recent turbulence and that I must glide down to an altitude of around 15,000 to 20,000 feet before I can get a relight. With the thunderstorms below me I had no choice but to glide through them and I let Dan know that it was going to be especially rough and to make sure he and Billy were belted in tight. Center told me that Hilton Head Island, SC was my best choice and started vectoring me toward it. I managed to get one engine started at 18,000 feet and the other one at 16,000 feet. I now had pressurization back and electricity, which before, I only had that small pneumatic standby attitude indicator. To say the glide down was interesting would be an understatement. When I landed in Hilton Head I had some mechanics check the Lear out while Dan and Billy went in to get something to eat. Everything checked out, just God and Mother Nature proving what a peon I was. Dan and Billy said they were not the least bit concerned as I didn't look concerned. I guess they weren't cognizant of the smell.

I had hired Larry, a cousin of my friend Teddy, who was killed in Vietnam. Larry had been a C141 pilot in the Air Farce so I knew he could fly. The Air Farce has a navigator to take their clearances and keep them on the correct route. Army pilots are trained to do everything themselves as are corporate pilots.

A typical clearance from Air traffic control would go something like this, and it had to be read back exactly.

"Lear 100EP you are cleared enroute to El Paso. Climb and maintain 5000 feet until Apple intersection, expect further altitude clearance 10 minutes after departure, contact departure control on 134.5 and squawk 6123.

I always copied the clearance as a backup in case Larry had trouble reading it back. I would be climbing through 25,000 feet and he was still back at the hanger figuring out how to start the engines. It was really frustrating. He was a nice guy married with two kids and had been unable to find a job after leaving the service. He was with me on the trip to Cabo. I took Dan up on his offer to charter a boat to go sail fishing. I picked out a fairly new 40 foot twin engine Uniflite and chartered it for the day. The ocean was a beautiful deep blue, with a gentle swell, but we no sooner left the harbor than Larry started to turn green. I had climbed up on the bridge, to sit in the sun and ask the Mexican crew, "Cervasa por favor" (Beer please), while they set me up for trolling. Larry lasted about 30 minutes and then proceeded to blow beats and call Buick over the side. If we went back to port the charter was over so Larry would just have to buck up. I caught a 12 foot Sailfish and had the time of my life. Larry on the other hand had a truly miserable day, going from green to gray and back again. He did manage to rebound for dinner that evening, probably because he was empty.

As is always the case no good deed goes unpunished, so when we returned to Houston, I found a note demanding I be in Joe's office by 9:00am on Monday. I arrived promptly and received a chewing out and was fired. I had no sooner arrived back at the hanger to pickup my stuff, when Dan calls and tells me to disregard Joe's rant and that by no means was I fired.

Disney World Florida

Acouple weeks later Dan and Billy wanted to fly to Disney World in Florida with friends. Always thinking of others, Dan says:

"Bob, why don't you and Larry bring your wives?" I checked with Larry and discovered his wife had two young kids and couldn't go. I informed Dan, and he said,

"Well Bob, how about Betsy?"

"Dan you are beyond generous and I appreciate your offer, but Betsy and I can't afford it and besides the Lear will be full!"

"Have all your previous employers been tight wads? I know the Lear is full, have Betsy come down on Delta, and Bob, send her first class."

Kick me in the balls, and make me a Democrat. I truly think I am in love!

Larry and I flew to Orlando, and Dan got us two suites in the hotel that the monorail ran through. They were very nice suites. I had a courtesy car drive me to the airport, and picked Betsy up about 6:00pm. We decided to have dinner at the hotel's best restaurant, a place guaranteed to get you laid. As we are having dinner, the maitre d' comes over and whispers:

"Mr Reynolds, I know you are incognito, but the lady over there would really appreciate an autograph."

I tried to explain it was a case of mistaken identity when Betsy and Larry chime in with, *"Go ahead Burt, give her an autograph!"*

Stuck with two collaborators both grinning like baboons eating banana goo, I signed *"Best always, Burt Reynolds."* (Sorry Burt!)

Grand Junction

Scotty, Me and Enterprize's Lear25D

A week later, with Scotty flying co-pilot, we were to fly Joe and his new bride to Grand Junction, Colorado. Joe had traded in his wife for one of the girls in accounting. She was rude, arrogant, and dumb as a rock. I tolerated her as best I could. At the time Grand Junction had a small airport about 5000 feet long located at an altitude of 5000 feet. The air is thin up there and performance is reduced. Scotty 's Dad had been an Eastern Airlines Captain and had retired in Grand Junction, building his dream house on the side of the mountain where you could ski out and back in to the ski lifts. Scotty invited Joe and his new wife to visit later that afternoon. About 5:00pm Joe and his wife show up.

The home was beyond fabulous and Joe's new wife made no pretense about how she wanted it. Eventually, Joe demands to know what Scotty's dad will take for it. Scotty's dad, as cordially as possible, says it's not for sale and that there are no other lots available, with this view, and that he had a good deal of his retirement money tied up in the house. Joe continues to push, offering to have Scotty's Dad call Joe's bank to assure him that he had the funds, no matter what it was. Joe then says he would want the house just as it sits, furnished, four wheel drive jeeps, snowmobiles, kitchen, silverware, etc. I tell Scotty to get his dad and go to the den. When his dad comes in, he wants to know who the hell this guy is, and he is just a little irritated. Scotty's last name was Davis, so I tell Captain Davis that Joe is what I refer to as *"new money"*. I inform him about the new wife, then tell him if he ever even considered doing it all again, to add up everything he had in the house, add 25% to it and as for the house its self, add $200,000 to the price.

"Are you shitting me?"

"No Sir, I am not. Trust me."

Scott and I dive into his Dad's scotch collection, Joe and his wife wander around the house, and Captain and Mrs. Davis retire to their bedroom to discuss this remarkable change in venue. An hour later Mr. Davis calls me into his room and shows me his price, and asks what I think.

"Sir, everything is relative. You really don't want to sell so you're not really obligated. So stack the deck and let Joe do the deciding."

We return to the living room and Mr. Davis gives Joe his number which Joe promptly accepts. Mr. Davis is nearly speechless, but not as much as when Joe asks him, "How soon can you be out of my house?" Unbelievable!

Atlanta

Next time I fly Joe and his wife, it is to Atlanta. We spend the night, and are to leave about noon the next day. Joe's wife has some of her girlfriends along and she wants to show off. She drops her bags at my feet and tells me to load them. While I am loading them they board the aircraft and the wife sits in one of the chairs and turns it around facing backwards to visit with her friends. **Does, all seats need to be upright facing forward, and trays stored,** ring a bell to anyone? I courteously, try to explain the FAA rules and politely ask that they please face forward for takeoff, after which they can turn the seats around.

"Joe honey, please explain to the pilot that you own the aircraft and he will do as we say." Did you catch the "we"! Joe being the pussy whipped guy he was, explains that to me. Whereupon, I promptly pack my flight kit and exit the aircraft. Joe follows me out, wanting to know WTF I think I am doing. I tell him that I was hired to fly this aircraft safely and within the FAA rules and I will not under any circumstances taxi right by the FAA offices with the seats turned backwards. I don't think Joe got laid that night but the seats got turned around.

Hattiesburg Mississippi

Larry and I were tasked to fly Dan and some associates to Hattiesburg, Mississippi. There was a cold front coming and the weather was miserable. Midway to Hattiesburg, I stop to fuel up in case the weather is really closed down, and I have to divert. When I get to Hattiesburg, we shoot an ILS approach and break out about 500 feet. The Lear is still fairly full of fuel, so I land as close to the end as possible. The landing was smooth as glass, but it had a hidden side. Almost immediately, I realize that we are hydroplaning. I pop the chute in the tail and try to maneuver the aircraft into the grass on the side. Once, you pull a jet engine to the stops on landing you are committed. It takes 8-10 seconds before the engines will again spool up enough to shove thrust out the back of the engine. We were committed and hurtling down the runway at breakneck speed. I had time to turn around and tell Dan that we were going off the other end of the runway and immediately shut down the engines . At the end of the runway there was a barbed wire fence and a shallow hill that ran down into a cleared field. I went through the barbed wire fence at about 60 knots. One of the posts put a 5 inch dent in the leading edge of the right wing and another post came up through the nose wheel, hit the rudder pedal jamming it to its full extent, thus saving me from being impaled. The aircraft continued on into the field and finally stopped a hundred feet out and settled into the mud. Everyone got out safely and there was no fire. The tower notified the FAA while Dan and group slogged their way out of the mud. In the meantime the cold front came through and one inch ice cycles formed on the flaps. Dan and group came back later and slogged out again to have their picture taken by the Lear. The FAA showed up, listened while the tower told them where I landed, where the chute came out, and why I hydroplaned. They had recently resurfaced the runway with asphalt but had not grooved it or put out a NOTAM (notice to airmen/pilots) about the resurfacing. No harm no foul except for a Lear Jet parked in the mud. They had an Army reserve engineer battalion stationed at the airport. As a former Captain I was able to talk them into lending me a Tank Retriever to try and get the Lear out of the mud. I called one of the engineers in San Antonio who had helped develop the wing modifications which would allow a Lear jet to stall and still recover. Prior to that development several Lear Jets flying at 45,000 feet had stalled, and because it was a T-tail aircraft, went all the way to the ground. One of those, Oh shit, Oh dear, moments. With the new leading edge mounted on a Lear one could intentionally deep stall the aircraft and it recovered quite nicely.

I brought the Tank Retriever over to the end of the runway. I had purchased some huge one and half inch ropes which, I intended to tie around the main gear and drag the Lear out. The engineer in San Antonio agreed to fly out and give me a hand. He was a great guy and didn't need to come but I was as appreciative as 12 year old girl with a padded bra. We tied the ropes around the main gear, taking caution not to pinch the hydraulic brake lines and started an easy pull with an 80 ton retriever. The Lear would not budge. Digging down, we found that the main gear had settled over a large stump. I had to dig way down under the gear, and place a large piece of roofing metal under it and try again. This time the aircraft began to ride up the roofing material, over the stump, and continue back up onto the runway. Once on the runway, we realized the nose gear had folded back under the nose, and would need to be welded in place, something the engineer said he could do. The engineer also riveted a piece of aluminum over the dent in the right wing. Once all this was completed I had the airport fire trucks come over and spray water into the front of the engine as I started them up making sure no foreign mud or material had settled into them. They worked as designed making us all very happy. I had to get a waiver from the FAA to ferry the Lear to San Antonio with the gear down, where I intended to replace the current leading edge on the wings, add thrust reversers to the engines, and polish the metal around the wind screen.

My co-pilots needed a break so I hired Luke to fill in for a trip to Chicago. We landed at Midway early morning. Not having a bathroom on the Lear for the pilots, Luke and I went into the fixed base operator to use their bathroom. We were both sending contributions to the democrats when this guy runs into the stall next to Luke whimpering loudly. Next thing I know he sneezes really loud and blew shit all over the wall under the partition and into Luke's pants crotch and onto his shoes. Even as I write this I can't quit laughing. I don't know why, just a sick sense of humor I guess. I had to leave Luke in the john, borrow a car and go find a department store and buy him new clothes, which included underwear, shoes and pants.

Flying with Joe

I was called into Joe's office to discuss buying a brand new Beech Baron. I had explained to him one time that the Baron had the best single engine performance. Joe wanted a new one, wanted to learn how to fly it, and take himself to Grand Junction on his own. He had a pilot's license but no multi-engine time and no instrument time. I did my best to talk him out of it but in the end he said, "Go buy me a new Baron with all the bells and whistles." I did manage to talk him into letting me instruct him in single engine work.

The new Baron was delivered and I marveled at the beauty of such a magnificent machine. My friend, Luke wanted to go along while I instructed Joe on single engine work flying a twin engine aircraft. We climbed up to 6000 feet and I told Joe, "I am going to pull one engine back to idle. You will recognize which engine it is by the rudder pedal on that side not having the normal required pressure. I had cleared our area for a block altitude so I knew I didn't have to worry about other aircraft. I pulled the right engine back and Joe stomped on the right rudder and we flipped into a spin.

"I've got the aircraft" I said as I pulled the other engine back to idle and recovered from the spin." Luke however was not thrilled with the spin. We climbed back up to 6000 feet and I again emphasized dead foot dead engine. I pulled another engine back and Joe stomped on that side's rudder again and we flipped into a spin again. This time Joe held onto the controls and we lost quite a bit of altitude while Luke, with both hands on the ceiling, yelled all the way down. On the third try, with another spin, Luke begged to be taken back. Joe was unfazed as he remarked that my instruction was worthless and engines very rarely quit. Dead man walking!

Hollywood

My attorney friend Don knew John Mecom Jr., a wealthy Texas Oilman and owner of the New Orleans NFL team, The Saints. John was not only wealthy, but incredibly handsome as well. He was big, rugged, and looked like Clint Walker. At any rate John wanted to borrow our Lear and the partners agreed. I was to pick John up in South Lake Tahoe and fly him back to Houston. Previously I had flown John over to New Orleans to watch his Saints play so we knew each other although I was so far from his status I might as well have been living on the streets. He was gracious with a superior intellect, and fun to be with. Arriving in South Lake Tahoe John informs me that he would like to take a quick side trip to Los Angeles. The airport only had one runway, running north and south. The elevation is 6200 plus feet and surrounded by mountains. It is an all weather facility which means flying an approach in snow or rain makes for a nice pucker factor. John's friends turned out to be Farrah Fawcett and Lee Majors. Everyone got on the Lear and I thought we were ready to go but John said we were waiting for one more. It was starting to snow increasing my anxiety as I had a full load of fuel thinking I was going back to Houston. A limousine drove up to the aircraft and Jim Nabors got out followed shortly by Roman Gabriel, the NFL quarterback. I was bowled over when they hugged each other followed by a long lingering kiss. I must have been shell shocked as Farrah snuck quietly up beside me, reached up and gently pushed my lower jaw closed. Got to admit I hadn't observed too many men kissing each other. Kissing another man with a mustache like mine makes my weed wacker disappear. A Lear Jet, at least a 25D model has one seat behind the co-pilot that sits perpendicular to the rest of the seats. Under the seat cushion is a small toilet which is lined with a plastic bag. There are curtains that can be pulled between the cockpit and the other passengers. Once I managed to takeoff and clear the mountains Farrah came up and sat in that seat leaning forward to talk to me. She was an incredibly beautiful woman. She had arrived at the aircraft with a full length white Canadian wolf fur, now she was in white jeans with a billowing white blouse that only had two buttons buttoned, no bra. I don't think she was flirting with me she was just curious what all the instruments were and how I knew where we were. On the other hand, trying to look her in the eye and not elsewhere, was harder than Chinese writing. She was interesting, intelligent and we had both grown up in Texas and were the same age. The group of them wrote a nice letter to my wife Betsy, about how they had hijacked me.

LAST FLIGHT

I had gotten divorced again, not for any legitimate reason, I was just dealing with PTSD, which I didn't even know I had. Betsy was an angel but certainly deserved better than me. I had dated several of the girls at work and of course Joe's wife had heard about it. She did everything she could to tell girls what an ass I was. I filed that away in my "give a rat's ass" folder. I was scheduled to fly Joe to Grand Junction again. The weather was marginal and predicted to snow. Not an altogether good situation for a relatively short runway and high altitude. By the time I got there it was snowing hard and we couldn't land. There was no tower nor was there an instrument approach system. It must be nice to live in Never Never Land. I had to divert to a field lower in the valley. Joe and wife were pissed off having to rent a car and drive back. I managed to pick them up several days later and Joe informed me that when we got home he wanted me in his office. Next day I arrived promptly in his office. He informed me that I was fired, that they were going to find a more mature pilot who could follow instructions. He said he could get any number of pilots for a $1000 a month. I agreed, but said, "Let me know how a $1000 dollar a month pilot works out in $4000 dollar weather." With that we parted ways. Dan called and requested I come back but I told him I had had enough of Joe as he was looking for a spot to auger into, and I already had another job. He wished me well as did Billy. A week later Joe had hired a forty plus year old pilot, allegedly more mature. This guy wanted his own pilots and got rid of Scotty and was working on Larry. He flew Dan, Billy and some friends to Amarillo, Texas. Once Dan and guests were unloaded, he made Larry move to the back and had one of his buddies fly. Dan liked to watch me takeoff because the Lear would climb so steep, and he was watching this time. Unbeknownst to the buddy flying, the 40 plus year old "mature pilot" decided to give his buddy a single engine on takeoff. They roared down the runway but before they reached rotation speed Mr. Mature pulled an engine on the guy flying. Some Jet aircraft have a V1 and a Vr which are the same air speed. A V1, being that point on a runway where speed, length of runway, and tempera-ture combine to make it safe to continue the takeoff roll despite losing an engine. Years of analysis have proved that more pilots die trying to stop than those who continue the takeoff. All aircraft are certified to continue a takeoff when losing an engine at V1. Other aircraft like the Lear have a V1 and then several knots faster a Vr or rotation speed. The flying pilot panicked and pulled the Lear into the air. It was not ready to fly and consequently rolled up on one wing tip dragging the wing tank and rupturing it. It caught fire then swept down like a falling leaf the other way, wiping out the gear while continuing up onto the other wing tip rupturing that fuel tank as well, causing it to burn. It then landed on its belly and with one engine screaming, started a horizon-tal spin down the runway, completely consumed in fire. As luck would have it, it slowed with its nose pointed down the runway trailing a 100 feet of fire and Larry was able to open the door and bail out followed promptly by the two mature pilots. It was such a spectacle that the tower rang the bell for the fire crew but told them they wouldn't need to hurry as it was most probably fatal. I saw pictures later of a big burn mark on the runway and two molten piles that had once been engines. Larry quit and quite frankly I couldn't care less what happened to the other two mature pilots.

Gulf States Toyota

My friend Luke was hired by Gulf States Toyota in Houston to fly a King Air. Gulf States was the first Toyota distributorship in America and was owned by an incredible guy named, Tommy_. The facility was approximately 100,000 square feet in which Toyota parts were stored. They had 346 dealers in five states. Tommy found a brand new Falcon 10 which had been ordered by a Mexican company who could not now afford it as they had devalued their currency in 1975. Tommy had picked it up at a good discount and was looking for a co-pilot with jet time to help Luke and cover the necessary insurance requirements. (*A Falcon 10 was a corporate jet, powered by twin TFE731 fan jet engines*) Barry was the manager and President of the Gulf States facility and Tommy had tasked Barry with finding a suitable co-pilot. Luke and I were friends so he took me to Barry's ranch located just outside Houston. Arriving at the ranch I not only found Barry, but his wife and two kids as well. We were doing the interview dance as inconspicuously as possible. We were outside the house looking at his vast pasture when this exquisite "Tennessee Walker" struts by.

"Damn Barry that is a stunning stallion."

"He's handsome all right but no one can ride him."

"Why not?"

"He is a stud, and considers a rider something to toy with."

"May I try?"

"Sure knock yourself out. After he bucks you off or drags you through the trees we will have to interview another pilot."

I was born with balls and a self confidence that sometimes, if it didn't put you off, made people wish, in this case, that the damn horse would trample me to death. His kids thought it would be great fun to see me try and ride the horse. Allegedly, the horse was broken but very high spirited and still a stud. I walked toward him cooing and speaking softly. He stood watching me approach but did not seem to be overly frightened. I stroked him, talked to him, and then grabbed his mane and swung up bareback. He just stood there until I dug my heels into his sides and we were off. I made a wide circle in the pasture and was coming back towards the group when Barry did one of those two fingers in the mouth whistles. The horse stopped as though he was stuck in cement and of course I didn't, flying forward and landing most ungallantly in a face first pile. Everyone was laughing so I joined in.

Monday morning arrived and I got a call from Luke that Barry wanted to see me in his office. I dressed in a suit and tie and drove to Gulf States Toyota. Barry ushers me into one of the most extravagant offices I had ever seen. He says *"After your visit to the ranch over the weekend, my wife and kids said if I didn't hire you, not to come home. So what will it take for you to work for Gulf States Toyota?"*

"Well sir, my last job gave me a new company car, paid for the gas and maintenance paid me $2500 a month and I would need at least that to work here."

"Done, now will you have a drink with me?"

"I'll have a scotch and soda please and if I knew it would be this easy I would have asked for $3000."

"I would have given you $5000. In life, a good deal is a good deal for everyone. Never go laterally with your salary. If it's not up, it isn't a good deal for you, which makes it a bad deal for both of us because you would be unhappy."

Having just left Enterprise I would probably have given him a kiss just to get back into jets, especially a Falcon 10.

We shook hands and he told me about the other perks which included getting a new Toyota (my choice of model) every six months as a company car. Further, I could buy any Toyota at Dealer's cost minus 10%, as long as it was for cash. He went on to explain the Falcon 10 deal and that we would be flying the King Air to New York the following week. We were to land in Newark turn the plane over to Flight Safety and begin a ground school and flight school with Flight Safety which would result in our attaining a type rating. Following the transition, we were to fly Barry to Geneva, where I would meet Tommy, spend a week, and then fly Tommy to South Africa and on to Botswana, where Tommy owned "Safari South", a 50 thousand square mile hunting preserve. Tommy had become a "Great White Hunter", a fete few men have ever achieved. Barry went on to explain that while we waited a week in Geneva he would take us to Amsterdam to see the new international car show and then on to Spain to see the sights.

I couldn't have been more excited if a perfect 10 twenty year old who was wealthy, owned a liquor store, was a nymphomaniac had GII corporate jet, and loved, really loved recreational sex.

FLIGHT SAFETY

Already having an ATR (Airline Transport Rating), and nearly 1200 hours in a Lear, I breezed through ground school. Training and check rides in a jet usually follow a basic pattern. You take off and get an engine failure either before V1, at which point you abort the takeoff, or after V1, in which case you continue the take off and **FLY THE DAMN PLANE.** (Statistics have shown that pilots who try to stop after attaining V1 speed invariably run off the other end of the runway thus they recommend that pilots continue the take-off) You then climb up to about 5000' and practice steep turns and stall series. Steep turns are designed to check your scan of the instruments. You slow to 250 knots airspeed and then roll into a 45 degree bank left and continue until you have made a 360 degree turn. When turning left the aircraft compensates for the engine torque, and you have to pull a little power off to stay at 250 kts. When you complete the left turn you roll right into another 45 degree bank to the right. Now you need to add power, because you are turning into the torque and you still need to maintain altitude and airspeed. Steep turns were my forte and I could hold altitude plus or minus 10 feet as well as bank and airspeed. After steep turns we started a stall series. There was a departure stall, flaps at takeoff, gear down. You pull up until the stall occurs followed by max power, holding your present altitude, and when you start to accelerate, gear up followed by flap retraction. The landing stall was all "dirtied up" flaps to 40 degrees, gear down. Once again, after the stall occurs, you call for max power and flaps 15 degrees, when you have held your present altitude, and start to accelerate, gear up and then "clean up"(retract flaps), at scheduled airspeeds. After stalls, we started approaches.

There are ADF, VOR, ILS, and DME approaches. All of these approaches have a front course and a back course. The important thing on any approach is **Flying the Damn Airplane** even if you are doing so with only one engine. After three days of familiarization on the Falcon 10 the instructor pulled me aside "Bob, you are a natural, but I am sure you can see that Luke is struggling. I wonder if I could get you to just sit in the back and give the rest of your time to Luke."

Steep turns ate Luke's lunch, stalls ate his breakfast, approaches ate his supper, and trying a single engine approach would have resulted in a crash. What I was sure Luke was thinking, was that as extroverted, cocky, and being as natural a pilot as I was, it wouldn't take long before Gulf States would offer his job to me. Combine that thought process and his mind could not focus on the job at hand, which was to **Fly the Damn Airplane.**

When check ride day came I passed with flying colors and Luke failed. The instructor was aware that we would shortly be flying to Europe and Africa and Luke was the chief pilot. In front of me he made Luke a deal, that as long as he never flew the Falcon 10 without me in the cockpit he would say nothing to Gulf States Toyota. That way Luke could build some time and confidence in the Falcon, come home and retake his check ride. He would also have time to stop sticking pins in his Voodoo doll of me. Luke agreed. That was the start of our eventual falling out.

Dealers

We flew the Falcon 10 back to Houston and Barry used it to take several trips. As I said, Gulf States Toyota was the first distributorship in America, and they had something like 356 dealers. The Japanese were very quality control sensitive and would not allow any of the shenanigans that one usually hears about car dealers. If a dealer got more than three written complaints, the Japanese hierarchy would fly to the US and we would fly them to see the particular dealer. It always amazes me when Americans look down their noses at other cultures as though we are somehow smarter and more intelligent. The Japanese businessmen never lost their tempers. One particular dealer was indignant that the Japanese would come and tell him how to handle his business. He actually resorted to calling them slant eyes and fish heads. The Japanese just sat quietly and when this guy finally sputtered out, the Japanese gentleman said, "One more written complaint, and you will not get any more Toyotas!" With that we got up to leave and the dealer again started cussing and fuming, and yelling, "You can't do that".

"Read contract", they replied and we walked out.

Secretary

Barry had hired an outstanding new secretary. Not only was she beautiful, she was very well endowed, and had a pleasant personality. We flew to Amarillo and Barry brought her along to show off the Falcon. He also proceeded to get her drunk which was working just fine until she blew beats all over Barry and the back seat.

Unbeknownst to me, Luke had started dating her. I told Luke he should just tell Barry, as Barry would not want to be made a fool of when he found out. Luke, still upset about his check ride failure, didn't want to hear anything from me. Our life and friendship had taken a definitively dark path. Next thing I know, Luke wants me to plan a trip to South Africa, through Geneva. He wanted three separate paths to present to Barry. He wanted to go through the middle of Africa, or down each coast. We had a week before we were to leave and each path had some significant pit falls. The biggest of which, was that most countries demanded a 30 day *prior permission* authorization. Luke just demanded I do it and Barry could find out the hard way. It was idiotic, superfluous work and time consuming. I managed to find a Shell Oil group that had contacts almost everywhere in the world, and for a fee, they would meet your aircraft and walk you through the various customs. Luke refused to present it to Barry. Frustrated, and at my wits end, I made an appointment to see Barry and walk him through the problems. His response, "Why didn't Luke just tell me?"

Departure

Barry made the appropriate calls, got our credit cards for fuel ironed out and we were off. Shell personnel would meet us at every stop outside the US. Our flight was to take us from Houston to New York, then to Sept Isles, Newfoundland, on to Reykjavik, Iceland, spend the night, on to Geneva, spend a week, then to Athens to refuel, cross the Mediterranean, parallel the top of Egypt, into Saudi Arabia, down to Nairobi, spend the night, on to refuel in Mozambique, into Johannesburg, South Africa, spend the night, and down to Cape Town, South Africa. For a 25 year old home from Vietnam, flying a Falcon 10 was the epitome of heaven. I switched off every leg and let Luke fly captain. Barry was his normal jovial self but Luke had turned sullen and quiet. We landed in Sept Isles on what turned out to

Sept Isles Newfoundland and Falcon 10

be, a giant British airfield. There were bombers there I had not previously seen. Once refueled, we headed out over the North Atlantic for Reykjavik. The flight was long and boring with nothing to see except endless water. Making an approach into Reykjavik, it again became interesting, as the airfield was a US military joint use field. The water was deep blue and the houses were all different shades of pastels. It was beautiful. We got a room at the BOQ, (Bachelor Officers Quarters) and I hitched a ride into town to check out the local color. Everyone jokes about a girl behind every tree in Iceland, but it was true. The girls were young, healthy and most had married early and gotten divorced. Alcohol was so expensive that to be an alcoholic you would need to be wealthy. What a lucky break as we had lots of alcohol on the aircraft. The sweaters and parkas made of sheep skin were plentiful and of excellent quality. I nearly wore myself out tasting the local color.

Geneva

We left the next morning vowing to return, and headed for Geneva. Another long flight, but once over Europe it was spectacular. The Alps are truly magnificent. Lake Geneva was a sapphire azure lake. The surrounding mountains snow capped and rugged, were monuments to God's creative hand.

We landed at the Geneva International Airport and parked at one of the private air facilities. Barry told us to go to the International Hotel where he had made reservations, and await his call to come meet Tommy and Tommy's wife. When the call came, Luke ordered me to stay at the hotel.

"Luke, you know Tommy will probably want to fly the Falcon and you're not supposed to be in the cockpit without me. If for any reason you have an incident or accident, with neither of you certified in the aircraft, the insurance company will happily disavow any responsibility."

Luke snapped, "I told you to stay here!"

I had absolutely no second thoughts about Tommy as his reputation as a pilot had preceded him, even if I didn't meet him.

Several hours passed and Barry and Luke returned. Luke did not want to go to dinner with us and begged off. Barry was furious. Barry and I had a quiet dinner, drank a half bottle of quality scotch, and retired. At nearly two in the morning Barry calls me and wanted me to come to his room.

I had barely sat down when Barry exploded. "What the fuck is wrong with Luke?"

Talk about having your dick in a wringer. I said," I can't tell you Barry".

I might as well have told him I just totaled his new V12 Jaguar, he wouldn't have gotten as hysterical and mad at that. He did however, go ballistic. He ranted, raved, made suggestions as to the marital status of my parents, and inferred what I could do with a donut, assuming I could catch it. He finally settled down and said he was firing Luke.

"You can't do that Barry."

"Well, you better start explaining why not, or you will be on the next plane home."

The cat was out of the bag, the shit hit the fan, the ball game was over, the fat lady was tuning up and he had my balls in a vice and had no qualms about squeezing whatever precious bodily fluids out of them I may need in the future. I was fucked.

He poured us both a scotch. It's amazing how well lips of any nomenclature loosen with a little liquid lubricant. We sat down and I told him everything including that I had promised never to take Luke's job. Barry seemed lost in a fog of reality until his secretary came up. Then, just as I predicted, he felt embarrassed, as though he had just kissed a transvestite at a party.

He said, "You know I wanted to take you guys to Amsterdam and then to Spain, but it's off now and you can thank your misguided loyalty to Luke as the reason you're not going."

Son of a bitch, beat me, hurt me, make me write a hot check, I lost the trip of a lifetime.

The Matterhorn

Matterhorn from Ski Village

With my dick dragging in the snow, Luke and I rented some skis and took a train to the local ski slope right outside of Geneva. Once there we rode a clog-wheel train nearly to the top of the slopes followed by a two person ski lift that at one point left us 1500 feet from terra firma. We were both beginner skiers and it showed. We got the requisite stares from the Swiss, as well as comments we couldn't understand. Something in Swedish on the order of, *look at those two assholes on skis!* Regardless, I had a great time and the weather was clear and cold.

We stayed nearly a week in Geneva. Barry went to Amsterdam and I trolled around the city.

Leaving for Africa

I finally met Tommy the day before we were to leave. He was handsome, extremely intelligent, witty with a charming personality. His wife was spectacularly beautiful. He said, "You guys are going to have to stop several places on the way down. I have business to attend to, so I will fly non-stop to Johannesburg on South African Airways, and meet you guys there."

Crossing Mediterranean Sea into Egypt

We filed a flight plan to Athens for a fuel stop. From Athens we flew across the Mediterranean Sea and paralleled the top of Egypt to an intersection that had to be crossed at exactly the time your flight plan called for, plus or minus

5 minutes. Once we crossed that intersection, we flew on to Saudi Arabia and landed at Jeddah. This was 1975, and while the airport was updated, once you went outside the doors of the terminal you were transformed back into the biblical times. Additionally, when I opened the door to the Falcon, the temperature outside was 134 degrees Fahrenheit. Being close to the eastern shore of the Red Sea the heat, the humidity, and the smells, rolled over me like Saigon in the heat of summer. Our Shell envoy met us, cleared us through the necessary paperwork and customs, and got us fuel. We departed for Nairobi. We arrived at night, bedded down the Falcon, and were escorted to a hotel, where we warned to stay off the streets at night. Just like today, in Harlem, NY

Nairobi Airport

you needed huge steel balls, a couple of grenades and an M60 (machine gun) if you had the stupidity to venture out. Anyone with a truck load of antiperspirant could have made a fortune there. We then flew to Blantyre, Mozambique. Not much there but they had the cleanest fuel, along with little wafers to show you that the fuel was not contaminated. Long as we didn't leave the airport which was just an asphalt strip with huts, customs was easily cleared. We then flew on to Johannesburg, South Africa. Tommy met us, got us a ride to the hotel, and again we were advised not to go out at night. Apartheid was in vogue and being a Lilly white American I would not be given a chance to display my sparkling personality without the possibility of a first-hand look at a flashing machete. It was depressing.

We flew to Cape Town, South Africa to pick up Tommy. Even in 1975, Cape Town was one of the most beautiful cities I had ever seen. Everywhere, were manicured lawns and every building was startlingly white. Not to let a great opportunity get away, I flew out and around the tip of South Africa which like South America's tip, has a nasty reputation among sea farers of being brutally nasty in bad weather. I climbed a hill and looked out at Flat Top Mountain, allegedly where their nuclear weapons were stored.

Southern Tip of South Africa

We picked up Tommy and with him flying Captain we flew to Gaborone, Botswana where Tommy owned Safari South, a hunting and photography preserve with somewhere around 8-10 separate areas to which customers could be flown who wanted to hunt or snap photos. I mentioned earlier that my mother had grown up in what was then the Congo. She loved Africa and talked about its beauty whenever anyone was interested. I began to understand her devotion.

With me flying Captain, Tommy directed us to an asphalt strip somewhere in the Kalahari preserve. The strip was the only thing in the area, there were no taxi lanes and fueling was done by hand pumping fuel from 50 gallon barrels into the Falcon. Tommy spoke several languages, so communication with the natives was no problem. As for me, I might as well have been deaf. There were 8 or so natives there to meet us. They had the requisite dirty undershirts and shorts, but were all smiles. Tommy had them allegedly looking through barrels used to fuel the Falcon for his wallet. However as they were rummaging through the fifty or so barrels that were there, Tommy says,

"Hey Bob, think you can go over there and help those guys find my wallet? I think I dropped it over there."

The natives were all jabbering and pulling barrels aside. Being the dumb ass I am, I went to join them`. The natives were trying to roust out a huge Cobra that had wandered into the barrels. I was about three barrels away when I heard this loud hissss and the cobra stood up just a little higher than the barrels. I sucked half my trousers up my ass and nearly broke my legs trying to get out of there. Tommy of course thought it was really funny and it didn't take long for me to see his humor, kind of like Luke in Midway when the guy blew shit into his crotch. Once fueled, Tommy pulls me aside and says

"Bob, these guys are our equivalent of the FAA. Could you take them up in the falcon, give them a low pass and show them what it can do? You can go by yourself and I will have one of them ride co-pilot. What am I going to say, No? Besides that was my kind of stunt.

Tommy filled the Falcon up and I had a guy in the co-pilot's seat. The entire aircraft smelled like dog shit freshly stepped in, it would nearly gag you. I taxied back down the runway to a takeoff position and turned around. The aircraft started bouncing and I thought WTF! I checked all the instruments, and then turned to look back in the cabin. All my passengers were waving their hands like they were flying. The one beside me looked like he was snake bit. I added power and took off, making an easy turn to a downwind. I cleaned up and accelerated to 280 knots, made a base leg from three miles out, and started a decent to arrive over the runway at 10 feet. I roared across the runway at 10 feet and at the other end, I pulled up steeply, climbing to around 22,000 feet. As I looked back over my shoulder all passengers including my co-pilot were out like I had nailed them between the eyes with a sledge hammer. G-lock, natures answer to cocky young aviators.

As soon as I let off the back pressure releasing the G-forces, the guys started flying again. I came back and landed glad no one had puked. Tommy was smiling like a dog in the neighbor's garbage.

Tommy said we could borrow one of the Cessna's he kept there and fly out to the Okavango Delta region where he had another hunting camp, and spend the night. He gave me good directions and Luke and I took off. I flew around 500 feet as we marveled at the game we saw over the Kalahari reserve. There were Water buffalo, giraffes, gazelles, wildebeest, elephants, with hundreds grazing together while lions rested in the shade of the trees, until the dinner bell. We found the area Tommy had described to me and I landed in open grassland. Soon as I shut down, natives materialized out of the adjacent trees walked to us grabbed our bags put them on their heads and singing, "What a fool White People are" started back toward the trees. We followed. Arriving under the trees, the place was amazing. Not a leaf lay on the ground. There were five or six tents set up with sewn in floors and mosquito netting on the sides. Each tent had two cots. There was also a big tent set up for dinners. I spent the afternoon wandering around the area and checking the scenery. At dinner time we moseyed over to the big tent to see what they had. Impressive hardly described the long table, white table cloth, polished silverware and to top it all off a leather bound menu with a wine list a five star restaurant would have found quite prestigious.

The menu included buffalo, gazelle, and other wild game prepared in an elegant sumptuous manner. In the middle of Africa, Tommy had made a first class hunting preserve.

Buffalo head

Waiting for the dinner bell

Next morning I was awakened with a slight shake from a native attired in white holding a tray with tea and coffee. I got up washed my face and proceeded to breakfast. I went down by the swamp which was crystal clear like an old Johnny Weismuller Tarzan movie. The swamp water had what looked like trails running through the underwater grasses which were about 15 feet deep. I asked one of the natives,

"Any crocodiles in here?"

"No Bwana."

So Luke and I dove in and swam around underwater following the readymade trails. When we flew back and met Tommy, I told him how first class his operation was and what a great swimming hole, the place had.

"You went swimming out there?"

"Yes Sir, I checked with one of the natives about whether there were any crocodiles in there and he said no Bwana".

"Bob that is my hunting camp for trophy crocodiles. Eighteen feet is not uncommon. Additionally, none of the servants speak English."

I think I flew home with a rusty zipper and yellow tennis shoes. We were to meet Tommy back in Geneva and he would then accompany us back to San Diego. Luke and I flew back to Johannesburg, took on a full load of fuel and took off hoping to make Blantyre, refuel and be on our way to Nairobi before dark. The weather was turning bad with giant thunderheads building. It was Africa's monsoon season. I climbed to 37,000 feet (max altitude for the Falcon due to overheating of the oil) and started picking my way through the thunderstorms. Enroute, Luke fell asleep and I was left to transit the weather. The thunderstorms probably topped out at 60-70,000 feet with lots of lightening, turbulence and heavy rain. I looked at my map, the little dog leg, which would take me to Blantyre was just about the same distance as it would be just to fly straight to Nairobi. The problem with just flying straight meant I would have to transit Mozambique, a communist country that supposedly had surface to air missiles. (Home from Vietnam, I just didn't give a shit.) Crashing around in the turbulence made up my mind. I turned off the transponder and turned left straight to Nairobi. I figured if the Mozambique population was as unsophisticated as some in Johannesburg, I would take my chances. Two hours later Luke woke up as I was on final for Nairobi.

"Where are we?" he asked.

"Final for Nairobi!"

"What happened to Blantyre?"

"Too many thunderstorms, I by passed it."

"Are you out of your mind, we could have been shot down!"

"Well Mr. Personality, as pleasant as you have been on this trip, I didn't think it would matter much!"

I landed in Nairobi, explaining that I got lost circumnavigating the weather. We spent another night, got up early and flew on to Jeddah. Luke was so hungry when we landed he went out the main terminal looking for food. Outside the efficaciously designed terminal of white marble, he found a guy making what looked like sloppy Joes and bought one. The guy's stand was literally covered in flies, as was Luke's sloppy Joe. Luke scarfed it down anyway. I was sure he would be regurgitating sloppy Joe all over the cockpit. He had a stomach of steel and managed to hold it down and we made it to Athens. Once refueled we flew on to Heathrow in London, where we picked Tommy up. We agreed that we would follow a three pronged flying schedule, Tommy Captain, Luke co-pilot, me in the back. Three hours later, we would switch, Luke Captain, me co-pilot, Tommy in the back, and so on. When Tommy flew with me, he handed me a big Cuban cigar which we enjoyed immensely for nearly two hours.

Following Sept Isles we flew nonstop to Minneapolis to clear customs. On the way Luke wanted to sleep so I flew with Tommy. At altitude, with autopilot on, Tommy hands me the Cuban cigars followed by a box of Dominican Churchill Cigars. I was to pull the wrappers off the Cubans so they looked like the Churchills. A_perfect modification for what at that time, were illegal cigars. In the process we both had another Cuban and told lies all the way to Minneapolis. Tommy was an amazing and interesting guy and an excellent pilot, and I enjoyed every minute with him.

We cleared customs and flew to San Diego. Luke and I got rooms at the Catamaran Resort and settled in for some much needed rest.

Robert Conrad

A couple of days later I was asked to report to Tommy at the Carlsbad airport. When I arrived, Tommy asked me if I had any time in a conventional gear (tail wheel) aircraft. I asked if an Army birddog, an Army Beaver, or a C46 would count.

"Ok wise ass, won't hurt your feelings if I get a friend to check you out in my Great Lakes?"

"Not a bit sir, where do I find him?"

"You'll find him strapped in the aircraft waiting on you."

Me and Tommy's Great Lakes

A Great lakes is a tandem two seat aerobatic, bi-wing aircraft. Tommy's was absolutely magnificent, painted in a sunburst pattern. His check pilot was a PSA (Pacific Southwest Airline) pilot maybe five years older than I was. We introduced ourselves and I climbed into the backseat, which is where you solo the aircraft. The check pilot had me takeoff and make two landings. I greased both landings on and he said that's enough let me out. Tommy walked over when we shut it down. His friend said, *"He's good to go,"* shook hands with me and left.

Tommy says, *"Do you know who Robert Conrad is?"*

"Yes sir, as a matter of fact I do, and told Tommy the story of meeting him."

"Mr. Conrad is making a commercial about batteries. If you can teach him to taxi, do so. However, do not let him screw up the aircraft and if need be, hunker down in the front seat and do what the director wants."

I took off and flew to the Ontario airport. I met Robert there and it wasn't long before he remembered who I was. The director of the commercial wanted Robert to taxi up to a specific spot, ground loop the aircraft, shut it down, jump out with a D-sized battery on his shoulder and give his pitch. Taxiing a tail wheel aircraft is hard enough if you know how to fly, impossible if you have no clue. I ended up hunkered down in the front seat, taxied up, ground looped the aircraft and shut it down, at which point Robert exits the aircraft and does his thing. I got an autograph and Robert got $400,000.

Robert Conrad and Me

Sky Diving

Tommy also owned a French helicopter. Looked much like a Jet Ranger, the difference being that the tail rotor was enclosed, and the main rotors turned right, where our Huey's and Jet Rangers turned left. That forces one to modify the emergency procedures. Tommy calls and asks if I would like to go to Lake Eloise with him to sky dive. Make me French kiss Miss America, hell yes. We take off in his helicopter and fly across the mountains to the lake bed. I don't have my gear so elect to ride up with the pilot in the jump plane. We get to altitude and the other sky divers jump. Tommy stands in the door and leaps out. I am leaning out watching him as he falls and notice he has surpassed the point where he should have pulled. His chute comes out but doesn't inflate. Close to 700 feet from the ground, he cuts away from his main chute and opens the reserve. It barely has time to open before he hits the ground. When I get back on the ground Tommy is smoking a cigar as though nothing untold happened. He says to me;

"You fly helicopters don't you?"

When I respond in the positive, he asks me to go get the helicopter, come over and pick him up. That he would trust me without checking me out was truly an extraordinary compliment. I walk over get the helicopter, having watched his start up procedure and hover over to pick him up. He climbs in and I turn toward home. Once clear of the mountains I am flying about 100 feet off the brush as we get close to the marine base at Pendleton.

"I'm starting to get a nose bleed, think you could drop it down some."

With that, I drop down with the skids just off the brush. Tommy doesn't even blink an eye. He leans back, puts his feet on a steel bar just in front of plexiglass wind screen and smokes his cigar. I was in seventh heaven.

When we get back to the Palomar airfield, Luke is waiting there. He wants to fly the Great Lakes. Tommy tells me to go check Luke out. Luke and I do the preflight inspection then get on board. There was a 15 knot cross wind about 25 degrees off our nose which would be on our right side when we land. I warn Luke that it is very easy to ground loop a tail dragger, and that if I say *"I've got it"*, please release the controls to me. No answer. We take off and Luke has a little trouble keeping it down the center. We come back around and Luke is having trouble keeping it straight down the middle, so we go around. On the next attempt we touch down but Luke loses it and we start to swerve down the runway. I yell I've got it, but Luke won't release the controls and subsequently rubs the left wing on the runway. I taxi back to the ramp and get out to inspect the damage. Sure enough there is a scrape that looks like we sandpapered the bottom of the wing and roughed up the mylar. I tell Luke:

"We need to go tell Tommy right now."

"I'll go tell Tommy, you go back to the hotel."

Luke was chief pilot so I leave, one of the biggest mistakes of my life. Luke never tells Tommy. Tommy's mechanic finds it, at which point who do you think gets the blame? A couple of years later Tommy's wife's secretary tells me the story and that Tommy couldn't believe I didn't just tell him. Screwed again, so much for loyalty!

Last Days

We fly back to Houston with hardly a word spoken. I decide to quit because I won't take Luke's job and I can't stand flying with him anymore. Before I can do that, Barry calls us in and tells us that Tommy's wife wants us to fly her to Palm Springs with her daughter. I haven't said anything yet, so I agree to go. Suzi was as beautiful as Tommy was handsome. Her daughter would make the Kardashians look like the chubby second class women they are. I flew out to Palomar and on arrival I asked the tower for a low pass. The tower informs me that Tommy was up in his P51 and waiting for me. I set up to scream down the runway at 10 feet. As I cross the boundary Tommy is coming the opposite way at 10 feet and over the radio he is mimicking a machine gun. We both break right and with my airspeed I climb up to nearly 18,000 feet before I can do a wing over and enter the traffic pattern. As I am landing, Tommy screams over my head in the P51 and machine guns me again.

We pick up Suzi and her daughter and make the short flight to Palm Springs. The two of them were so beautiful it was very hard to breathe

The next day at the pool I informed Suzi that I was quitting, the reasons why, and how much I enjoyed flying for them. It would be a year later before I met Suzi's secretary and she would tell me how Luke screwed me with Tommy.

The Airlines

Without a job I return to Houston and start updating my resume and sending them out to every airline I can spell. I eventually get an interview with Delta Airlines in Atlanta. One of my friends says that Delta is so conservative (anal retentive) that I should shave off my mustache something I haven't done since before Vietnam. I shave it off and fly to Atlanta. I feel like I am naked standing in church. Delta supposedly had a shrink who would ask you into his office where he had an overstuffed chair and a rocking chair. Allegedly, there was supposed to be some psychological inference attached to which chair you sat in. Delta was conservative all right the pilots walked around like someone had shoved an air hose up their ass. They gave us all a printed sheet upon leaving as to what Delta was looking for. It stated: A pilot with 1500 hours, a wife, two and a half children, and an ATR. *Two and a half kids?* Go figure, they had one of the highest divorce rates. American Airlines wanted a company physical. On my interview, the doctor pointed out my former broken bones from the motorcycle accident at Fort Huachuca on an x-ray and denied me. Years later, American would have one of the highest number of pilots, on long term disability. After those two interviews, which were really the airlines way of clearing out their hundreds of applicants, I moved to Burbank and lived with my kinky haired Jewish friend. Every Monday, Wednesday, and Friday I would make the trek to the Los Angeles airport and drop a letter off to Western, Flying Tigers, Evergreen, Continental, United, Hughes AirWest and TWA. A nice secretary told me after several previous visits, that without a letter to put in my file, they would forget me the minute I left the office. I took her advice and typed out a simple letter. ***This*** *letter will serve to update my file with my continued inter-est in a future job as a pilot for,* whomever. My kinky haired Jewish friend from Ft. Lewis was working for NBC. He got me a job monitoring the sound levels of commercials during programming.

Mark my best friend

I started to run to stay in shape after years as a corporate pilot. Running in Burbank was like sucking on the tail pipe of a car. The crap in the air actually burned my lungs. I lasted about five months living with Mark until I made the unforgiv-able sin of eating his girlfriend's cereal. Additionally, they got married and I was not the sort of influence on Mark she wanted. Looking back I can't blame her. It was downhill from there. Mark informed me that the president of Con-tinental and Bob Hope were good friends. He said" why don't you write Bob Hope, it couldn't hurt". So I sat down and wrote Bob Hope, giving him my particulars, telling him I had seen him in Bien Hoa in 1969 and asking just for the chance to get an interview. Two weeks later I got the interview. With that said, I can't say that Mr. Hope intervened on my behalf, but I can't say he didn't either. Part of the interview included a miniature flight physical. Part of that physical involved checking your lung function. For the uninitiated this required getting as big a breath as you could and then blowing through a tube the size of a toilet paper roller and continuing to blow as long as you could. They had a device that looked like a weight scale with a needle that had to go up to the acceptable level and hold there. The nurse giving the test was young, good looking and a nine on the man scale. One of the guys huffed and puffed and when he tried to blow, he farted loud and long. He had to try it three times with the same result every time. The rest of the interview went well and I got hired. It was what I had wanted since I was 12. I was ecstatic. At Continental you were required to wear a coat and tie to class. I had used the remainder of my GI benefits to get a Flight Engineer rating before I went to Lear Jet school. So this was the second time I was in school for a 727 flight engineer rating. One day the Chief Pilot and several other management types saw me with one of my albums and invited me to come eat lunch with them. That did not sit well with the man in charge of Second Officers Training. This guy was a former Marine Major; I'm really sorry for the men that had to salute him, a Richard cranium if ever there was one. He was short, arrogant, and had a temper. I was in the simulator taking my check ride when the phone that was installed inside the simulator rang. I heard the instructor say "now!" They shut the simulator down and I was told to report to J. J. Moren's office, that prick of a Marine Major. When I knocked on his door he turned around and said. *"You have 5 minutes to get your ass off this property."* I asked for an explanation only to hear him say. *"Now you have 4 and 1/2 minutes."*

I left feeling like I could dangle my legs off a cigarette butt. Stunned would be a massive understatement. I went back to the apartment several of us shared. They were scared shitless and wanted to know why. I couldn't answer them. Just before I had gotten hired at Continental I had received an invitation for an interview with Pacific Southwest Airlines in San Diego. Realizing I had nothing to lose, I called PSA and inquired if the offer was still open. They replied "absolutely", please be here Monday morning at eight. Feeling somewhat better I called Continental's chief pilot and asked for an explanation. He replied, *"Bob, when we hire someone, it is with the intent of one day you being a Captain. We just couldn't keep you with that record!*

"What record, I asked?"

"You weren't told? It has to do with all the violations and accidents you had."

"What violations and accidents."

"J. J. informed us that you have numerous violations and accidents."

That frigging prick! I told the chief pilot that I would have all of my recent employers write a letter about my conduct and record with them and that I would have them sent to him in care of me so I wouldn't see them first. He told me that if what I said was true, I would certainly get my job back. I didn't tell him I didn't know anyone under the same circumstances that would want to work for them, except maybe to kick J.J.'s ass up around his ears and pop him so hard in the mouth he could eat apples out the back of his head. I then called everyone I had flown for and asked them to write the letters. They all readily agreed. I then focused on PSA.

PSA

Monday morning eight o'clock sharp, I was sitting in the office at PSA dressed in a nice pressed shirt, coat and tie. There were probably nine of us. We were told our interview would include several tests, some of them timed, a physical, interviews with guy in charge of Second Officer training, the guy in charge of all training, and the Chief Pilot, followed by a lie detector test, and a check ride in a 727 simulator. The tests were interesting. They would give us small blocks of different colors and as fast as you could, you had to name the color. Following that test, they gave you the words of the color but they were in a different color and as fast as you could you had to say the colors even though words were in a different color. If you got through that, you took a mini physical, eyes, weight, blood pressure and balance. After that you were sent to take a polygraph test. If you have never taken a polygraph, you feel like you are lying when they ask your name. They sat you down and explained that they were going to give you all the questions and then break them down to just Yes and No answers. Anything that had to do with Vietnam was not to be considered. Sounded okay to me and they plugged me in. I was skating through until the guy asked me if I was a pervert. I said, *"If we are talking about twosomes or threesomes, I could be in trouble."*

He said, *"Anything between two consenting adults, be they male and male or male and female in the privacy of their own homes was considered morally okay."*

So I said, *"That certainly leaves a lot of room, what then would be a pervert?"*

Without missing a beat, he says *"Do you fuck dead bodies, animals or children."*

"How old are the children?" I asked. He just smiled and said I was done. I was then sent home. If I passed I would get a call that night to come in for the other interviews.

Nervous as a whore in church, I spent the afternoon running around in ever tightening circles trying to jump up my own ass. Five o'clock came and went, and I felt like I had just been kicked by a mule. At five ten I got the call to come in the next day.

The following morning I was to meet with the head of Second Officer Training. As I was ushered into his office, he was all smiles and made me feel really relaxed. He started to say something when I interrupted," *Sir, I don't want to waste your time, but I was fired Friday from Continental Airlines."*

"Son, I couldn't care less. We gave you a polygraph, and nothing came up that would have us worry about your integrity."

Unbelievable, I was really starting to like PSA. After about 15 minutes I was told to report to the guy in charge of all PSA training. I walked into his office and was asked to sit down.

"I'm interested in how you got the DFC (Distinguished Flying Cross)."

"Well sir, if it's all right with you, I would just as soon not talk about it. I have found that when I got home from Vietnam all those awards and $1.25 would get me a cup of coffee."

He got up, leaned forward on his knuckles and said *"If you have any intention of working here I suggest that you start talking about it now!"*

Scared the shit out of me and I proceeded with the normal pilot war story, "There I was....."

Next, I had to go see the Chief Pilot. He informed me that I had the job and that only I could screw it up. He then scheduled me for a check ride in their 727 simulator. I reported to the simulator and a Captain Bill Hall ushered me into the Captain's seat.

"We are going to see if you can fly. We realize that while you have jet time you have never flown a big jet. I will act as your co-pilot and if anything comes up you don't know about just ask for a check list."

Sounded simple enough, so I adjusted myself in the seat and prepared to fly the damn aircraft.

"I'll start the engines you just fly the airplane."

In a simulator the instructor can just gang start the engines or have you start each one per checklist giving you different problems as you start. He just gang started them and had me taxi out to the active runway. Everything is night time in the simulator and they can make the weather anything they want. You have a movie screen out the windscreen and it's so realistic you can feel the bumps between sections of the taxiway as you taxi out. Waiting for takeoff, he gave me a clearance and had me read it back. So far so good, I was given clearance for takeoff, centered the aircraft down the centerline of the runway, spooled the engines up, checked all the gauges and started the takeoff roll. (Spooling the engines up is an aeronautical term. Jet engines have a compression stage about 8-13 tiny fans in a row that compress the air down to a really tight batch of air. From there it goes into a combustion chamber where fuel is added and a 20,000 volt spark of electricity ignites the engine. The engine will then basically idle. In order to get thrust you have to advance the throttles above 20% N1 (compression stage on an instrument.) At approximately 20% N1 there are bleed bands around the inside of the engine that are open while it is idling and above 20% they automatically close down to shunt all the compressed air out of the turbine section at the back of the engine that gives the engine thrust. The bleed bands are designed to let the engine *spool up* before diverting air out the back. Kind of like a clutch in a car to let you rev up an engine before you feed the torque to the wheels. Big thing is that a jet engine if pulled to idle on landing and you need to go around, won't give you any thrust for 8-13 seconds while you run out of airspeed and ideas all at the same time. Right at V1 (the 727 had a V1 and Vr that were the same speed, Vr being rotate speed) a friggin red light comes on the instrument panel and a loud bell starts ringing.

"What the hell is that," I said as I continued the takeoff.

"APU fire light, fly the damn airplane and ask for a checklist."

Soon as I ask for the checklist the problem goes away and he tells me to climb to 5000 feet and hold 250 knots. Once there he tells me to do a left 360 degree turn at 45 degrees of bank, and once back on the heading I started with, roll immediately into a right turn, same bank, same airspeed same altitude. The idea was to check a pilot's instrument scan which meant not losing or gaining any altitude, keeping the 45 degree bank constant, and holding 250 knots. As I said earlier steep turns were my forte. I held it plus or minus 10 feet. When the steep turns were completed, he said he would talk me through a stall series. The controls in a 727 were nearly identical to the Falcon 10 as were the stalls, so once again I did well. Pilots are trained to do **departure stalls, climbing stalls, and landing stalls.** Departure stalls involved keeping the gear down until reaching 800feet and flaps at takeoff setting. You could get a departure stall by losing an engine or by not being able to see out of your glass navel or flying into a micro burst. Recovery was **MAX** power, nose up to go-around attitude, flaps immediately to 15 degrees, leaving the gear down until a positive rate of climb was achieved followed by normal after takeoff check list. Climbing stalls or turning stalls or stalls encountered due to micro burst simulated a clean airplane, no flaps or gear down. By being unable to see clearly out that glass navel one might inadvertently stall the aircraft which required **MAX** power leveling the aircraft with a nose up attitude, not losing any altitude and holding the aircraft like that until it accelerated. In the last 20 plus years they discovered that during a nasty thunderstorm an area with an intense downdraft could develop out the bottom of the thunderstorm. When it hit the ground the downdraft would of course act like water poured out of a glass, and disperse into a three hundred and sixty degree pattern. If you were taking off into a micro burst you would have anywhere from a 20 to 40 mph additional headwind. However, flying through a micro burst, which have been clocked at as much as 250 mph, you could have a zero headwind followed by a tailwind of 20 to 40 mph which would stick the baseball bat up your ass. It would require instant attention to detail if you didn't want to kiss your big rosey red ass goodbye. I was then given a clearance to San Jose for an ILS approach. In the simulator they can put you at any airport they want, but the feeling and operation of the jet is just like the real thing. In fact, simulators today are so sophisticated that pilots never actually fly the real plane until passengers are on board. I set up for the approach the weather was ½ mile visibility with winds from the right. Just as I break out of the clouds there was a small truck heading for the runway, so I call out "go around". I had no sooner started the go around procedure when he cut an engine on me. If the engine is either the right or left engine, there are multiple problems as both control the air conditioning hydraulics and one of the generators. I called for a checklist and asked to go out and hold somewhere. Both requests were granted and we worked through the checklists. When I had completed the checklist I was given a clearance for a back course ADF approach. I shot a good approach but coming out of the clouds there was that damn truck again. I was going around when he cuts one of the generators. Again, I ask for a checklist and to go hold while we complete the one generator checklist. With the checklist complete, I get a clearance for a VOR approach. I'm sweating now, not from being scared, just due to the work load involved with these problems. I shoot the approach, damn truck again, and I go around. On this go around I lose the co-pilots instruments. I get a clearance for a back course ILS. Breaking out of the clouds, there came that damn f—-ing truck again. Calling for "go around" I lose the center engine. Given a clearance to hold at a specific intersection, left hand turns, two minute legs, I'm really sweating and getting tired of that damn truck. I enter holding with a tear drop turn back to the intersection and start my left hand turns. Into the first left hand turn, all the <u>off</u> flags on the instrument panel come on. I ask him to check the circuit breakers. He responds that they are all in. Now I'm flying with one engine, a small two inch pneumatically controlled standby attitude indicator and all the other instruments are frozen in a left hand turn mode with "off" flags. I start looking around between my legs and he says,

"What the hell are you doing?"

I said *"I'm looking for the ejection handle, I'm going to punch out of this piece of shit and you guys can buy a new one."*

He starts laughing so hard we stop. He shakes my hand, says well done and I leave. Two years later I learned two things. One: the guy in charge of all PSA training was a Marine Corps Sgt Major that had spent thirty years in the Corps with another Sgt Major, who just happened to work for Continental. After I left his office, he calls his buddy at Continental and asks why I got fired. His buddy informs him that Major J.J., the world's biggest prick, was an embarrassment to the Corps and that PSA was lucky to have me. Two: Bill Hall was the senior instructor pilot at PSA. After my simulator ride he went immediately up the stairs to the Chief Pilots office and tells him to hire me on the spot. Bill and I became great friends. He told me later, that I was doing so well, he just kept loading me up to see how far I could go.

That evening I got a call from Bobby, an impressive secretary for the management guys upstairs, who told me I had been hired. Once again, my spirits went through the roof.

I called the Chief Pilot at Continental to inquire if he got the letters. He tells me that they were exceptional but that he has been advised by legal not to talk to me. I told him that I don't really want to work for an outfit that automatically believes lies without checking, but to tell legal I do indeed, plan to sue. I didn't but I wanted that to ruin their day.

The following Monday I started Second Officers Training for the third time. While I was in class there was a young guy, Stansberry, who was having trouble in the simulator. He had never flown jets and they had paired him with two complete ego maniacs who were upgrading to copilot. These two guys were very intimidating, yelling at him for all the checklists and yelling at him for being slow. He had never been put in such a position and the intimidation was getting to him. I liked him and asked him to move in with me and I would tutor him. We got paid $700 a month before taxes for a period of 18 months. I was able to rent a one room studio with a kitchenette on one wall, and a bathroom. It was 500 square feet so a little tight with both of us. I tutored him on the 727 and tried to tell him how to handle the two maniacs. He came home one day and told me that they had fired him. He had a wife and two kids. I drove over to the company to see the former Sgt. Major in charge of all training. I explained the problem with the maniacs (which he was aware of) and told him that, if he would switch me to fly with the two maniacs, I would guarantee that Stan passed or they could fire me too.

"Bob, do you know what you are saying? You don't owe him anything!"

"Please sir, give me the opportunity."

"Okay, I will make the switch but you sure are hazarding your own job"

Next time the two maniacs entered the simulator they found me sitting at the engineer panel. They didn't know me from Joe Schmuck the rag man and thought they were going to buffalo me too. After they got the start list completed and a takeoff clearance I was basically just along for the steep turns and stall series. But once we started approaches, **big difference!** When you get an engine out, they needed a single engine checklist, a one generator checklist, a one engine out prelanding checklist and a one engine out landing checklist. To prove what aces of the base they were (aces spelled with two SS), they started the intimidation tactics if they didn't get the checklists fast enough. It was more to impress the instructor than to intimidate me but either way as far as I was concerned they had unzipped their pants and I was going to help them step on it.

"Gentlemen, there is no hurry, just slow down, ask for a holding pattern somewhere until we are all on the same page."

The instructor who was sitting right beside me got a huge grin on his face, and said *"Good call. You guys fly the airplane, trying to hurry gets people killed."*

Got their arrogance slapped and the rest of the time we worked together.

Stan, the guy I switched places with, got hours of tutoring a day from me and subsequently passed. Prior to my graduation in the middle of my check ride I was summoned to the Chief Pilot's office. Shit #*.@, not again please. I arrived at his door and he motioned for me to be quiet and sit down. He pointed to his phone pushed the conference call button and began to speak.

"I apologize for the interruption I had to put out a fire. Now what were you saying?"

"Well, I work here at Continental and we heard you guys had hired Bob Boyd. We just thought you should know that we had fired him as incompetent."

"That's a hell of an accusation which may cause Mr. Boyd to lose his job. However, we have found that when we get anonymous unidentified callers that have some beef with one of our pilots, they're usually old girlfriends, wives or such. If you would give us your name, it would lend a great deal of credibility to your call."

"No, all you need to know is that I work at Continental and that we fired him."

"Well you know J.J. Bob is sitting right here in my office, he told us about you and we checked up on you from another source we have, and Bob's right, you are a chicken shit asshole."

"CLICK"

I couldn't believe what a dick he was. The chief pilot says "listen when you finish your check ride the main training boss wants to see you."

I went back into the simulator and finished my check ride for the third time. Then I drove back to the Company to see the former Sgt Major who was our director of second officer training. Our simulator was out near Miramar about a 30 minute drive from the airport in San Diego.

"Bob, you graduated top of the class. I want you to be a simulator instructor after your line time and check ride. What do you say.....?"

At this point I would have walked his dog, mowed his yard, and waxed his car.

"Okay sir."

Line Time

With the airlines, line time means flying with an instructor and a regular crew. As luck would have it, I got one of the maniacs from the simulator. No matter what I did, he would yell "no" at me and if I reached for anything like setting takeoff power or setting cruise power, he would literally slap my hand. As they say, pay back is a bitch. However, the Captain, Don Coney, who spent two thirds of his adult life as a mercenary, was kicked out of Africa in 1961 by the State Department, (check Time Magazine, I think the June issue) and who was bigger than a truck, was not enthused with my instruction, and finally turned around and said,

"Son, get yourself another instructor, this guy is going to get you fired."

When I finished my line check this instructor actually wrote a letter to the Chief Pilot demanding I be terminated while I was still on probation.

Chief Pilot called me at home and asked me to come in. Here we go again.

Up in his office the Chief Pilot handed me the letter and asked my opinion. Not as yet diagnosed with PTSD, I guess I turned red and gripped his chair so hard I left an indent in it.

"What do you think, Bob?"

"Since, I am still on probation I think I will put the word out that as soon as I am off probation, I'm going to kill him, and tell God he died."

"He's not a bad pilot, just has a mountain of an ego, and thinks he's God's gift to women. Don't let it bother you I'll take care of it."

Simulator Instructor

Soon as I had my finished my line check, I was given some business cards that said, **Pacific Southwest Airlines, Flight Simulator Instructor,** with the other BS so associated. A plan developed in my head. I went to a florist and ordered a dozen red roses. Mr. J.J. Moren (I puke if I call him Major) was now stationed in Denver. I had the order sent to Denver with an envelope signed by a girl. Inside I placed one of my business cards and a note that said, **"Thanks again for everything you did for me. You are living proof, the Indians fucked buffalo!"**

The friends from my class told me the roses sat on a desk in Continental's Operations for about three days before J.J. arrived. Since, he was married (at least I think he was married, probably on a bet) everyone was giving him the oolala business. They said he strutted up to the flowers, forty to fifty guys around him to see who the card was from, and opened the envelope, then the cocky little bastard threw a shit fit. He threw the flowers across the operations room, turned bright red and stomped out of the room making crude comments about the marital status of my parents. Revenge is sweeter that an eighteen year old hard-bodied flight attendant.

One of my students from the simulator was Sully, from Hudson River fame. I remember a company picnic where I got so drunk I did a pirouette off a picnic table and Sully took me home. I had to be in the simulator at 5:00am. I made it, due to superior training in Vietnam. Sully was a quiet studious person and an excellent pilot. To this day I give him high marks for being married and staying that way. Most pilots I know could take a lesson

Flying the Line

I was dating a great girl I had met at a local bar and grill. Ellen had taken a week off to go snow skiing at Steamboat Springs in Colorado. She was an expert skier, but while standing at the top of the slope to clean her goggles, she slipped and spiral fractured her right leg. It was a freak accident. She called me that night from the hospital crying to tell me that she had no insurance and that the orthopedic trauma surgeon refused to fix her leg with no insurance. "What's his name"? I asked. I told her to try and stay calm and she would be fixed in no time. I was still on the $700 a month salary and had nothing but an American Express Card. I called the doctor and demanded to know why Ellen was not being taken care of. His attitude was that of that prick J.J. Moren until I told him my attorney (my buddy Don from Belize days) would be suing him for violation of the Hippocratic Oath and neglect. I told him to look up Don, and while he was doing so, I would have Don get in touch with him. In the mean time I would give the hospital an American Express Card for the fees, and by the time I get hold of Don, Ellen better be scheduled for surgery. When I called later Ellen had been in surgery and the doctor's attitude had a brand new ring to it, even telling me he was going to reduce his normal fee. The surgery required three plates and eight screws. It took me several years to pay off that card. That same year Ellen and I went to a Halloween costume party. She went as an animal trainer and I went as a gorilla under her control. The gorilla costume was like a scuba divers wet suit which made dogs unable to smell me and it was great fun to growl at dogs and look at the expression of people as I drove my car.

Ellen Me and Halloween Party

Burbank

Burbank is a relatively short runway with approaches over the San Gabriel Mountains. I considered it to be one of four challenging airports we flew into and out of. The other three were Orange County, Long Beach and Monterey. Orange County, because of the noise abatement procedures that had to be adhered to on takeoff. When they built Orange County virtually no one lived near the airport. Now they had expensive homes all around the damn airport and the people living in those homes complained constantly about the noise. **Duh!** As a result, our noise abatement procedure was to hold the brakes, go to max power, then run down the runway until we got to Vr and yank the airplane into a 20 degree nose up attitude. Reaching 800 feet we were to pull as much as 20% of the power back. Not too hard unless you lost an engine right at or above the 800 feet. Long Beach we called the Doctor-Lawyer crash site because of all the small airplanes flying all over the place. Monterey was short and you had to use the runway to back taxi to the terminal. John Denver killed himself at Monterey.

One day at Burbank one of our Captains was pissed about something. Taking off on runway 25 there is blast fence at your tail protecting the road right behind it and on other side of that road is a liquor store. The 727-200 had an engine in the tail that was just a little higher than the blast fence. We were never suppose to do a *rolling* takeoff but this Captain did just that, jamming the power forward while he was still rolling out of the turn. As a result he blew the entire roof off the liquor store. Southwest Airlines was landing toward the blast fence and unable to stop ran through it and ended up on the road behind it. Nobody is infallible!

My Half Interest in Sea Rey

Me and buddy Scott

The summer of my probation I spent water skiing, scuba diving and dating several absolutely gorgeous girls. If I asked a girl out and she started to give me the *"who were you with, where did you go"* jealousy gig, I would circle around several blocks then end up back at her place. I would say *"The dates over, you're a good looking girl, but I have been married and now as a bachelor, I do not need the jealousy routine. I date girls that like to do things I do, like sky diving or scuba diving or skiing. If we happen to end up in bed, it will be a mutual desire, and not a notch on my bedpost."* I never let a girl leave anything at my house. Women are like wolves, they like to mark what they think is their territory.

During this time PSA was hiring lots of flight attendants. I had purchased a ½ ownership of a 19 foot Sea Ray with one of my classmates from Continental, Scott. We used it to water ski and scuba dive. I had it one afternoon out on Mission Bay in San Diego. Part of the bay could be accessed by driving under a bridge and entering another bay that was used primarily for water skiing. The water was a lot calmer and the beaches were great. I pulled into the calmer bay one afternoon and ran into

19 foot Sea Ray and friend

two of our co-pilots who shared a nifty 17 foot silver metal flake ski boat. With me was a new hire flight attendant who could easily compete with Bo Dereck. When I had pulled up on the sand the two co-pilots immediately walked over to check out my date. During the conversation they asked if I wanted to ski behind their boat. It was a two prong attack, one, they could separate me from the girl, and two, they could get her to ride with them. I said, *"I don't really know much about skiing but I will give it a go, What kind of skis do you have?"*

"We just have a single ski, that's all we use."

"Okay, can I try it?"

"Sure, it's a Maharajah Competition slalom ski."

"Well, throw it to me and I will give it a shot."

They ask my date if she would like to ride along with them and watch. They then throw me the slalom ski and escort her to their boat.

"How do you guy's start, sitting in the water or stand up until the rope gets taut?"

"Oh we start from the beach, you want to try that?"

"Sure. By the way how fast will your boat go?"

"About sixty miles per hour faster than you will want to go."

"If I give you a thumbs up will you go faster?"

I could hear them as they escorted my date into their boat, *"Boy are we going to yank this sucker on his ass"*. I put on the ski and coiled up several loops. When they had taken up what slack except for the coils I had in my hand, I told them to hit it. They were grinning like two escapees from a nut house. As the boat accelerated I dropped the coils

I had until the rope got taut, then I stepped onto the ski and we took off. When they got to about 35 mph I swung out to one side of the boat made a turn almost dragging my shoulder in the water, hauled ass toward the other side, jumping the wake as I went and gave them the thumbs up sign. When they hit the gas I kicked the ski off and started to barefoot from one side of the boat wake to the other. When they turned and headed back to the shore I swung out toward the shore letting loose of the rope and skied right up onto the beach and sat down. They of course had to go retrieve their ski before returning to the beach. After parking they got out helped my date down and then sheepishly walked up to me.

"You sure pulled one on us."

"Yes I did. When you assume something, you make an ass out of you and me."

The Menu

PSA at this time could only fly within the State of California, much like Southwest in Texas. In fact before Southwest became an airline they came to San Diego studied our pilot manual, flight attendant manual, maintenance and operations manuals, then went back to Houston and copied PSA's business structure. We basically flew two day trips. As much as twelve take offs and landings followed by one trip home to San Diego after an overnight. I had been advised to go to my room and lay low as one never knew who was bonking who and all it took was a Captain to want you fired and you were out of there. I was in my room as advised, in Oakland. My phone rings and a flight attendant asked me to at least come have dinner with them. What the heck, I go down to the restaurant and find four of them sitting there.

"Oh, good evening Bob, perhaps you can help us. We are having a discussion about how to give the best blow job."

Choking on my salad I remembered being told that the flight attendants were very good at pulling your chain.

On another trip a beautiful girl knocks on the door of the cockpit and we let her in. I'm still flying engineer, so she sits on the edge of my desk and says;

"You're new aren't you? Has anyone given you your good luck fuck yet?"

Trying to untangle my tongue from cockpit floor I answer like a deer in the headlights, *"Well no!"*

"Great, then I can be the first. I'd like to give it to you now those guys there won't mind, they all got theirs. Let me lock the door." She locks the door and with her hand on the top button of her blouse, she leans down and says, *"Good luck, fuck!"*

Didn't I just say something about assumptions?

Flight 182

September 25th, 1978 I was flying engineer on a flight from Sacramento with a stop in Los Angeles and on to San Diego. It was a favorite "dead head" for other crew members returning to San Diego. Just before landing I was notified that I needed to exit the aircraft in Los Angeles and call the Chief Pilot. Telling the Captain I would be right back I ran into operations and called the Chief Pilot.

"Bob, your brother called, your mother died while camping with your dad in Colorado. He is driving your dad back to Texas, and requests that you meet him at home. I managed to get you a jump seat on an American DC-10 leaving in 30 minutes, can you make it?"

"Yes sir."

An hour later the American pilot turns to me and says, *"You guys lost one in San Diego!"*

PSA 182, a 727 200 series was involved in a midair collision on a sparkling clear azure summer day over San Diego.

That was a very sobering event in my life as well as everyone else's life at PSA. No one ever thinks such a thing will happen to them otherwise you wouldn't willingly fly every chance you get. Whether that flight was the continuation of my scheduled trip would be speculation, but the times were the same and I can only wonder.

The papers were full of headlines detailing, **Lackadaisical Crew kills 144, or Laughing PSA Pilots Cause Crash.** It would be nearly 6 years later that the FAA would accept responsibility. Approach control had warned the pilots of one aircraft but not another Cessna that was nearly 1500 feet off its assigned altitude and heading. Our 727 hit the small Cessna with the nose gear which then impacted the right wing's underside and flaps, exploding the fuel in that wing and causing a huge fire. The impact also took out both hydraulic systems which left the crew unable to maneuver the aircraft. Five pilots in the cockpit, and 39 other crew members riding in the back, died in the ensuing crash.

Engineer Experiences

Flying along at 33,000 feet on the way to Sacramento we get a sound like a truck tire losing air followed by smoke coming in the cabin and the aircraft shaking violently. Soon after the number one engine, (one that normally runs one of the hydraulic systems, and the air conditioning), indicates compressor problems. Captain calls for a checklist and while he and the co-pilot shut down the number one engine, I transfer the air conditioning and generator to the number two engine and we now have one hydraulic system. No big deal but lots of brown underwear in the back.

As an engineer you had many duties, one of which was to make a walk around at each stop. You checked the tires for cuts, the fuselage and wings for hydraulic or fuel leaks, and the general condition of the aircraft. We landed in Burbank after a heavy rain storm. I went out to do the walk around and couldn't immediately understand why the wings looked different. However, within seconds I realized that the flaps were missing. I called a mechanic out to look and he was astounded as well. We had noticed nothing unusual on approach or landing except there was a huge water puddle at the intersection of Burbank's two runways. The mechanic took a truck and drove out there, finding not only our inboard flaps, but in addition, another pair as well.

Long before we had to submit to random alcohol and drug testing we would party on overnights as long as we didn't violate company policy. PSA's drinking rule was no alcohol within 8 hours of flying. That was the FAA rule at the time. Rest on overnights according to the FAA was 8 hours. The company interpreted that as being 8 hours from the time the parking brake was set until we taxied out in the morning. No time was allotted for driving to our hotel or for reporting to work an hour before flying. Today the rules are much more stringent, the FAA having gotten its tit in a ringer. However, we had fun on overnights whether it entailed drinking or not. We were also hiring a class of new flight attendants nearly every week and they wanted to chase the pilot's wallets so they partied with us quite regularly. Dealing with girls 19 to 20 was fun even though most of them knew absolutely nothing about where their tolerance ran when drinking. Several times the flight attendants woke up walleyed and we had to take care of them. Since PSA only flew two day trips, usually 8-12 legs a day followed by 8 hours of rest then one leg home to San Diego, the girls figured they could hack one flight home. Unfortunately, that was not always the case. When a new flight attendant woke up wondering where she was, we would put her up in the overhead bins and lock the door. PSA crews were allotted the last two overhead bins on the 727-200 to store our suitcases. These bins would lock so passengers would not put a five finger discount on our stuff. We saved many a flight attendant from making a scene by falling down in public.

PSA was such a fun airline to work for that when first hired, I told my dad I couldn't believe they paid me for such a fun place. Periodically the company would provide a 727 to fly crew members up to Sacramento for a three day raft trip. First night we got bused to a park where we camped and partied. Next morning we would have rafts, inner tubes or air mattresses tied together and float the river while drinking copious amounts of beer. A lot of romances were kindled and flamed out at these events.

In the winter all the airlines would have a ski week some-where. These were sponsored by either Vodka companies or Bacardi companies or any one of a myriad of alcohol brewers. There were parties every night and the liquor was free. Cheryl and I were going to drive to a ski week in New Mexico. We were both working at the time and planned to leave Los Angeles airport as soon as our flights were done. We were then going to drive back to my house in San Diego pick up our skis and drive to Phoenix to spend the night with my younger brother. Cheryl liked to drink what she called "Champagne Kiers". This was Korbel Champagne with Crème d' Cassis mixed in giving it a cherry flavor. The two of us drank two bottles just driving to San Diego. After storing the skis on top of my 1982 black Toyota Celica, we bought two more bottles and headed for Phoenix. It was after mid-night so if we felt a little tipsy we would roll down the win-dows and let the cold air snap us awake. We got a little frisky and Cheryl was sitting on my lap while I was driving when we flew through one of those border fruit check points on interstate 10 entering Arizona. Arizona is pretty anal about any fruit coming into the state due to the infestation of bugs that have a tendency to hide out in the fruit. Those check-points are like toll booths in New York. There are usually 8 of them about a car width apart. We forgot Arizona had them and went roaring through one at 75mph. It was dark as we went through, but as we passed the whole world lit up with sirens and bells and loud speakers. I stopped and backed up with Cheryl still in my lap. Stopping back at a guy's booth he just stared at us and asked if we had any fruit. "No Sir" we both replied and he sent us on our way. I won't lie to you and tell you we were both sober as choir girls but I wasn't weaving either. My brother lived next to the South Moun-tains of Phoenix and I could see his front porch light from the freeway. I was still smoking along about 75 when I noticed several sets of red and blue lights in my rear view mirror. I was still in my uniform, at least my uniform shirt that had my pilot stripes on the epaulets. I pulled over on an overpass and we were both busily trying to get dressed when the officer knocked on my window. I rolled the window down and asked him to wait while I got dressed. While I was doing that two more patrol cars pulled up and it looked like a crime scene with all the lights. The officers were all my age and grinning because I had to get dressed and was obviously toasted. I got out and walked back behind my Celica and tried to rest one foot on the bumper to look casual and cool. My foot missed the bumper and I fell face first, into the trunk lid. They had my PSA ID and my Military ID as well as my driver's license.

"Where have you been Mr. Boyd and where are you going?"

I had sobered up pretty quick thinking about the news headlines, but I forgot to inform my legs.

"Gentlemen, I got off work tonight in Los Angeles after flying 8 hours. Then Cheryl and I drove to San Diego to pick up our skis and were driving over here to stay at my brother's house which you can see right over there."

The officers could not keep from laughing having watched me put on my pants then fall into my trunk lid trying to rest my foot on the bumper.

"Well Mr. Boyd do you think you could make it to your brother's"

"Vy theringly, sir!"

"Okay Mr. Boyd we'll follow you over there to make sure you make it, but you must spend the night there tonight. We

*have to admit that you have given us the best laugh in a
year."*

"Thokay"

With an escort of five car police cars with all the lights flashing I was followed to my brother's house, not arriving incognito by any means. Thank you God, I know I am an asshole.

Scuba Diving and Sailing

Doc's 38' Sailboat

One of the guy's I interviewed with at Continental was called Doc. Not his given name but his call sign in the Navy. His real name was Robert White but he made such a great drink in the Navy they nick named him Doc, as in Dr White's feel good drink. Doc had spent his first tour commanding a River Boat. He wanted to go to flight school which he did and spent his second tour in an F4.

Doc was an excellent pilot, but when Frank Lorenzo bought Eastern Airlines he then started transferring all Eastern's assets to Continental. When he left Eastern with nothing he let Eastern go bankrupt. Moving to Continental Lorenzo told all the pilots they would take a 50% paycut or go find another job. (Some folks are alive only because it's against the law to kill them). The pilots went on strike rather than take a 50% paycut. Doc had been left with some holdings that he and his mother took care of so Doc said screw it and never went back. As a result we spent one summer revarnishing his sailboat. It was 38 feet long and had a 50-75 foot main mast. Since we both scuba dive, he would sail us out to the Coronada Islands, a couple of bare desert rock islands off San Diego about 30 miles. Doc took Pam and I out to the Coronado Islands one day to scuba dive. Following my divorce from Betsey, Pam and I had been dating, she did scuba, sky diving and running. Doc had told us there was a cave in the islands near the bottom. When we arrived at the islands the swell was gentle so Pam and I went searching for the cave. However, while we were down, the swell had picked up quite a bit creating a surge effect near the mouth of the cave. When Pam and I got close to the mouth of the cave we got sucked in and then out and then back in again. The cave had a small opening through the roof out onto the island. We had to swim for all we were worth in order to make the coral just above the water line in the cave. I had to take my fins off and physically pull Pam up onto the rocks as the surge wanted to pull her back out. We nearly got beat to death in the surge. Once up on the rocks, we had to tenderly drag our gear with us up through the roof and out onto a ledge about 15 feet in the air above from where Doc had anchored the boat. Doc then had to take his gear off and pull our gear back to the boat as we threw everything to him. It was damn near a disastrous experience.

Pam

Doc and I also took a trip to scuba dive Truk Lagoon. It was the site of the Japanese Navy's Pearl Harbor. The US had sunk more than 80 Japanese ships in that 200 square mile lagoon. We were there a week and did two dives a day and a night dive. The water was incredibly clear. Everything was just as the ships had sunk. The holes of the freighters were full of tanks, airplanes, Noritake china, live ammunition, and in some cases bones. It was a great trip.

One time Doc and I sailed out to the Islands while Doc tried to teach me how to sail. After scuba diving the afternoon away we started back to San Diego. As we got out of the lee of the Island we found ourselves embracing a strong westerly wind with huge black clouds racing towards us. As we got away from the islands, more or less out in the Pacific 18 miles from San Diego the winds were blowing 30 mph and the seas were rapidly building. We had all the sails up and we were hauling ass. At some point you need to tack the boat in a different direction. Sailing is like zig zagging toward your destination. By this point the waves were 10 to 15 feet high. Doc tells me that he was going to start his engine and use it to help us come about. The engine had a small two bladed prop. He tells me to go to the bow and anchor myself in the bow sprint and be ready to help pull the big copper ring around the cable that was attached to the main jib sail You could tighten the jib with the ropes (Doc called them sheets) which were attached to a sewn in copper ring at the end on the sail. There were two ropes attached there, one for each side of the boat, which were run through pulleys that could be cranked down to make the sail tight. My brain tumor was acting up so I make my way to the bow and anchor my legs around the chrome bow sprint. Doc said he was going to turn into the waves and crank the opposite rope to pull the sail around the cable that ran from the bow sprint to the top of the mast. I'm looking at these monster waves sliding under the boat when Doc yells *"Ready"*. I heard the engine rev up and the boat started to turn back into the waves. When we were facing the waves we rode up one wave and then dropped nearly 60 degrees into the trough behind it. I was looking at a wall of water that was 15 feet tall. Next cognizant thought I had was that of being under water where it was very dark and I could hear the theme to "JAWS" reverberating in my head. The wave washed over the boat which shed the water like a dog after a bath. I surfaced again and found that the ring was caught on the cable and Doc yelling at me to pull it over the cable. It took all my strength to pull it over the cable. We're talking about a 50 foot tall sail that was some 30 feet wide. As soon as I got the ring around that cable the wind caught the sail and I found myself flapping in the wind at the end of the sail, desperately hanging onto that small ring like a woman with a credit card. I was flapping some 15 feet in the air and 20 feet from the boat. Every now and then the sail would flap me over the boat but at 15 feet I was loath to let go knowing I was going to bust my ass on the deck. Swung out over the ocean again I had an epiphany, a very clairvoyant thought that hit me like a two-by-four. If I got shaken loose with no life preserver on, Doc would never be able to come get me and I might very well end up as a snack for a great white. When I again flapped over the boat I said fuck it and let go. I hit hard and skidded to a stop on my hands and knees leaving nice impressions of teak decking on my extremities. I know some sailors would have considered such an event laughable but I would much rather date an ugly woman before going through that again.

Home in San Diego

I always liked running around in my own home naked. If, I was to be gone for several days on a trip, I would let other pilot friends of mine, use my car to go to training and stay at my house. I had left on a trip and had told Matt, a great guy who shot down two Migs in Vietnam on the same mission, that he could use my car, (a new 1982 black Toyota Celica), and stay at my house. I arrived back in San Diego three days later to a huge group of pilots gathered in operations. Matt was there telling the pilots how they should never underestimate me. He said, *"Not only did Bob let me use his car and stay at his house, but when I arrived at the house, I could hear someone running a vacuum cleaner. I didn't think anyone would be there and since whoever it was didn't hear me knock, I opened the door and went in. You won't believe this, but there buck ass naked vacuuming his house was Jill,(under the circumstances, a made up name to protect the innocent). She sees me, turns off the vacuum cleaner, and says, "Hi, you must be Matt. Bob told me you were coming so I was just tiding up a bit. He also said you like scotch. I have one all made up for you, so just relax while I finish up and I will be gone. I swear that's the truth."*

Another night I was sitting in my living room naked of course, reading. I love books. Around 10:45pm my doorbell rings. I walk down to the door and look out the peep hole. It was a flight attendant I knew well. She asked if I felt like company and I told her sure come on in. I had three steps from the door to my living room. I was on the second step when I hear her say, *"It's okay."* I turn around and six of our flight attendants file into my house. I was an Officer and gentleman, the gentleman by an act of Congress, so I will just leave the rest of the story to your imagination.

I had a San Jose overnight with a late check in the next day. The flight attendants call me and want to go across the street from the hotel and have Chinese food. Since we had a long layover, we consumed a good deal of rice wine. On the way back to the hotel the girls wanted to go get their bathing suits and get in the hot tub which was located in the hotel lobby surrounded by fake palmettos. I had not thought to bring a bathing suit so I wrapped up in a big towel. I make my way down to the hot tub and get in. I informed the girls that I was naked which got a big laugh and then they got in. Soon after, I had a flight attendant sitting on each leg while we told jokes. It was late, the Cajun, one of our Captains and a good friend comes strolling along. Hearing the joviality he goes and gets his suit along with two other co-pilots and they all come and get in the hot tub. Serious competition! However, try as they might they couldn't break one of the girls loose. Imagine the picture me naked on one side and three guys sitting together on the other side when along comes the night watchman, a huge black guy, probably 6 foot 6 inches and 300 pounds. One of the co-pilots does that-two- finger- in- the- mouth-whistle and calls the watchman over. He saunters over and the co-pilot says, *"That guy is naked."*

"You naked, boy?"

"Yes sir, I am." I could see the headlines the next day, **Naked PSA Pilot Found in Hotel Hot Tub.** I'm doomed, screwed, damned, unlucky, cursed, and a bit pissed off.

The watchman looks from me to the other three, and says *"At least he ain't queer,"* and walks off.

Drunks, fools, and idiots, saved again!

Duties of a Flight Engineer

As a flight engineer you did everything but fly the aircraft. You started the engines, set takeoff power, set cruise power, read all the checklists, did the walk around after every flight, managed the inflight air conditioning and heating, got the aircraft first thing in the mornings and had the APU fired up and checked everything in the cockpit for air worthiness. You also checked with operations for every flight and brought the Captain the recommended fuel for his okay. Los Angeles was probably our biggest hub at the time. Our crew room was big enough to handle 50 to 75 flight crew members and flight attendants waiting on their flights. One of our Captains had a reputation of really picking on copilots and engineers. One day I walked into the LAX crew room looking for a Captain Oransky. I said " Is there a Captain Oransky in here?"

A Captain sitting on one of the couches with several flight attendants in attendance says "Who wants to know?"

"I do Sir"

"And who are you?"

"I am the flight engineer and I need approval for the fuel load."

"What's your name Flight Engineer?"

"Sir it's Bob Boyd"

"Oh great, I have heard about you!"

"Are you Captain Oransky?"

"Yeah"

"Well Sir I have heard about you too"

"Yeah what have you heard?"

At that point the entire crew room got quiet. "I heard you were the biggest asshole we have flying here as Captain, Sir"

Oransky jumps up off the couch, comes over puts his arm around my shoulders and says "Come on boy, we're going to get along just great"

JUMP SEAT

Every airliner has at least one and sometimes two jump seats in the cockpit. They are there to accommodate FAA inspectors if they choose to monitor an airline's standards. They can also be used at the discretion of the Captain to allow other pilots even those from different airlines to ride and get to or from work. I was down at the Spokane airport trying to get a jump seat on Northwest Airlines to Chicago. The Captain had agreed and I was sitting in the cockpit watching as they started the engines. When the pilots pull down on the start switch the engineer should notice a drop in the pack or air conditioning manifold pressure indicating that the start value opened. When the start switch is released, the pack or manifold pressure will rise to indicate that the value has closed. Most airlines flying the 727-200 will start the right hand engine first. Number three as it's called will give the pilots a generator as well as air conditioning. When the pilot on this particular aircraft tried to start the right engine there was no movement on the pack pressure indicating that the start value had not opened. They started the other two engines and then came back to number three. It still would not start. They had a full aircraft so they shut the other two engines down and called maintenance. Maintenance could not figure out the problem and they were going to cancel the flight. I said, *"Captain I don't mean to butt in but at PSA all engineers are required to start an engine manually in the event something like this happens."*

"Are you shitting me"

"No sir, you are on your way to your maintenance base in Minneapolis where they can figure this out and you won't have to cancel the flight."

"That would be great Mr. Boyd but it is against company regulations."

"Well sir I certainly won't tell anyone and if you can trust the mechanics, I'll need a maintenance stand and a set of ear phones so I can talk to you"

They called the maintenance man up and discussed it with him. He said if I could start it let me try and they could write it up in Minneapolis.

"Well Mr. Boyd I sure hope you know what you are doing let's try it."

I left the cockpit and walked back to the number three engine. The mechanics pushed a maintenance stand back beside the engine and gave me a set of headphones. There are several plug- ins around an aircraft from which the Captain can communicate with the maintenance crew. I plugged into the receptacle on the engine and got a commo check with the Captain. With communication established I opened the access panel on the engine and stuck my arm in and found the manual start valve lever and called the Captain.

" You are cleared to start number three sir, advise value opening and closing." I heard the engine start to turn rpms, at twenty percent N1 the Captain said okay push the start valve. I pushed the start valve in and heard the engine get its electric spark and start to speed up. When it had reached the designated rpm, the Captain advised me to close the start valve which only required me letting it go.

I let it go and the Captain relayed that it had closed. How many times have I said no good deed goes unpunished? Every jet engine has a little puddle of oil that accumulates overnight in the bottom of turbine section. When an engine starts up the engine will expel this little puddle now turned to black soot, out a hole next to the access panel. I forgot to bring a towel to cover that hole, so consequently the black soot blew out chest high on my nice white uniform shirt.

Another time I arrived in Spokane about 5:00am in order to be the first to ask for the jump seat to Minneapolis. I went to operations checked in and filled out the paperwork for the jump seat. With time to spare I decided to hit the john. I had a clip on black tie. That would prevent some unruly passenger from grabbing my tie pulling my head down and handing me my ass. Finishing my business I leaned forward to finish the job and as I did so the tip of my tie got caught under my thigh. When I sat up to flush the toilet my tie pulled off and was gone in a heartbeat due to the tornado that flushes those toilets. I had to go out to the airplane and ask the Captain if I could ride his jump seat. He turned around and noticed my open uniform shirt and said, *"Well Hollywood, what can I do for you?"*

"Sir, I realize how this must look but if you give me a minute I can explain" When they heard the explanation they started laughing so hard we had to shut the cockpit door.

Underestimated

Since I was a kid I loved to water ski. I taught myself how to barefoot by nailing a tennis shoe to a small piece of wood that looked like a small boat. I would stick the piece in my bathing suit, once up skiing on a slalom ski I would slip on the tennis shoe and put my foot down in the water until it would take all my weight and then drop off the slalom. After that, it was simple to just put my barefoot in the water until it could take my weight. At any rate, at PSA we found a ski jump in the San Diego bay. We were anxious to try it but short the necessary funds to buy a **safe** pair of jump skis. By safe, I mean a pair of skis which had foot pieces mounted on stainless steel then mounted to the ski in case the ski split or broke. We however, settled for an antique pair of jump skis for a $100. Normally, a skier in jump competition is only allowed to have the boat pull him at 35 mph. The idea being that the skier would pick up speed skiing to opposite side of the boat away from the ski jump and then make a hard cut back across the boat wake and up the ski jump. That was normal, not a word located in my lexicon. I would have the guy driving the boat pull me as fast as the boat would go at which time I would make the cut hitting the ramp at 50 to 60 mph getting maximum "air time" in the jump. It wasn't long before the $100 jump skis began to crack. We wrapped them with gray tape until the tape became an impediment. When we went to the water ski shop, the manager was astounded that grown men would not understand the possibility of wood splinters being driven into our feet once the ski broke. Somewhat humbled, we elected to purchase the $800 set of jump skis and returned to our jump.

I went out one day with my buddy Rodger, an American Airline pilot. Both of us being the quiet, subdued, shy guys that we were, we of course took along the requisite four or five girls to awe and amaze. In our haste I had not fully briefed Rodger on how to drive the boat. The inlet where the ski jump was located had just enough length for a boat to pull a jumper, let him hit the water and then make a 180 degree turn to go back and make another run. With anticipation and balls too big for my brain I did a magnificent jump, only to hit the water with a slack rope, leaving me nothing to pull against. Rodger had started his turn before I even hit the water. I tumbled through the water wrapping the ski rope round and around my right arm until the boat took up the slack. At that point the rope handle got caught between my arm and body, tightened down until it stopped the boat, then broke and flew forward and got caught in the boats propeller. I thought it had ripped my arm off as I couldn't feel or find my arm. I finally found it floating behind me, and a quick check revealed it was indeed still attached. It did not feel right though so I called Rodger to come get me. Rodger of course, was still trying to get the rope out of the propeller. Once clear, Rodger motored over to me and put the ladder down. I used my left arm to climb in the boat. There were audible gasps and a few beets were blown. Rodger looked at me, *"you look just like Popeye"*. As the rope had tightened down on my arm, it actually split my right bicep into two pieces. One piece snapped down into my wrist, and the other piece snapped up under my arm and into my pectoral area giving me a 34D look. Some of the girls were upset but quickly recovered to "take care of me."

Rodger drove me to the hospital. The surgeon for the San Diego Chargers scheduled me for surgery that evening. It was presently 8:00am. The San Diego bay is not the cleanest environment and I desperately wanted to rinse off and drink some water. Guess again, Cheecho, no water and no food before surgery.

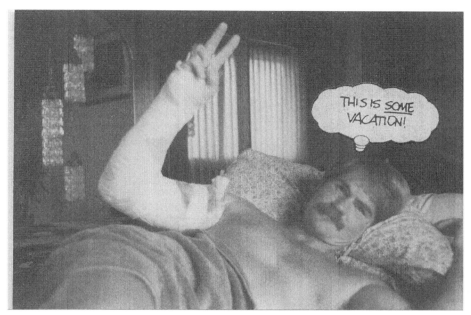

Results of Ski jump accident

I wake up the next morning with a cast from shoulder to wrist and a good deal of pain. I'm hungry, thirsty and nervous about my arm. The doctor comes in and orders a 100 cc's of morphine.

"How did it go Doc?"

"Son, your bicep was split into two pieces. I sewed them back together but will not know the outcome for several weeks."

"Uh, you know doc I'm an airline pilot."

"No son, you were an airline pilot. Best scenario I can give you is that at least you have your arm. With the bicep mus-

cle ripped in two, I cannot tell you if the nerves will grow back so that your brain will be able to tell it stretch out or pull in."

Man that wrecked my day.

The morphine was making me feel like a million bucks when my buddies showed up. They had a dozen red roses, and a Playboy.

"Don't you want to smell your roses?" They chided.

"What, did you guys stop at a gay bar on the way and get the flowers?"

Rodger brings the roses closer, *"I think you will love these."*

The vase the roses were in was filled with Jim Beam. We got a couple of diet cokes and were all having a drink when Nurse Kratchet walks in. Apparently, she had a nose like a grizzly bear and it took less time than it takes to write this for her to find the Jim Beam, pour it out, throw the Playboy in the trash, kick all my friends out with orders never to return and tongue whipped me until I was bleeding. I of course was on morphine and didn't give a shit.

My friend Roger was a hound dog. At the time he was dating a girl he met at Nordstroms. She was fishing him in and had the hook stuck in his mouth. I tried to tell him what was going on but *Love is blind.* We were jogging together one morning in San Diego when he asks me *"You have been married before, can you tell me, (yelling at the top of his voice), why the hell anyone would get married again?"* He stayed with her though and is married to this day.

With my arm still in a cast, PSA allowed me to go back to being a simulator instructor while I recovered, a period of nearly six weeks. I could watch my bicep muscle move through the top of the cast by rotating my wrist back and forth, and said "Thank you God." I don't think God believed me as he would continue to try and get my attention.

On my first flight back on the line, I was flying with my friend Coney, the former mercenary. We were nearly to San Francisco when one of the older flight attendants lets herself in the cockpit crying. By older, I didn't mean age wise, I meant she had experience in dealing with the Richard Craniums that plied our airline. Her blouse was ripped and she had fingernail scratch marks across her chest. When Captain Coney got off the radio we learned that a Mexican American had ordered a drink and then gotten pissed when she didn't immediately give him change. The flight attendants always serve everyone first before returning change. When Captain Coney saw the scratch marks, a look came over his face that would have scared Satan himself.

"Bob, go back there and sit with that asshole until we arrive in San Francisco and do not let him off this plane until I talk to him."

I make my way back to the last third of the aircraft as casually as possible. The guy was sitting near the window with two empty seats beside him. I sit down next to the aisle lean over and tell him the Captain wants to speak to him when we arrive in San Francisco. As I sit there, I notice a long red fresh scar on his left forearm. Great, I'm sitting next to a crazed lunatic who is probably sporting a blade. We arrive at the gate and like all airline passengers everyone jumps up as though they are late for picking up their lotto winnings. Ass wipe beside me gets up as well. I tell him to sit back down until the Captain gets there. There are people in the aisle and he gets up again and starts pushing on my legs to get by. He was getting wound up and clenching his fists. I knew it was coming. He tried to back hand me in the face but I ducked and tried to get up. I still had the damn seat belt on. You can't get much motion between airline seats but he was getting ready to try and hit me again. I managed to undo my seat belt just in time and kneed him in the groin. I would have been whimpering like a baby, but he comes back at me scratches my face and rips my shirt off. That did it, now I was pissed. Using my index finger and thumb spread wide I straight armed my hand into his throat, and hit him in the chest with a straight arm powered from my shoulder which pushed him against the window. He slipped and started to go down face first in the seat when I kneed him in the ass. His head hit the seat and I heard a loud crack. I thought Oh shit I killed him. As I stood up I felt hot breath on my neck. I turned around still breathing like a teenager viewing his first set of bristols and there stood Captain Coney. (Bristol is the British term for breasts).

"Thanks Captain, first day back with my arm out of a cast and I get into a fight with a lunatic."

"Yeah, but you always bring an extra shirt."

Turned out the guy had just gotten out of prison that morning in San Diego, so we helped him get acquainted with the prison in San Francisco.

Letting off steam

My brother had a Mastercraft ski boat in Phoenix. I went over to see him shortly after my arm had healed, as least the best it was going too. They had a special oblong circular manmade lake over there that had a ski jump and smooth water on either side of an oblong island. Both of us tried to impress the other with our skiing. I brought my jump skies and asked my brother to pull me over the jump. He agreed and I hit the jump at about 40mph. I crashed when I hit the water coming up only to find one of the skis heading for my face. I tried to duck under water but the ski hit me in the face right below my right eye. As I pulled myself up into my brother's boat a deluge of blood fell out on his carpet. When he looked at the cut the ski had made he said it was a tear more than a cut and he could see the yellow cottage cheese of fat squishing out the tear. He took me to a hospital and the doctor there cut the edges smooth and sewed me up. Back at my brother's house we called my Dad to keep him in the loop. This was a Sunday. After explaining what had happened, my father says," **What was a ski jump doing in church?"**

Passengers

I have no idea what happens to people let loose in public without supervision. They suddenly are elevated to star status, become Einsteins, get diarrhea of the mouth, suddenly become comedians, haven't taken a bath since the cavemen roomed the earth and still demand their rights when all those around them just want to cold cock them, want to get off the plane, or they simply become what they always were, complete assholes. Last flight of the day from San Francisco to San Diego, a gentleman in a three piece suit walks on board goes into the small galley in the front, pulls the curtain, and takes a dump right there on the floor. Couples get on, take back seats and engage in sex as though no one else is around. Women take their babies into the lavatories, change them, leaving shit and diapers right on the sink. A man brought a python on board stuffed in his pants. Another brought a giant lizard on board that got away and damn near freaked out the entire plane. I actually had a mother put two kids on board that had measles. During the flight, a flight attendant comes into the cockpit and tells me there is a near riot going on in the back from all the old folks

I flew into San Jose one evening. Just as we are about to land, I see a huge owl fly into my field of view, and I hit it right on the nose cone. Parking at the gate I get out and expect to see some damage. However, what confronted me was the perfect outline of the owl, complete with the eye sockets, emboldened on the black nose cone. It had been covered in dust.

PSA was a small regional carrier. We had approximately 451 pilots when I was hired. We had our own in-house union. Management was entirely made up of former pilots with a bunch of bean counters thrown in. After years of telling the line pilots that just as soon as this or that happened they would renegotiate a competitive contract, the pilots had finally had enough. The highest pay grade was as a 12 year Captain, and that pay grade was about 30% lower than other comparable airlines. Eventually, this situation came to a head and the pilots voted to walk out. I found myself on a picket line outside Los Angeles International airport. I was embarrassed as it was quite clear that Joe Schmuck the rag man, didn't give a big rat's ass about our contract, and I hated walking a picket line. So as not to look morose, I reverted to my Fuck It, It don't mean Shit, attitude. Mike my former nemesis, was wound up so tight you couldn't drive a ten penny nail up his ass with a sledge hammer. Western Airlines had at the time laid off hundreds of pilots as had Continental Airlines. I would sidle up to Mike and whisper," *I just heard several hundred Continental guys are going to San Diego to take our jobs.*" With his blood pressure blowing the mercury out of a blood pressure cuff, he would drop his strike sign and literally run to find the nearest phone. Sick sense of humor but I enjoyed it. I walked that picket line for two days before I couldn't stand it anymore. I returned to San Diego and offered to man the phones at the union strike center. I was answering the phones when the guys suggested that maybe it would be a good idea if I didn't answer the phones as some of the pilots thought I was too

Me 2nd from left Mike on the right end

radical, to be working the phones. Radical meant I wouldn't bullshit the pilots for the union's position. I hated unions and their manipulation of the truth. So I asked to borrow the phone and called a former boss I had flown Lear Jets for to see if he needed a standby pilot. As luck would have it, he had a position open. I went back to Houston and never missed a paycheck while the union kept the pilots riled up. The CEO of PSA had been a Captain himself. He called some of the really senior Captains and told them he was going to replace them if they didn't come back to work. The senior guys started to cross the picket line. To be fair and balanced, some of them crossed at 2:00am and shot the finger at the guys managing the picket line. That did not sit well with the strikers, especially since pictures were taken.

At another time in my life I used to steal airplanes back from people who had stolen them first. Usually it was Mexico, or other South American countries. It is remarkably easy to steal an aircraft. Since we were on strike my contact called me and wanted to know if I was interested in stealing a Lear back from a South American country. I told him I was, but under certain conditions. I told him I would get back to him. I called my buddy Coney, the former mercenary, to see if he would go with me. He wanted the names of the principles and he would call me back. Thirty minutes later he calls back and announces that the principles checked out. He said to tell them that we wanted $200,000 each, $100,000 now and the other $100,000 when we delivered the aircraft. He also informed me, that he had a shooter who would go and if necessary, be left behind to get his own way out. I rung off and called my guys. They agreed to everything including first class airfare and wanted to know how soon we could go. I called Coney. He said *"Bob, I couldn't possibly be ready to go before midnight."*

Couple of hours later they settled the strike. We decided that while it was good money on the Lear deal it held significant risks which returning to work did not, so we bowed out. The strike ended with the guys getting less than the first offer.

Basics for flying a big jet

Most of us who claim to be pilots have never really flown an airliner or a jet for that matter. The physics of flying an airliner run contradictory to small single engine aircraft. In small aircraft when landing you pull the power off and flare the aircraft to settle on its wheels. In an airliner, the wings are swept back which causes a very different airflow over them. Jets also have very different power systems. If you pull the power all the way off a jet engine the bleed bands that surround the compressor section will open up. These bleed bands are designed so that the engine, can spool up fast before they snap shut and force the air out thru the turbine section creating thrust. Pulled to idle the jet engine will take as much as 8 to 13 seconds to spool back up. Additionally, when landing you can't flare an airliner from its descent, you have to add power to stop the descent and basically parallel the runway. Our company policy called for never reducing to idle power until the landing was assured. Hard landings were the result of not following that rule.

Following our strike, PSA bought the MD-80, a stretch version of the DC-9. Most of our pilots were already settled in San Diego and didn't want to commute to Burbank, which is where the company was going to base the MD-80. I bid a co-pilot's slot and got the bid. It turned out to be a very senior slot as nobody wanted to commute. Additionally, PSA was now allowed to fly out of state. I was slotted to fly with one of the senior Captains who had crossed the picket line in the middle of the night. Since, all blocks (monthly flying schedules) were published in operations everyone knew who was flying with whom. Some of the pilots noticed who I was blocked with and wanted me to really make the trip miserable. *"Don't talk to him, fuck with him every way possible, spill coffee in his flight bag, put his flight bag under the tires, don't help him while flying."* I don't believe in that kind of harassment, especially while flying. I had already watched the dissension from guys who made nasty and threatening phone calls to wives and kids. I put the word out that anyone I could identify making such phone calls to wives or kids would retire medically. To me, that kind of treatment is shitty and cowardly. Anyway, back to Bob the Captain in question. When I arrived on the aircraft he was seated and was looking out his window. I said hello to the flight attendants ,then entered the cockpit, closed and locked the cockpit door.

"Captain, I'm Bob. I am here to fly this trip. If you want to talk about women or how best to fly this machine, I'm your man. I couldn't care less what you did during the strike everyone had their own row to hoe when they play you-bet-your-job. I'm here to have fun and to learn the best approach to flying this machine as smoothly as possible."

To this day we are good friends while others let anger and hatred eat them up.

I invited my mercenary buddy Coney and Bob (the Captain the others wanted nothing to do with from the strike), over one night to play craps. I should also mention that Bob had been Chief pilot for a number of years, so his take on the strike was somewhat biased. At any rate, we were drinking scotch and rolling dice. These guys were older than me but I highly respected them both and they always gave me sage advice. When one of us crapped out the dice would move to the next person. We had three sets of dice and they all belonged to me. Starting a new game, the roller would place whatever he wanted to bet in the middle of our little circle. The next guy clockwise would then cover the entire bet or leave some which would allow the next guy to cover, if he wanted. We had been playing several hours and having a good time. We started to get somewhat shit-faced, and as we did, the bets went up, probably why in Las Vegas they serve free drinks at the tables. At one point Coney throws out $500, I take a $100 of it and Bob takes the remaining $400. Coney's first roll is Little Joe, or a four. He makes several rolls without rolling a seven, and eventually rolls his little Joe. For the uninitiated, rolling dice requires that "you talk to the bones," if you want to win. Having been drinking scotch for several hours, we all were talking to the bones. Judy, my girlfriend was in my bedroom, tucked under the covers of my massive water bed, and told me later they could probably hear us down town. Coney is still the roller and decides to let his thousand dollars ride. I'm broke, so I pass, but Bob, covers the whole thousand. Coney rolls and gets an 11, an automatic winner. Coney pulls a thousand and leaves a thousand. Again, I pass and Bob covers the whole thousand, remarking *"You will never roll another winner."* That proved to be famous last words as Coney rolled another 11. Remember, those were my dice, so I knew they weren't loaded. Coney pulls another thousand, and leaves a thousand, with the same comment by Bob. Dip me in brown mahogany Coney rolls a seven, another automatic winner and so it went until Bob had lost $7000, and we quit.

Parties and Fun

One of our co-pilots Roger sent out wedding invitations to most of the pilots and flight attendants. It informed us that he was getting married to a Trish Caan. No one had heard of this girl nor could any of us believe Rodger would get married. The wedding was to be held at one of PSA's favorite bars, The Brigatine, across from Shelter Island. Everyone showed up on time and had a couple of drinks to ease the pain of seeing a good friend bite the dust. Most of the guys wore tuxedos and the girls were all T & A. (You can figure that out). The" Here Comes the Bride" music started and we all stood up. Through the back door comes Rodger with a decorated trash can, Trish Caan. A marvelous expensive practical joke that left most of us with death defying hangovers.

On a flight with Dave as the pilot and Gary flying on the jumpseat, the conversation turned to toys. Gary had a new Rolex, self winding. Dave says, *"May I see it, I'll wind it for you."* On 727s there are trim tabs on the elevators. These allow a pilot doing .80 mach to trim the aircraft which he would be unable to do at that speed without help. The electric trim tabs have a fast and slow rate. If you lose electric power to the trim tabs you can manually trim the aircraft with a handle that folds up into the trim tab. On the 727 the trim tab is located on the control yoke where the manual trim is next to the pilot's right leg mounted on the center console. The manual trim is a wheel about a foot in diameter, and in the fast mode on the ground, if the handle is out, it will spin so fast that it can break your arm. Dave takes the watch pulls out the handle of the manual trim and wraps the watch band around it. He then engaged the trim wheel electrically and spun the watch so fast that it stretched out the band which hit the foot rest below the instrument panel (we rest our feet on that while on autopilot) and instantaneously flew into a 1000 pieces. The best laid plans for mice and men!

Later at a party in Tom McDonough's condo, Tom takes my buddy Coney's Rolex and drops it down the garbage disposal and turns it on. Coney in turn takes Tom's dining table and sticks it sideways into Tom's living room wall complete with the chairs. I forget just how Tom retaliated but next thing I know Coney and friends go outside and turn Tom's Volkswagon upside down in the driveway. No one got upset, they just played rough.

The Cajun had some wild parties that usually involved lots of women and lots of liquor. Discretion being the better part of valor, I must leave the details out

I was dating a particular vivacious, slender, fun loving flight attendant, named Cheryl. Her bidding buddy, (someone with whom they always fly), was Keith. Keith was gay but had none of the characteristics people normally associate with gays. In fact, I had no idea until he told me. We had an overnight in San Francisco on Halloween night. The Captain had absolutely no desire to associate with the peons so he went to bed. Keith and Cheryl talked me into renting a car and going over to Castro Street in San Francisco. Keith agreed to go rent a car while the rest of us went to the hotel to get out of our uniforms. I was big into my Texas cowboy ways at the time, so I had on jeans a lavender shirt, boots, and a cowboy hat. Keith pulls up in a pink Ford town car and swears it was the only car left. With Keith driving, Cheryl and I in the front seat with him, I enquire as to where and what Castro Street was. They both look at me grinning and inform me that Castro Street is the gayest part of San Francisco. Oh great and I'm in a lavender shirt. There is something to be said about gay men, I'm still trying to figure out exactly what that is. On the other hand, to each his own and I was willing to live and let live. Keith takes us to a club we had to walk up stairs to get into. The interior was floor to ceiling mirrors and I think Cheryl was the only female there. Guys would walk up to Keith, put their arms around him and say *"Who's your friend?"* Keith would just say, *"Leave him alone, he's straight."*

"What a shame," they would reply."

After several drinks I needed to go to the rest room. It was hard to orient yourself with all the mirrors, so I asked Keith how to get there.

"Bob, you do not want to go there."

"You want me to just use a glass?"

"Trust me you need to go outside around the corner and into the alley."

"You're shitting me right?"

"No!"

We had crew busses which would pick us up after a trip at the jet ways, and take us back down the airfield to our operations in San Diego. Normally, a noisy happy go lucky crowd with about 30 to 40 crew members on board. One day as we arrived at PSA operations, Keith was about to get off when one of our homophobic pilots standing on the ground says, *"You think we should help these ladies with their luggage?"*

Without missing a beat Keith replies, *"You know you left your panties at my house last night. Do you want to come get them or should I give them to you here?"*

The guy immediately goes bright red and starts for the bus stairs. I quickly step in front of Keith, *"Unless you want to come through me, back off."*

Several weeks later Cheryl and Keith were visiting me in Hayden Lake, Idaho. Keith says he wants to give me something, explaining that his dad was a cop and couldn't stand him and never once had anyone ever taken up for him. His gift was a beautiful numbered print of wolves standing under snow covered trees looking out into a field. I have it to this day.

Cheryl and I went to a movie but Keith wanted to stay home with my dog. I had a 7/8th wolf that had the markings of a timber wolf and looked like a huge German shepherd. His name was Lou Neige, or white wolf. I called him Louper. Smartest dog I ever had. I also had a Siberian Husky I had rescued from an abusive home. Her name was Sierra and she had a tendency to wander. Keith ordered a pizza to be delivered. When the pizza got there Keith went out to pick up Sierra who had wandered off around the block and was being held at someone's home. When Keith got back he opened the pizza box and found it was empty. He said he looked around the floor, downstairs, upstairs, but could find not a smidgen of pizza anywhere. At that point he called the pizza place and accused them of delivering an empty box. Later that evening when Cheryl and I got home Keith was still irritated, but settled down as we all went downstairs to watch TV. It wasn't long before Louper, who was sleeping on the floor, cuts an insanely nasty fart, kind of had a pizza tinge to it, so I quickly checked his mouth. Sure enough he had tomato topping around his lips and gums. While Keith had gone to get Sierra, Louper had somehow pulled the pizza out of the box, leaving the cardboard bottom, and eaten the entire pizza without leaving a single clue. I can only imagine the conversation at the pizza place when Keith had called.

Another time I was downstairs when the doorbell rang. Cheryl went to see who it was, calling me to the door. One of my neighbors from down the street was standing there.

"Your dog has been harassing my pheasants!"

"How do you know it was my dog?"

"He left his dog tags stuck in the fence, here"

I put Louper on a chain and walked with the guy back to his house. In his backyard he had a 20 X 20 foot area enclosed in a hurricane fence, including a top. Outside of that he had another two foot area of hurricane fence, top included, around the entire area. Impregnable. I sat Louper down scolded him and returned home. A week later door bell rings again. Again, Cheryl goes to the door. She comes downstairs and tells me the neighbor is back and really pissed off. I meet him at the door and he wants me to follow him. We walk back over to his backyard, he shows me a two foot round hole which had been dug under both his fences and into the main enclosure, where Louper had emerged and eaten 19 of his pheasants. The guy was as amazed as I was because he had checked the area two hours before due to his pheasant's expected chicks hatching. I was dumbfounded and had to pay $350 for the damage. I walk back home where Louper is lounging on the floor cutting farts. I check his mouth and sure enough he has pin feathers stuck in his muzzle.

San Francisco

It was near Christmas in 1982, I had upgraded to Captain and Cheryl and I were in downtown San Francisco celebrating. There was a guy on the street with a cart loaded with Roses. Enquiring how much it would be for a bundle, he replied *"25 dollars"*.

"Okay, I tell you what, I'll flip a coin you call heads or tails. If I win I get the whole cart. If you win I'll pay for all the roses you have left." I have always been lucky flipping coins so for the next hour Cheryl and I had fun passing out roses to every man we saw. As we walked by Sax Fifth Avenue they had a mannequin in the window dressed in a tux with a full-length dyed black fox coat thrown over its shoulders. Cheryl says," you have to try that on". I had on my western gear again so in we went looking for the furrier. As luck would have it, it was right next to the women's lingerie section. The salesman tells us that that is the only coat they have. Cheryl asks him to go get it. When he gets back with the coat not only Cheryl, but several women in the lingerie section come over and tell me I have to have it. Asking how much, I am informed that it is a Vermillion fur and costs $11,600. It is beautiful but I would have to be dead drunk and dipped in brown mahogany to consider that. I tell the manager that if he still has it after Christmas I'll give him $5000 and he has to ship it to Idaho. Two weeks after Christmas I own a full length dyed black fox coat, which I still have.

Black fox coat

Lingerie Party

Just before St. Patrick's Day I get a call from one of my all time favorite flight attendants, Susan. She informs me that a bunch of flight attendants would like to have a lingerie party but that they don't want to have it anywhere near any of their homes. She asks if they could have it at my house. I said sure, but I have to be there. They didn't want any men there mainly because lingerie party is part of the lexicon of sex toys. I told her that I would act as a bartender and stay in my kitchen. She had to check first. The deal we worked out was that I could be there so long as I agreed to wear whatever they wanted me to, stay in the kitchen and make drinks. They wanted me to wear black pants, no shirt, white cuffs and a collar with bow tie. Make me stand on my head and gargle peanut butter, I'm in. St Patrick's Day arrives and the girls start showing up. I had a gallon of tequila, several boxes of frozen strawberries and cans of limeade. Mixed together the ingredients made for a wicked but very tasty margarita. Susan had found a mold for making ice cubes. This particular mold made 4" ice cubes in the exact shape of a phallus. She brought dozens of them ready-made. After 30 minutes of tequila lubrication the show started. I never saw such a variant of things vibrating, making music, or buzzing, dancing across my dining room table. It was somewhat ironic to watch the girls happily sucking on the ice cube while drinking the margarita since once they say *"I do"*, they will never do it again. Following the vibration demonstrations the hostess started bringing out lingerie pieces which were really quite extraordinary. I told the girls I would buy them any one of the pieces as long they modeled it there. It was a site to see. Then the hostess brings out men's lingerie. One of the girls said she would buy me anyone of the skimpy things if I would model it. Susan pipes up and says *"don't buy him anything just tell him to try it on!"* It was a remarkable party. Of course in fairness, a great many guys traded in mom and the kids for one of these hard bodied young ladies, only to find later, that they had married a runner up to Homeland Security and their constant location and every aspect of their lives were under tight scrutiny. Without the camaraderie of the other girls and the tequila, the girlfriends and wives were exactly the same. Like the **Lion King,** it was the circle of life.

Lingerie Party Susan middle

My friend Judy called me one day crying and informed me that she was pregnant. It wasn't from me, but she was a good friend. She told me that she had gotten involved with a guy from Fresno who turned out to be married. When I asked what she was going to do she informed me that she had an abortion scheduled that day, but that the father had washed his hands of the affair and told her good luck. I do not adhere to the Liberal way of approaching such a problem. They think it is an abomination to fry a murderer but okay to kill a baby. However, I volunteered to take her, I'd take care of the loser later. Arriving at the doctor's office I found it full of young girls, very nervous and very unhappy. Not a man in sight. In this case I have to admit men are truly assholes. They came for Judy and I was left sitting there like a turd in a punch bowl. I told a joke and got some smiles, so I told jokes for the next 45 minutes. The nurse came out and said the doctor wanted to see me. I go in to see him and he says, "*I don't know what you are doing out there, but can you come back tomorrow.*" Mr. Fresno man found himself in the paper, along with his other sordid affairs. Lesson: Don't mess with my friends.

Judy

Every pilot wants to be a Captain. It is true however, that the time you spend in the other seats hopefully helps prepare you for the position. Contrary to what the public thinks, that we all sit on our asses, chase flight attendants and watch the autopilot fly, the reality is vastly different. As a Captain, no matter what happens, it's your fault. Flight attendant screws up, it's your fault. Co-pilot screws up, it's your fault. Maintenance, operations, guys fueling the aircraft, unruly passengers, it's your fault. There was a time, when Captains were highly respected and kids and passengers looked up to them. Not so today. You are merely a pawn or a number to some bean counter who can barely drive a car, much less fly a 100,000+ pound aircraft in a three dimensional world through all kinds of weather and survive the incredible array of problems that creep up all too often.

At the time, PSA had not received their MD80 simulator, so checking out as a co-pilot made it mandatory to use an actual aircraft for training. The MD80 was certified by the FAA to be flown on the autopilot. The reasoning was that, since there would only be two guys in the , both pilots would have time to keep an eye outside to prevent mid airs. Once I had finished training I was assigned a Captain who would check me out flying with passengers. Susan, my good friend and senior flight attendant, was riding the very back of the aircraft. The weather was shitty,(I mean inclement), low ceilings and rain. We were taking off out of Oakland, California to the south. That direction would put you right into the traffic arriving into San Francisco. The departure called for an immediate right turn of 180 degrees and level at 1500 feet until air traffic control could route you north out of the traffic area and then left out over the Pacific. The Captain wanted me to takeoff and immediately turn the autopilot on, use the heading bug to make the 180 degree turn, and the preprogrammed altitude, to capture the 1500 feet. The throttles were controlled by a push button array which could give you TO for takeoff or CL for climb. Once altitude was captured, the throttles would retard back to the speed you had selected digitally on the autopilot. We took off and the aircraft roared through 1000 feet while in the turn with a 20 degree nose up attitude. I put my hands on the yoke to punch off the autopilot. The Captain yelled at me to leave it alone. We went through 1500 feet like shit though a goose with no sign of trying to capture that altitude. We were accelerating through 250 knots, which is max airspeed below 10,000 feet, and again I wanted to punch the autopilot off. Because, we were accelerating through normal flap retraction speed, I called for flaps up and climb power. We were already at 2200 feet. The aircraft then recognized that we had overshot the preprogrammed altitude and started a gut wrenching negative-g to get back to 1500 feet. The aircraft was accelerating through 300 knots and shot through 1500 feet in the blink of an eye. I punched off the autopilot and told the Captain not to even think about reengaging it or touching the controls. I managed to stop the decent at about 700 feet out over San Francisco Bay, still in the clouds. I was beyond pissed off. Air Traffic control called and asked if we had an emergency, a sure sign they noticed the altitude bust and the airspeed bust. Airliners must maintain their assigned altitudes or risk a midair collision. The Captain, begged me not to say anything to anyone. I told him I'm going to tell every swinging dick I know, as we came damn close to busting our ass or getting a violation. When I talk to Susan, she tells me what a wild ride it was at the back of the aircraft. Because I told everyone, PSA looked into it and found out that as long as the aircraft had TO entered into the auto throttles, all the aircraft would do was takeoff. None of the other functions would operate. Sort of nice to know, flying a new aircraft.

A pilot takes a first class flight physical every six months. Additionally, we go to ground school for a week once a year. We endure two simulator check rides, which if failed means you are off the payroll until it is passed. And, we have a company and or an FAA inspector ride a trip with us at least twice a year to insure we are following company procedures.

Me and Cockpit of MD80

Initially, I was checked out as Captain on the MD80, an upgraded stretched DC9, with the latest in cock pit hardware. Soon however, PSA bought the BAE146, a British made high wing four engine aircraft, with a trailing gear that unless you were the worst pilot in history you could land so smoothly no one would know you were on the ground. Our PSA pilots went over to Britain to train and pick up the first BAE146-200. Britain is highly unionized as our pilots soon found out. At PSA a new hire, training as an engineer, had to know how to manually start a 727 engine, how to start the APU, check every system on the 727, and do a walk around prior to the Captain and first officer getting on board. To start the APU, it only requires the flip of a switch. In Britain, our guys went out to the new BAE146 and started the APU. It caused an immediate strike. British unions required that one man flip the APU start switch, another man would put the APU on-line, another man, would check a certain instrument and so on and so forth. Easy to see why Britain is broke and the USA is on its way.

The BAE 146

PSA's 146s were to be stationed in San Francisco. I was living in Hayden Lake, Idaho which was a one leg commute on Alaska Airlines to Spokane. I bid the 146 and became a fairly senior Captain, due to the lack of interest of other more senior pilots. It was a great aircraft to fly, although it did have its problems. I would bid trips that took me up through Oregon, landing in airfields like Eugene, Medford, Klamath Falls, and Bend. Going to Bend if the weather was good, I would request altitudes of only 11,000 to 12,000 feet. In that way, I could give the passengers a great look at Crater Lake flying in a left hand turn all the way around the lake, followed by a right hand turn all the way around the lake again. With the wing over the fuselage, passengers had a remarkable view out the windows. PSA had a very lenient rule regarding your last flight. If your last flight could be flown by another Captain, who would still be legal to fly his own trip, you could get off the airplane and still get paid for the last trip because the Captain taking over was basically getting a guaranteed ride to San Francisco, and not have to be standing in line with the other commuters. December 7th, 1987 I was in such a position as my last flight was to be from Los Angeles back to San Francisco. There were several Captains commuting to San Francisco, so finding a Captain willing to fly that leg was easy. As a result, I got off and ran over to Alaska Airlines which had a flight leaving shortly for Spokane, and asked the Captain if I could ride his jump seat. We were some where north of San Lius Obispo, in central California, when the Alaska pilot turned to me and said that gun shots had been reported to center from a PSA 146 enroute to San Francisco.

Whether that was my last flight I will never really be sure, but the timing was right. Cruising at 22,000 feet, an employee recently fired by USAIR, (which was currently in the process of merging PSA into USAIR) for a $69 petty theft, had gotten on the flight with his unsurrendered PSA ID and a borrowed .44 magnum. The USAIR manager who had fired him was also on the flight. The employee, David Burke, had worked for USAIR in Rochester, NY and had been suspect in a drug smuggling ring. He moved to Los Angeles to avoid further suspicion and was caught stealing cash out of the in-flight drink receipts. He had met with the supervisor early that morning trying unsuccessfully to get his job back. Once at cruising altitude PSA reported two gunshots in the cabin.

Seconds later a flight attendant entered the cockpit and told the Captain *"We have a problem."* When the Captain asked what kind of problem, David Burke pushed into the cockpit stating *"I am the problem."* Mere seconds later, three gunshots are recorded on the voice recorder. There were three crew members in the cockpit. The voice recorder then picked up the sound of increasing engine revolutions followed by loud wind noise outside the cockpit windows. A split second before impact there was one more gunshot. The aircraft crashed into the side of a hill on a cattle ranch near San Luis Obispo. It was estimated that the aircraft was going somewhere near 700mph when it hit the ground. At that speed virtually nothing was left, save for some feet in shoes. However, the investigators found a note written on a barf bag, apparently to Burke's supervisor which said, *"Hi Ray, its ironical we ended up like this. I asked for some leniency for my family, Remember? Well I got none and you'll get none."* They surmised that Burke then shot his former supervisor, hence the first two shots fired in the cabin. Burke had then burst into the cockpit, shot the three Captains riding there and pushed the four throttles full forward. The autopilot which couldn't handle the extra speed, kicked off and the plane went into a 70 degree dive. A split second before impact the last shot was recorded. They think Burke chickened out and shot himself. They found the handle to the .44 magnum along with the chamber for the rounds. Additionally, they found some skin on the trigger, which once rolled out by forensics, had Burke's finger print. He had also left a goodbye message to his girlfriend on her telephone. No other passengers were ever identified.

Before USAIR moved all the MD80's to Pittsburg, I bid back to the MD80. I was flying a trip out of Los Angeles to Seattle. There were probably 30 aircraft waiting in a taxi line to take-off. Because, I was going to push back from a gate that was less than 500 feet to the threshold of the active runway, I was going to be number two in line for takeoff. As I made the corner of the taxiway just prior to taking the active, a flight attendant comes in and says there is an old man that has to use the bathroom. I ask her if he can't wait 5 minutes and we would be in the air. She tells me that even his wife says he has to go. Unbelievable! I call ground control and tell them I need to pull into the penalty box, a wide concrete area next to the last taxi way. They clear me into the penalty box and inform me I am now number 29 for takeoff. Shit, that was going to be close to an hour delay. I shut one engine down to save fuel and begin to contemplate my luck. About three minutes later, I hear coughing and gagging in the cabin. I call for the flight attendant to come up. Huge mistake, the smell intrudes into the cockpit and we both nearly gag. I have never smelled a shit that smelled that bad. Not even a cat would come close. Next thing I know, half the passengers are rebelling and want off the aircraft. I am astounded. What kind of excuse, other than the truth, am I going to tell operations? I get clearance to taxi back to the gate. As I pull in the Chief Pilot is waiting. As soon as we open the door, the Chief Pilot's nostrils are attacked to such a degree he has to step out the jet way door to remain upright.

When I met Sally she was working in Bend, Oregon as a ramp rat. She would direct the aircraft in and then help load and unload the bags. As soon as our shut down checklist was complete I would exit the aircraft and tell the co-pilot that I would do the walk around. I would do everything but stand in her way and still she would not make any attempt at communication. After several weeks, I did stand in her way and ask her if I had bad breath, as I knew I had taken a shower that morning. She says, "I've heard about you. You have slept with every girl at PSA."

"Not true, you're a girl and I haven't slept with you. Besides, I don't make checks on my bedpost. I date girls that like to do things I like to do. If we end up at my house, it's because it is a mutual desire. On top of that, I have a lot of girlfriends I date and don't take home."

"I'll think about it."

It was the start of an impossible romance.

Sally

Flying into Burbank one night with nasty thunderstorms everywhere, I had a new co-pilot with me. If you are flying in from the north, you transition from altitude over the San Gabriel Mountains. It is normally a very rough ride. Following a downwind approach over the San Gabriel's with constant lightning, we are struck directly on the wind screen. What looked like a huge ball of fire passed through the cockpit, out the cockpit door, through the passenger cabin, and exited out the back of the aircraft. Once on the ground, maintenance found some rather large burn holes on the tail section and an unusual smell in the cabin due to lots of brown underwear. The co-pilots instruments had also fried.

Another time, again coming in from the north, having started our descent, we miss a guy hang gliding up at 15,000 feet. He was so close I was afraid our turbulence would upset his hang glider. I'll bet his shorts looked like my grandsons diaper, after a nice load.

Move to Pittsburg

Once USAIR had completed their purchase of PSA, they moved all the MD80s to Pittsburg. Seeing the handwriting on the wall, I bid back to the MD80 and started commuting out of Spokane to Pittsburg.

When I arrived in Pittsburg, I discovered that USAIR considered their pilots superior to PSA's pilots, and as such, they made their DC9 pilots instructors on the MD80. The MD80 was far superior to a regular DC9, with nearly the exact cockpit of the DC10. I had nearly 3000 hours in the MD80, but I still had to take a line check with one of their instructors. First takeoff, the USAIR guy reaches up and turns the autopilot off, stating that we don't use that. These superior pilots didn't use the autopilot as they didn't know how. I put up with this arrogant ass all day until our last leg. Prior to that, I went in and called the FAA and requested one of their pilots to give us a line check back to Pittsburg. All the FAA has to do is walk on board and show his ID and he can ride anywhere anytime in our jump seat. The Captain was so captivated by his position that it would have been beneath him to do a walk around. I left the cockpit and went up to the gate agent and asked if she had seen an FAA inspector. She had not, so I requested that if one were to show up would he meet me under the aircraft, as I was doing a walk around. Very shortly a man comes up and identifies himself as an FAA inspector who would be riding our jump seat. He follows me around while I do my walk around and we chat. I inquire how much about the MD80 he knows, and he informs me that he had just moved from San Francisco where he was the inspector for PSA and Alaska airlines. Perfect. Soon as I takeoff, I engage the autopilot and the Captain reaches up and turns it off. I ask him again why he does that and he tells me that he has already told me, that USAIR doesn't use it. Bingo. The inspector speaks up and asks the Captain if he is aware that the airplane was certified to fly with the auto pilot. His reply was not what the inspector wanted to hear. He asks the Captain if he was an instructor. When the Captain says yes, the inspector informs him that he is no longer, and will not be allowed to fly the aircraft until he can prove he knows how to fly the autopilot. The inspector says he will approach USAIR management and tell them the same will go for any of their pilots who cannot demonstrate the proper function of the auto pilot. Retribution for contemptuousness, conceit, and superciliousness has such a sweet flavor.

I was flying from Erie to Pittsburgh, the weather sucked, heavy rain, thunderstorms and lightning. USAIR allowed maintenance men to ride the jump seat and I had one with me. Arriving in Pittsburgh it was raining so hard that even with windshield wipers going full speed, you couldn't see a thing. We broke out of the clouds about 300 feet and with the hard rain I could barely make out the runway. Additionally, it was really turbulent with constant thunder and lightning. I was paying attention to the aircraft instruments for the ILS we were shooting. About 200 feet I notice out of the corner of my eye that the maintenance man is white as a sheet and sweating profusely. Barely able to see a half mile down the runway due to the rain, I make a super smooth landing. Any pilot can make a great landing in a rain swept runway. The trick is not to hydroplane. With engines reversed I managed to make the taxiway in the middle of the field. As I was taxiing to the gate the maintenance man says *"Captain, in the maintenance hanger we all bad mouth you pilots as bunch of over paid, egotistical, arrogant ass-holes. I would like to thank you for getting me on the ground safely and I think you need to make a lot more money."*

I was flying a trip from Siberacruse (my name for Syracuse) to Boston one afternoon. The weather really sucked and we were in the clouds from takeoff to landing. Level at 35,000 feet, still in the clouds, we hear a Continental Pilot, declare an emergency as being out of control. I find out he is just ahead of me and had run into severe turbulence. Pilots never declare an emergency just for turbulence, but out of control is something else. Air traffic control informs us that he was able to recover and is apparently okay. It still rests in the back of your mind and you are conscious of the possibility to your aircraft. Arriving in the Boston area we proceeded with our normal descent and contacted approach con-trol for an instrument approach into Boston International. The co-pilot was flying. Approach asked us to slow down to minimum approach speed as we were following a twin engine corporate aircraft. The weather radar was on and was painting a screen full of green or light rain. Weather radars can indicate clear skies, green for light rain, yellow for heavier rain, red for rain in excess of 2" an hour and ma-genta for severe turbulence. A note here for future refer-ence, the weather radar cannot pickup ice.

We configured the aircraft, meaning flaps to approach speed, airspeed at recommended plus 5 knots, and gear down and locked, spoilers armed. I was watching the ra-dar, when we encountered a couple of good bumps. I asked approach if the corporate aircraft ahead of us had reported any turbulence.

"No sir, they report smooth sailing."

We were 2500 feet off the ground when the radar displayed complete magenta. Within seconds, we experienced se-vere turbulence, like dropping the aircraft off a two story building. Additionally, we started to descend past 1500 feet and the aircraft was rolled up nearly 110 degrees. The tail of the aircraft was trying to slew sideways, a condition that it was not designed to take. Everything in the cockpit, books, dirt, uniform coats, and the microphones began to bounce off the roof and my face. We were out of control. Descending through 1000 feet I declared an emergency and told the co-pilot to go around. I turned on the ignition override in case the turbulence flamed out an engine. His instruments had frozen so I took control. When you declare an emergency, approach control is required to ask how much fuel you have on board and how many passengers. Sounds simple enough, but when you can't grab a flying microphone and you are desperately trying to save your ass those questions become one more distraction that you don't need. I had already pushed the power up to mcx and hit the go around button which immediately gave the command bars a 20 degree up indication and yet we were still going down. This particular approach to the East put us somewhere over downtown Boston, not a particular great place to be descending out of control. We were advised to make an immediate left turn and climb to 7000 feet. I couldn't answer as I fought the aircraft. I had the nose up to "go around" attitude and full power and we were still rolling nearly 110 degrees and descending. All of a sudden we flew out of the turbulence and the aircraft reacted to the nose up attitude and I was able to make the left turn and start cleaning up the aircraft, i.e. gear up when indicating a climb, flaps up on required speeds, and able to capture the microphone. I requested to climb to 25,000 feet and return to Syracuse at a slow cruise. I didn't know if we had damaged the aircraft from the severe jolts and didn't want to put any undue strain on the airframe. The co-pilots instruments eventually returned to normal and I gave the aircraft back to him. Once level at 25,000 feet I told the co-pilot I was going back to check on our passengers. Smiling like I had not a care in the world, I walked back through the cabin assuring the passengers everything was all right. One gentleman and his wife or girlfriend (you quickly learn never to make assumptions) who were holding each other tightly, asked out loud,

"Did you shit in your pants, Captain?"

"I actually don't know I haven't had time to look."

We landed in Syracuse and the FAA met us to get a report. Maintenance wanted to x-ray the wing roots, and the engine mountings, which would take about an hour and a half. Operations still wanted us to fly back to Boston and on to Miami. When maintenance cleared the aircraft, and we were boarding for the trip back to Boston, every single passenger got back on. I took it as a sign of confidence.

One thing that pilots forget is that the passengers have no idea what's happening. A quick PA is very encouraging. At this point I should also mention that there are no air pockets. There are different wind currents at different altitudes. So if you have a 250 knot jet stream at 30,000 feet it's like water over rocks creating rapids. The air on either side of that jet stream is rubbing against it creating turbulence. You can either climb over the jet stream or descend out of it.

My crew and I flew a trip from Pittsburg to Fort Myers in Florida. We spent the night and the next morning the bus was late in picking us up. This was shortly after the incident with the Northwest crew that had pushed the limits of alcohol consumption on an overnight. As we walked up to the gate a flabby dude in a Hawaiian shirt unbuttoned to his waist with enough bling around his neck to insure his eventual depredation, loudly made an observation about us being too drunk to show up on time. I sent the flight attendants on down to the airplane and I walked over to the gate agent.

"Do you have the tickets for the loudmouth over there?"

"Yes I do, and he has been bitchin for the last half hour."

"Well, will you give me his tickets please? I suppose the menagerie with him is his family?"

"Yep, there are four of them."

"I gathered their tickets, tore their boarding passes into and walked over to him."

Everyone was watching me as I walked over to him. Loud enough to keep everyone in the loop, I addressed him, *"Sir, your comments pissed me off. In all fairness I should cancel this trip and go have the entire crew tested. I am a professional, something a big teenager like you probably can't understand. However, I am returning your tickets to you because you are not going to Pittsburg on this aircraft. To have you on my airplane now would so irritate me that it would be a safety of flight issue to have a loudmouth like you on board."*

With that I walked back to the cockpit. There wasn't another flight to Pittsburgh until 7:30 that evening.

The east coast, especially the Florida panhandle, is notorious for its thunderstorms. They rise in height up to and above 70,000 feet. These are severe thunderstorms and only an idiot would fly into or close to them. Lightening has been known to hit aircraft from as far as 30 miles from a thunderstorm in clear air. Pittsburgh is another thunderstorm breeder. Scheduled to fly from Pittsburgh to Minneapolis, operations had briefed us on a line of thunderstorms developing along a cold front coming in from the north. Taking off after dark the lightning was visible every three to five seconds as far west as we could see. Traffic control allowed us to modify our flight path south of the line thunderstorms and give the passengers a smoother flight. The constant lightning just to our right made a beautiful show at night, but one I knew was Satan's own playground. The weather radar depicted serious cells located within these thunderstorms. As I got closer to Minneapolis it was obvious that I would have to fly further west to get around the nastiest of the thunderstorm line. Talking to air traffic control I learned that most airliners were flying as far west as Sioux Falls and coming in around the back side of the front. When I got to Sioux Falls, I heard a Delta pilot ask for help with vectors, (heading directions), through the back side of the storms as his weather radar had gone tits up. Air Traffic control acknowledged the request but told Delta they were far too busy to give him that aid. I asked Control where Delta was and discovered he was following me 15 miles in trail. Knowing Delta was listening, I asked Control if they would vector him right behind me and I would take him through the rough stuff. Control and Delta both enthusiastically agreed. I made the right turn to start the transition back through the tail end of the front. We were still in the clouds, occasional lightning now, but the static electricity was all over the aircraft in the form of miniature blue lightning bolts on the windscreen and along the nose cone. We were in our initial descent when suddenly a brilliant spot light appeared right in front of us. The co-pilot yelled out that I was descending on another aircraft. Remember the necessity of flying the other seats to get experience? I told him it was just a symptom of the static electricity, but when it left the aircraft there would be a huge thunder clap. It remained on the nose for about three minutes and then with a tremendous crack of thunder it left the aircraft. A lot of brown underwear occurred with that thunder. I led Delta through giving him updates on the static electricity and we both landed safely.

On another trip, Pittsburgh to Minneapolis, we again were in the tops of thunderstorms. We were hauling ass as we were late. I had the radar on a 100 mile sweep. Starting our initial descent, still running right on red line speed, I had the co-pilot switch the radar to a 30 mile sweep. Immediately, two huge cells popped up directly in front of us with a small area between them. We banked for that small opening and backed off the throttles. Within 30 seconds we ran into hail stones the size of baseballs. Because the windscreen is heated, they would momentarily appear. The sound, as hail that size hit the aircraft, was enormous. The co-pilot and I both ducked at the same time and nearly knocked ourselves out after hitting our heads together. Remember, weather radar doesn't depict ice, so we flew right into a sucker hole. When we landed in Minneapolis, the leading edge of the wings, were severely dented as were the engine intakes and the tail. They grounded the aircraft.

During this time it was discovered that a majority of U.S. Senators and Congressmen had been writing, hot checks and never making good on them. I pounced on that news while doing my PA announcements. Flying into Washington D.C., I would make a goodbye announcement as we started our descent.

"Ladies and Gentlemen, your Captain Speaking. I want to thank all of you for choosing USAirways. I hope you found the flight not only safe but comfortable as well. We have started our descent into Washington D.C., should have you on the ground in 20 minutes. Not only is Washington our Nation's capital but it is probably the only city I know of where tonight you can take all your friends and family out to dinner, write a check, and never have to make good on it. I would pause, and then continue. *Actually, I really don't want to see you good folks get in trouble, you do need to have the word **Honorable** in front of your name."*

After landing I would stand at the cockpit door and say goodbye a 100 times. Following my announcement one day, Senator Howell Heflin of Alabama, stops in front of me and says,

"I didn't like your humor Captain."

"Well Senator, if the shoe fits I guess you have to wear it."

If the co-pilot was flying and had not yet mastered adding a little power to stop the descent and made a rough landing, I would help him out on the PA as we taxied to the gate.

" Ladies and gentlemen I would like to apologize for that rough landing that the co-pilot made. To be fair, just as we were about to touch down a stray dog wandered onto the runway and froze at the sound of us landing. The co-pilot, being the great humanitarian he is, managed to hold the aircraft off the runway long enough to miss the little dog until airspeed and ideas caught up to him and we bumped down." Shutting down at the gate nearly everyone stopped by to thank him for saving the dog.

Responsibilities and Mentoring

Flying back from Florida one winter evening, I had to make stops in Charlotte, N.C., Pittsburgh and on to Syracuse. The weather was extremely low ceilings and rain. On the last leg from Pittsburgh to Syracuse the weather was reported as low ceilings ½ mile visibility with winds of 28mph gusting to 30, with blowing snow. The active runway would have the winds at almost 27 degrees from the right. It was the copilots turn to fly but he didn't really want to. I asked him why he didn't want to fly his leg?

"Sir, most of the Captains I have flown with would never let me fly in this kind of weather"

"Is that your only reason?"

"Actually, I wouldn't want to screw it up."

"Son, when you check out as Captain you will have no choice. I don't want to be sitting in back knowing you are the Captain and don't have any experience in this kind of weather. So, you are going to fly the leg, I will not let you hurt me, basically because once we shut that passenger door, the most important person on this airplane is me! I will talk you through the approach and landing, you just need to follow my instructions.

Arriving in the Syracuse area, I listened to the weather and discovered the runway is packed ice and snow, braking at good to fair. The braking is determined by driving an automobile down the runway and hitting the brakes. My copilot is obviously very nervous. All U.S. airliners are required to have their landing lights on below 10,000 feet. We were descending through 3000 feet when we broke out of the clouds and into a nasty snowstorm. As air traffic control centered us up on the active runway, the landing lights brought out just how hard it was snowing. Normally rain or snow looks like it is coming right at you, but in our case, every two or three seconds it would appear perpendicular to us, due to the gusts. I instructed the copilot to keep the aircraft down the middle of the runway, letting it crab into the wind as necessary to keep it lined up. We approached with a 30 degree heading away from our line of flight. I instructed him to let the airplane crab all the way down to us crossing the numbers, (referring to the runway designation), and then with the right aileron turned into the wind to keep the right wing down, push in enough left rudder to bring the nose around to the center of the runway.

"You will be landing on the right main gear first. Don't let the wing tip hit the ground."

He made the best landing of his life and was so relieved, that he quit **Flying the Damn Airplane**. As a result, before he could get the nose wheel down on the runway, the wind picked up that right wing and we were blown 30 degrees off the center line. He immediately hit the brakes and we started a sideway slide down the runway in the packed ice and snow. You have never quite lived until you have experienced a big airliner sliding sideways down a runway. I said, "***I said, I have the airplane, get off the brakes."*** As he did so, I quickly yanked the right engine into reverse, and pushed the control yoke forward to keep the nose on the ground. Once the nose centered up, I brought the left engine into reverse, and slowly started adding the brakes. We were able to stop and turnoff the active about 1000 feet from the end. The copilot was eaten up with conflicting emotions. One, he made a great landing, but two he forgot to continue to fly the aircraft until it stopped.

"Shit happens son, don't beat yourself up. However, if you never learn anything from me, remember to **Fly the Damn Airplane** *until you are stopped.*

"Damn sir, I wish we could go back up and do it again."

On a New Year's Eve, we were flying down to Miami. Two breath-taking young ladies got on with rather large Bristols. That is the name the British use to describe breasts. They were Playboy Bunnies on their way to a party. They even had their layouts in the Playboy Magazines they carried. They were vivacious and flirtatious and a tiny bit toasted, okay a lot toasted. Half way to Miami, after several more rounds they wanted to come show the Captain their Bristols. One of the flight attendants came up and asked if the girls could step into the cockpit and show them to me. I've been accused of a lot of things, (most of them unfortunately are true) but stupid is not one of them. I'd seen lots of Bristols in my life and at the possible loss of $161,000 a year, two more sets were not worth the risk, even though they were magnificent.

As a single man, I always volunteered to fly on the holidays, Christmas, New Years, Valentine's Day, Easter and Thanksgiving. I wanted to give the married guys the time with their families and of course, the junior girls were always left to fly on those days. Christmas Eve 1990, I was flying from Pittsburgh to Miami. On descent I made the following announcement, *"Ladies and gentlemen have a merry Christmas, but while doing so, please don't forget our troops currently massing in the middle east."* After landing one of the flight attendants entered the cockpit and said there was a disgusting hippie guy, who smelled worse than a week dead goat with all kinds of piercings, demanding to use the microphone to talk to the passengers. He didn't believe in war and the military was a fascist organization and he loathed them. I got up to talk to this guy, a young apparent college student who couldn't get laid with a handful of pardons at a women's prison. What is it about smelling bad that makes these kids think it is cool? He had enough steel in his nose, ears, and lips to outfit a small foundry. I ushered him out of the aircraft into the jet way, and then outside the door normally used for the crew to access the ground in order to do their walk around of the aircraft prior to every flight. To this day I have never gotten over the wonderful welcome I got from Uncle Sam's free Southeast Asian vacation so I was already spring loaded for this asshole. No one could see us out behind the jet way door, so I tell this punk, *"You wouldn't make a good pimple on a soldier's ass. You smell worse than my dog's asshole, and if I could think of good place to hide your body, I'd put you out of your ignorant misery and tell God you died."* Of course the little shit for brains calls the airline and when I get back to Pittsburgh the chief pilot meets me and wants to give me two weeks off without pay, and give ass wipe a free 1st class round trip on the airline. I said I can use the two weeks off but in fairness to Useless Airways (USAirways), as soon as I get home you will see this event in the papers and the fact that Useless caters to pricks like him versus our men and women in uniform. So much, for the two weeks off and the free 1st class ticket.

Half Wits

Flight attendants have to put up with a lot of crap, but when flying with me, I took care of them. Out of Baltimore one day a jerk and his two kids get on board with huge 3' X 2' bags. They wouldn't fit under any seat or in any overhead. Why the agent let them out the door was beyond me. At any rate, he was cussing the flight attendants who told him he needed to check them. When I heard the commotion I got out of my seat to go see what was happening. As the flight attendants were trying to explain, the jerk starts to tell me how fucked up USAirways is for not just allowing him to strap them in empty seats. I explained that that would be a violation of FAA rules. *"Well fuck you and the FAA."* That was it, end of Bob's Courtesy lesson. I told him he could pick up his bags and get off my aircraft or I could have security do it for him. *"How am I going to get to New York?"*

"Well if you are real nice, there is another flight in about 5 hours, but you are not riding on this aircraft!"

Sputtering with almost uncontrollable rage and yelling about how he was going to sue, he left the aircraft. Once he was gone, the entire Cabin started clapping. I told you how at one time a Captain was respected. Well, this asshole called the company and they gave him a free round trip 1st Class ticket. Great lesson in backing up your people! Very few people understand the FAA regulations, but they are multitude. As an example, merely standing up while the aircraft taxis to the gate, or putting a small child next to an emergency exit, can garner the Captain a $10,000 violation and the company doesn't pay.

Last flight of the day from San Jose to San Diego with the plane full, a three piece suit guy gets on. Just about ready to push back the lead flight attendant comes to me and says a passenger refuses to buckle his seat belt. She said I figured he was having a bad day, so I left him and finished the rest of my walk through and came back to him. Now these were senior flight attendants, been there, done that, had the t-shirts. When she gets back to him he still refuses and says "*What's the matter with you, you having your period?*" They are taught not to get into confrontations, just go tell the Captain. So I make a PA announcement apologizing for the delay, that when everyone is buckled up and seated, we can push back. Couple of minutes, go by and the flight attendant returns with the word that he still will not buckle his seat belt. I said," go tell him I said to buckle his seat belt or I will have him removed". She is back in 30 seconds, "he says to tell you to go fuck yourself, and if you try to remove him he will sue". Ok, have it your way. I call security and explain the situation. Couple of minutes later, a big black woman from security comes into the cabin. I take her to the passenger. She says, "*Sir, you will have to exit this aircraft.*"

"*Go fuck yourself*", he says. At that point, faster than a cobra strike, she whips out her night stick, puts it under his neck and with a hand holding each end and her thumbs in the back of his head, she lifts him out of his seat, down the aisle, and off the aircraft. I return to the cockpit, turn around and look back into the cabin. Every passenger is leaning out sideways looking at me. I tell the ground crew they can push us back. I do the checklists and start the engines. While taxiing out I make the following PA:

"*Good evening, this is your Captain. On behalf of PSA I want to apologize for the brief delay. What you have just witnessed, was a man with an alligator mouth that he let override his lizard ass. On that note, drinks are on me, thank you for your patience."* There was a roar of hand clapping from the cabin. I got 75 letters on that flight. Not one for the free drinks, but all of them, praising me for having backed up for the flight attendants.

I was flying out of Hartford, Connecticut one evening in a severe snowstorm. Our company policy stated we were not allowed to take off with more than a 1/4 inch of slushy snow or water, or anything above 2 inches of dry snow. It was very cold and the snow was accumulating at a rapid pace. It was a full flight. Our gate was only about 400 yards to the active runway. When we buttoned up the doors I called for the de-ice trucks. Once they had accomplished their job we started the engines and taxied out for the runway. Being first in line for takeoff I inquired of the tower how deep the snow was. The airport was running snowplows down the runway, letting an aircraft take off, and then repeating the procedure. The tower told me the snow was nearing another four inches. I thought about it and decided to wait for another plowing. However, behind me a Continental MD80 responded that they would take the active. Asked if they could get around me, they were cleared for takeoff. Having turned around taxiing back to our gate, I watched the Continental MD80 roar down the runway. He didn't seem to be going fast enough to take off and eventually put in max reverse and tried to stop. Unfortunately, he didn't make it and slid off the other end of the runway. The snow had been too deep and kept the aircraft from reaching takeoff speed.

Don't Wet Your Pants

I was flying back into Pittsburg from Florida. Air traffic control would usually start us down, about a 100 to 120 miles out. I got cleared to 15,000 feet which put me solidly in the clouds. From 15,000 feet we would be vectored onto a downwind leg and cleared to 10,000 feet. Ask a pilot and he will tell you that landing at an airport normally comes with a downwind leg, a 90 degree crosswind leg, followed by a turn to final, basically ½ of a square. I got the clearance to turn left to 260 degrees and descend to 10,000 feet. When I went to roll out on the 260 degree heading, I felt the aircraft turn but both of our attitude instruments, and the DG (directional gyro) just froze, still showing a left hand turn no airspeed and no altitude. I had one pneumatic standby attitude instrument that was 2" in diameter. I advised air traffic control that I needed a no-gyro approach. I then asked the copilot who was already saying his prayers to get up, check and pull the circuit breakers that controlled the instruments. He did and said that they were all in, so I had him start the APU and we tried switching the engine generators to the APU. It didn't work and I was somewhat amazed that I had no "OFF" flags on the instruments. Concentrating on a two inch instrument with two 7 inch instruments indicating a left hand bank is not only is unnerving but also prone to giving one, vertigo. I just flew the airplane and figured some homitron was running around in the electrical system blowing fuses. Air traffic control would give me turns when to stop a turn and read out my altitude. Long story short, we landed okay. Maintenance found a short in DGs that affected out attitude instruments. They could not however account for the lack of "OFF" flags.

GROUNDED

I had been having problems with my blood pressure. It would go up and down like a yo-yo. I had been to seven cardiovascular heart physicians trying to find out why. Blood pressure is controlled by several organs. Your kidneys, your thyroid, tiny bit of pancreas, being overweight, stress, PTSD and lack of sleep are all contributors. I had ultrasounds as well as angiograms performed on my organs, which passed muster. I had an angiogram done on my heart and surrounding arterial vessels. All were good no heart disease was evident. Not wanting to lose a $161,000 job I went to a physician recommended by a friend. This Doctor had been a Navy Seal in Vietnam. He told me that he had seen this before from other Veterans who had sucked up a good deal of Agent Orange. He explained that Agent Orange was a powerful Dioxin and would screw up your bodies normal functioning. There is no cure. He told me that if I contacted the Veterans Administration, they couldn't even spell Agent Orange and would deny any problems. He was right. On November 16, 1994, I was stopped by our chief pilot outside a gate in Pittsburgh. I was on my way to get something to eat.

"How is the blood pressure Bob?"

"I don't think you want to know."

"Please come with me and have it checked at the clinic." We had a clinic in the Pittsburgh airport, so I followed him to it to have them read my blood pressure. It was 248/176, or a bit HIGH.

"Bob, please call in sick, we can't afford another accident." USAirways had recently lost a 737 approaching Pittsburgh.

"Technically, I still have a flight physical good until January 15th. I still have a roundtrip to Miami, but if you will guarantee me that USAirways will never try to intimidate me because I retire on long term disability, I will fly to Miami and back and you will not see me again."

I flew to Miami and back to Pittsburgh and retired. In order to retire on long term disability, a pilot must have doctor's reports followed by a review from a board of pilots who will determine if you will be placed on long term disability. Our contract called for a pilot on long term disability to receive 50% of his last 12 consecutive month's salary for life. I was making $161,000 a year.

Prior to getting grounded I had married my third wife Sally, in December of 1990. She was 25 and I was 42. My fourth wife says I always chased the wrong real estate, go figure. Within six months, we were having problems. She wanted to go to counseling, which I agreed to, and let her find the counselor. Upon arriving at the counselor's office he saw us both for about 10 minutes and then said he would like to see each of us separately. I was to go first. This guy was 61 years old and had been a psychiatrist for 45 years.

"Bob, look at this chart and tell me where you would place your wife's drinking." The chart looked like an upside down horseshoe, with half an eyebrow on each end. It had remarks written down every side less than a mm apart about how much a person drank. I read down all of them and then choose one on the bottom of the horseshoe, discretion being the better part of possibly being wrong, rationalizing that she didn't drink any more than I did. He takes the chart back.

"Bob, your wife is so far off this chart that we would have to have two charts to get anywhere close to her drinking."

"Get the hell out of here! You only just met us, how can you tell that in 10 minutes."

"I would never presume to tell you how to fly an airliner, this is my profession, I know what I am talking about."

I was appalled.

"Let me tell you how your life will play out. You will stick with her basically because you don't believe me. You will have children, hoping that changes things. It won't. The drinking will affect her moods, her ability to concentrate, and behavior. She will lie constantly. If she gets into trouble, you will bail her out, thus making you an enabler. For the sake of the kids, you will stick with her until it is untenable and then you will divorce. I give you 10 years. When she comes in here and I tell her she is an alcoholic, she will make an excuse not to see me again."

That guy was reading my mail. Everything, exactly as he had predicted, came true. It was probably the worst 10 years of my life. We had two beautiful boys. She wrecked two brand new Forerunners, and each time I bailed her out. She went to AA I went to Al-Anon. She went to a 28 day recovery clinic where she admitted drinking a fifth and a half a day. Less than a week after coming home, she was at it again. We divorced January 20th, 2000. We lived the movie "**When a Man Loves a Woman**". Today we can communicate and talk about our boys.

Following the divorce, I got custody of my boys. Being grounded gave me the opportunity to be with my boys while flying did not. A year and a half later I married Margaret, my fourth. She was very

My Best Friend and Wife, Margaret

Spiritual, less than 7 years my junior, and had been married for 21 years to what she called a very controlling man. Both of us being newly divorced found common ground. We refused to date for a year after our divorces. Margaret got me to return to church and eventually to go to the VA, something my dad was never able to get me to do. The psychiatrist, who did the interview, told me I was certifiable. I think it was a joke but it was close to the truth. He told me I had PTSD and recommended I attend PTSD classes. I didn't believe I had PTSD and refused to go until Margaret intervened. Being a member of the sex without partners club was not my idea of a good time. I attended two 12 week classes just for veterans and Margaret and I attended two 12 week courses for couples. It brought back a lot of stuffed memories. PTSD is characterized by drug and alcohol abuse, multiple marriages, hyper alertness, high blood pressures, stress, inability to sleep, nightmares, bursts of unexplainable anger, flash backs, night sweats, and numerous sexual liaisons. For nearly 40 years I had no emotions. When I asked the VA shrink when this will go away, he says, "Never."

Adding to my stress, anger and frustration, USAIRWAYS stole the pilot's pensions in 2003. The CEO and lawyers filed for bankruptcy and at the same time took over $30 million dollars for themselves. During the bankruptcy hearing they told the Judge that the pilot pension plan was only 64% funded. Air Line Pilots Association, whose job was to monitor and keep each pilot updated on the status of the pension plan, sat quietly and never said a word. You could smell the stink of it for a thousand miles. Our representatives had at the time written each pilot a letter stating that the membership would vote on the pension plan's future. Then at 3:00AM those same pilot representatives allowed the company to terminate the plan. I can still smell a rat. Following that betrayal the same representatives discovered that pilots on long term disability who were drawing 50% of their former salary would be making more than the pilots would be paid from the Pension Benefit Guarantee Corporation, the government agency that takes over a company's pension plan. With ALPA's help the Company terminated the Long Term Disability Plan. Sleazy, fraudulent and cowardly, the pilot representatives aided and abetted ALPA and USAIRWAYS ability to screw the pilots. The PBGC awards a retiree only a fifth of his normal earned retirement monies. Can you think of one reason why the representatives would have taken this path? (factual, honesty, integrity, or payoff, you decide). In the aftermath of this debacle, USAIRWAYS was sued by the PBGC and after several suits it was discovered that the pilot pension plan had been funded at 100%. Watching the success of USAIRWAYS, the other airlines followed suit. It was total bullshit but with ALPA sitting quietly during the bankruptcy hearing, there was nothing that could be done.

I don't give too many *"your ass"* looks at Richard Craniums as the VA has medicated me. In fact, when friends say *"you're crazy"* I can respond with, *"Certifiable."* I have a t-shirt that says **This Veteran is highly medicated for your protection.** Is the VA helpful? They have written on their paperwork heading *"**Making a Difference.** What a crock! If you file a claim with the VA regarding any diability, you can expect years and years of delay. First time I went to the Spokane Veterans hospital they gave me a C&P (an exam to see if you qualified for benefits). I had submitted a claim for my right ACL that had been ripped out at the football game while at Fort Huachuca. I took my 13 year old son with me. A fat ugly nurse, and that's a compliment, with a nasty disposition called for me. When my son Cody and I stood up she barked at Cody that he was not welcome at the hospital. She took me to a room and wanted me to extend and retract my right knee. This was prior to having both knees replaced due to damage from 30 plus years without an ACL and my joint was now bone on bone. When I had trouble pulling it all the way back, she grabbed my foot and shoved it against my ass muttering that *"you vets are a bunch of con men working the system"*. My knee had virtually no meniscus left between the knee joint and it hurt like hell. If it had been a man, I would have knocked him clean out of the 7th story window. I wanted to file a complaint but my service officer told me that if I did, my file would end up in the *never to be found area*. I submitted several claims and it has now been over 10 years with the VA still claiming DENIED, that there is no proof in my records. Recently Margaret found the microfilm the Army had given me upon my release. It had a record of every physical, every school, every OER, and everywhere I had been stationed. Sending it to the VA to show them proof, they still denied the claim. I despise the VA's VARO department in Idaho like I do child molesters. I could write an entire book on soldiers that have been denied legitimate claims for having served this country.

I have never claimed to be a straight arrow. On the other hand without these experiences I would not be where I am today. For all eternity I do not want to be a charcoal briquette. When I witnessed my son's birth I don't know how you could be an atheist. Furthermore, knowing that every human cell has 7 meters of the DNA spiral boggles my mind. I don't think that came about from an electric shock on some unknown bacteria somewhere in the Universe. Course we will all get the chance to plead our case eventually.

Epilogue

Vietnam sucked I did more things than I really needed too, frankly because I wanted to analyze my own reactions. With Betsy, my second wife, I was gone as long as 6 weeks at a time leaving her in a strange city and all alone. She was a beautiful, kind, intelligent, loyal wife who should not have had to put up with a PTSD stranger. Sally, my third wife, while a serious alcoholic, has today, been sober for nearly 11 years and currently married to a former alcoholic and clean to the point that my oldest son works for them full time. I take my hat off to her. With Margaret, we had initial problem as well until she gave me an offer (or order) I couldn't refuse and sent me to the VA. Her love and spirituality have amazed me in a time where I was extremely cynical and devoid of emotions. I have to take 15 pills a day, forget them and Margaret can tell in a heartbeat. They all come with some nasty side effects, but what the hell I'm upright and taking nutrition.

The following was written to my two boys from my kinky haired Jewish friend, Mark Corwin. *Bob was literally a "wild man" in the service. At first, I thought he was a rather cool guy and I was drawn to him, as were many others. What else could you want in a guy? But then, I noticed he couldn't turn this off, almost like a sickness, it grew and nurtured itself. His spontaneity blossomed into outrageous behavior. I truly thought the guy was out of control and I feared for him. I tried at times to discuss this with him until I became aware of his nightmares.*

It was just before Christmas when I came back to our apartment after duty. It was very late and I was getting ready for bed. Bob was in his room, a scotch bottle sat on the counter half full, when I heard Bob scream. God it literally scared me to death. I ran to his room and entered without even knocking. He was curled up on his bed in the fetal position, sobbing like a baby. His words were unintelligible, but it seemed they had a theme of fear and loss of life. The dream was horrible, and for the first time I realized that this man was truly tormented, and, that perhaps these dreams were what was driving him in the conscious world. I tried to talk to him, but he blew me off.

As a pilot, I always felt that he was unsurpassed in skill and prowess. He was part of any airplane he flew.

I have been married to Margaret for nearly 11 years. I am medicated like I run a pharmacy. On my off time I use to drink like a fish. It covered up some nasty things. My teenage boys were worried about me so I quit cold turkey maybe wine with dinner. Scotland's Scotch industry is pulling their hair out. While I still refuse to talk about some experiences or what may be driving my nightmares I am happy have renewed my faith that I had given up on while in Vietnam and my family is my life. I guess I am as happy as I can be. If I could have made a VARO bureaucrat walk point in Vietnam, I would be just peachy especially if he stepped on a bouncing Betty. I give Margaret all the credit seeing as how I wake up in the morning with her standing ready to pour my drugs down my throat.

Most of the girls I dated are still my friends. My special friend Susan even invited Margaret down to San Diego to spend a week with her. They got along great and Margaret learned where all the bodies are buried.

Alpa was sued by the TWA pilots for Alpa's betrayal of the TWA pilots in their merger with American Airlines. The award was for some $600 million dollars. Alpa appealed but just recently lost the appeal. A great example of *what goes around comes around.*

My buddy Bill Hall, the senior check pilot at PSA died of a stroke. My buddy Don Coney died of a rare disease picked up as a mercenary. A good deal more of our PSA pilots have made the last flight west.

My two boys are now 18 and 20 years old. The youngest is going to attend a two year college in Portland and get a helicopter rating and then join the Army. All of the girls pictured in this book are still my friends, still upright and taking nutrition. I am privileged to have known them all.

Robert Boyd

Captain U.S. Army OV-1 Mohawk Models A,B,C,D/ OH58, Huey Pilot

Captain Pacific Southwest Airlines/ US Airways727-100,200, BAC 146, MD80, Bac111,DC9

DFC, Bronze Star, 16 Air Medals, Army Commendation Medal, Army Good Conduct Medal, Vietnamese Service Medal, Vietnamese Campaign Medal with three leafs

"Fuck It, It Don't Mean Shit"

22676173R00222

Made in the USA
Charleston, SC
27 September 2013